# Industrial Economics

# Industrial Economics:
## Theory, Applications and Policy

**Richard Stead, Peter Curwen and Kevin Lawler**

**McGRAW-HILL BOOK COMPANY**

**London** · New York · St Louis · San Francisco · Auckland · Bogotá · Caracas · Lisbon
Madrid · Mexico · Milan · Montreal · New Delhi · Panama · Paris · San Juan · São Paulo
Singapore · Sydney · Tokyo · Toronto

Published by

## McGRAW-HILL Book Company Europe

Shoppenhangers Road, Maidenhead, Berkshire, SL6 2QL, England
Telephone 01628 23432
Facsimile 01628 770224

**British Library Cataloguing in Publication Data**
Stead, Richard
  Industrial economics : theory, applications and policy
  1. Industrial organization (Economic theory)
  2. Microeconomics
  I. Title II. Curwen, Peter J. (Peter Jeremy)
  III. Lawler, K. A.
  338

  ISBN 0077092236

**Library of Congress Cataloging-in-Publication Data**
Stead, Richard.
  Industrial economics : theory, applications, and policy / Richard
Stead, Peter Curwen, and Kevin Lawler.
    p.    cm.
  ISBN 0-07-709223-6 (pbk. : alk. paper)
  1. Industrial organization (Economic theory) 2. Industrial
policy. I. Curwen, Peter J. II. Lawler, Kevin. III. Title.
HD2326.S75  1996
338–dc20                        95–50819
                                     CIP

# *McGraw-Hill*

*A Division of The McGraw·Hill Companies*

Reprinted 1997

Typeset and illustrated by Keyword Typesetting Services Ltd, Wallington, Surrey
Printed and bound in Great Britain at the University Press, Cambridge

Printed on permanent paper in compliance with ISO Standard 9706

# Contents

# Acknowledgements

The authors are grateful to Mr Marcus Ling, research assistant at Sunderland Business School, for his invaluable help in checking large parts of the manuscript and other tasks. Mr Ling's unstinting and indefatigable efforts have contributed much to what is good in this volume. All mistakes remain ours, however.

# List of abbreviations

| | |
|---|---|
| DGFT | Director General of Fair Trading |
| DGIV | Directorate General (of the European Commission) IV — responsible for competition policy |
| ECPR | Economic Component Pricing Rule |
| FDI | Foreign Direct Investment |
| FTC | Federal Trade Commission |
| IRC | Industrial Reorganisation Corporation |
| LB | Line of Business |
| LBO | Leveraged Buy Out |
| MCR | Merger Control Regulation |
| MES | Minimum Efficient Scale |
| MMC | Monopolies and Mergers Commission |
| NAFTA | North American Free Trade Agreement |
| NEB | National Enterprise Board |
| OFT | Office of Fair Trading |
| PCM | Price-Cost Margin |
| PLC | Public Limited Companies |
| RCA | Revealed Comparative Advantage |
| RPM | Resale Price Maintenance |
| RTA | Revealed Technological Advantage |
| SMEs | Small and Medium Enterprises |
| SOP | Standard Operating Procedure |
| TFP | Total Factor Productivity |
| TFT | Tit For Tat |

# PART I   THEORY

# 1 Introduction: industrial economics

## 1.1 Introduction

Industrial economics (IE) is 'the study of the supply side of the economy, particularly those markets in which business firms are sellers', to quote Richard Schmalensee (1988, p.643), one of its foremost practitioners. Industrial economics thus offers us ways of understanding the world of real industries and their markets. This, however, is white water. While other branches of economics show the typical firm as operating a single plant, making one kind of product and engaging in perfect competition, industrial economists have to work with the reality that firms are often multiplant, multiproduct, multinational oligopolists, who compete against each other by differentiating their products or by locking customers into entire ranges of products, who shield their innovations behind walls of patents while trying to reverse-engineer competitors' products, who reshape entire industries by buying up their competitors, who lobby extensively for preferential treatment from government and generally engage in strategies which differ widely from the notion of perfect competition.

This focus upon oligopolistic markets in which differentiated products are sold sets an agenda of core issues for industrial economists: its prime elements are market power, competition and efficiency. Questions for analysis include: what are the market structures which best promote efficiency? Which, by contrast, are most conducive to efficiency-sapping collusion? What kinds of markets best promote technical progress? Within this research programme, one puzzle is to find ways of gauging the strength of competition in such markets: while economists often take the view that in oligopoly, competition is muted, businesses normally assert that competition is unrelenting, with the effect that only the efficient and dynamic can prosper. Who is right? As Schmalensee (1988, p.660) puts it, 'The Holy Grail of research in oligopoly theory has been the ability to use observable quantities to predict the intensity of rivalry in markets dominated by a small number of sellers'. As yet, the Holy Grail remains unfound.

Besides its significance for students of business behaviour, industrial economics is of much importance for governments and those who would understand and advise upon their policies. Most governments are concerned to raise the industrial performance of their economies; all accordingly require an analysis of the inter-relations between industrial structure, organization and efficiency: in both the static and dynamic senses. If, for example, certain kinds of industrial structure are associated with rapid technical improvement, then a government could take steps (for example, by controlling mergers, privatizing or regulating) to establish or to create those structures.

In recent years, industrial economics has changed dramatically. Theories have been extended and developed, partly in response to new ideas such as 'commitment', partly to new empirical findings (which often derive in turn from the use of new sources of empirical evidence such as share prices) and partly to the arrival of new tools such as computer simulations. In part, of course, such developments have also been driven by policy initiatives of governments such as privatization and deregulation: though these in turn can be attributed to the earlier theoretical work of certain industrial economists. At the same time, the field is also populated by contending ideological factions (interventionists and free marketeers) who put conflicting interpretations on their own and others' findings. The aim of this book is to guide the apprentice industrial economist through the rapids.

## 1.2 Overview and history: structure, conduct and performance

Let us begin with a brief historical sketch of the subject. The pre-history of IE lies in case studies of single industries, which frequently drew evidence from US anti-trust investigations. A pioneer of such work, which dates from the late 1930s, was Mason of Harvard University. A student of Mason's, Professor Joe Bain, gave the field its modern shape by using inter-industry comparisons (1951, 1956). Of the core issues listed above, Bain focused upon the relationship between the organization or structure of industry and profit. In brief, the hypothesis from which he began was that more concentrated industries should show higher profits than those with a lower concentration. This basic idea was, in due course, systematized and extended to become the principal theme of IE. Among the additions was the idea of an industry's 'basic conditions', so that it would be more correct, if less elegant, to speak of the 'basic conditions-structure–conduct–performance (S–C–P) hypothesis'. Its principal component, however, remained covert. This was its *determinism*; the idea that the performance of an industry was determined by the conduct of firms, which was in turn determined by structure, itself determined by basic conditions (Fig. 1.1). Let us now look at these elements in more detail.

**Figure 1.1**  The S–C–P model

### 1.2.1 Basic conditions

These operate on both supply and demand sides of the market. On the demand side, the basic conditions refer to the size of the market, and its growth as well as its dependence on seasons and the economic cycle. Of critical importance is the elasticity of demand and the availability of substitutes, since these affect the strength of competition from other industries. If substitutability between two products is easy, then the two industries should be treated as one. On the supply side, basic conditions begin with technical factors such as the technology of production, the perishability of the product and its value-to-weight ratio. Production, of course, includes all aspects of supply such as distribution, advertising and marketing as well as manufacturing or mining. Perishability and value-to-weight ratio influence the number and location of production sites and the competition between them: valuable, transportable items such as perfumes compete in a single world market while cheaper, heavier products such as cement sell in large numbers of separate local markets. The technology of production can generate economies of scale; which can occur just as easily in advertising as in manufacturing, of course. Economies of scale in turn mean that larger firms will be more efficient, so that an industry with scale economies will tend to be concentrated.

Other basic supply-side conditions include legal and social factors such as the regulatory framework (for example, the obligation, if any, to acquire a permit or a qualification before one can commence trading, and the role, if any, of trade unions). Another factor is the availability of vital inputs. If their supply cannot be guaranteed, would-be producers will feel obliged to integrate backwards in order to control them.

### 1.2.2 Market structure

This has two aspects: internal aspects (the number and the sizes of buyers and sellers) and the external aspects (the conditions of entry and exit). At one extreme stands monopoly, in which one seller, sheltered by insurmountable entry barriers, faces a myriad of buyers. More common, however, are concentrated markets in which large proportions of output are in the hands of small numbers of sellers, in which entry barriers are significant so as to isolate the oligopolists from new competitors, and in which buyers are numerous and unorganized. Firms in such circumstances may possess market power, so that such situations are of substantial interest to industrial economists. If, however, buyers are themselves concentrated, then they may have countervailing power to balance that of producers.

The role of entry barriers is important in that without them even the most complete monopoly is open to competition from new entrants. Such barriers may take a number of forms. Some are literally insurmountable, such as a government decision that it is going to buy its warships from a particular shipyard. The market then has entry barriers: no other yard can compete for orders and the favoured yard is a monopolist. Other barriers can be surmounted given sufficient funds and ingenuity, thus effectively limiting the population of those able to enter an industry. For example, economies of scale may demand that a new competitor enter either on a large scale (with heavy outlays) or not at all. The absence of such economies in the building trade, as an illustration, means that entry is easy. Partly in consequence the industry has an army of small producers alongside the large companies. Patents, advanced technology and brand images can all be considered barriers to entry, though it is only fair to note that this description is controversial in that some groups of industrial economists; notably those of the neo-Austrian school (see below) argue that a barrier which is surmountable is not truly a barrier. Recent work in IE has drawn attention to the effect of exit barriers, which are just as effective as entry barriers: a firm which has to buy or create a specialized asset in order to enter an industry would stand to lose its money if it then decided to reverse its decision and leave, because it might not be able to find a buyer.

Some of the devices noted above such as branding are often not so much entry barriers for an entire market as forces protecting one firm's section of that market. Their purpose is thus product differentiation, and their effect is to make the producer a quasi-monopolist with a degree of market power, again, attracting the attention of industrial economists. A proliferation of brands can, however, collectively make a market difficult to enter. A final element in structure is the organization of firms in terms of their degrees of vertical integration and of conglomeration, because these factors enhance producers' room for manoeuvre, in particular the ability to cross-subsidize one subsidiary from another.

### 1.2.3 Conduct

This refers to the decisions and policies of producers (and, in principle, of buyers, though in practice attention focuses upon the former). It thus relates to companies' pricing policies, such as any attempts to segment a market by setting premium prices for some groups of customers and offering discounts to others (e.g. publishers selling hardbacks, softbacks and, later, remainder copies). Collusion (concerted action by producers to suppress competition and raise prices) is a form of conduct which attracts the attention of both industrial economists and the competition authorities such as the Office of Fair Trading. Also included under this heading are attempts to create entry barriers, either deliberately or inadvertently. Brand creation, for example, will make it more difficult for a new entrant to attract customers from existing firms ('incumbents') while research and development (R&D) and innovation may also make entry more costly because a more advanced product is more difficult to imitate. A policy of low prices will likewise discourage entry (and benefit consumers) while collusion-induced price rises will, all else being equal, encourage new entry. Investment and mergers are further aspects of conduct which influence potential entrants.

### 1.2.4  Performance

This relates to the record of the industry in terms of the benefits which it generates for its various stakeholders. Formally, of course, companies are owned by shareholders and thus the first aspect of performance is the industry's profitability. Since profits can arise from market power as well as from efficiency, care must naturally be taken not to equate high profits with good performance. Analogously, normal profits cannot be taken to indicate a competitive and efficient industry, since monopoly revenues may be frittered away in high costs such as excessively-high salaries. Economists are thus interested in the efficiency of the industry as well as its profitability. Also of interest are its ability to provide stable, adequately-paid employment and its technological progressiveness (in terms both of developing new products and of using new technology). A final aspect of performance is an industry's record in the field of international trade, that is, trends in its exports and of foreign imports into the home market and, of course, the net trade balance for the industry.

### 1.2.5  Determinism

The full model of S–C–P includes the proposition that the elements are linked in a deterministic way. Thus an industry's basic conditions determine its structure, which in turn determines conduct; and conduct determines performance. For example, the basic conditions relating to the construction industry are that the technology used is largely simple, that there are few economies of scale and that demand is sensitive to the economic cycle. Entry is thus relatively simple, so that the industry has a large number of small enterprises. Conduct takes the form primarily of price-based competition, that is, there is little scope for differentiation of products since they are usually designed by (or for) the client: the construction firm simply builds to specification. The performance of the industry thus shows fluctuating profits coupled with a relatively limited rate of investment and technological development compared with other industries. By contrast, beer production is dominated by three factors. First, most beer is made using large-scale continuous-flow processes in which large plants have a cost advantage over small ones; that is, there are economies of scale. Second, there are also economies of scale in advertising and marketing beer. Third, there are barriers to entry into the retailing of beer (in pubs and off-licences) in that both require licences. These combine to dictate the structure of the industry: economies of scale mean that companies are large so that the industry is oligopolistic, while licences compel breweries to integrate forward and own their own pubs so as to ensure sales outlets.

This integration creates another barrier to entry, because it means that the wholesale market for beer is very limited in size since most beer bypasses it. It is thus difficult for a new beer producer to find customers. The conduct of the industry is characterized by muted *price* competition; but there is vigorous competition in terms of the development of new products, brand promotion, pub decor and entertainment and, in the period 1960–80, by frequent mergers as a means of growth. The performance of the industry shows good profits for the largest five firms (averaging over 13 per cent return on capital in the 1980s) but a persistent and growing trade deficit due to rising imports of foreign beers, caused in part by differences in tax rates between the UK and other EU countries. Concerned about the apparent lack of competition in beer supply, the Monopolies and Mergers Commission (MMC) reviewed the industry in 1989. To stimulate competition, the Commission recommended that the brewers' so-called 'tied estates' of pubs be reduced in size and that landlords be permitted to offer 'guest beers' from other brewers. The MMC, as implicit followers of the S–C–P tradition, sought to improve the performance of the industry by altering its structure. In the event, the MMC's recommendations were adopted only in part and were then in large measure evaded by the industry: some firms elected to end beer production and so kept their tied estates, while those which disposed of pubs did so by a combination of closing the smaller, under-used ones or imposing harsh terms on incoming landlords. Landlords were easily discouraged from exploiting the 'guest beer' option. Competitive pressure was, however, raised by the entry of small-scale brewers, often with only one or two pubs, who brewed on pub premises. From outside the industry came further pressure in the form of imported beer and new forms of entertainment which competed with pubs.

## 1.3 S–C–P: problems and perspectives

The S–C–P approach or paradigm suffers from several major problems, to which economists have responded with both criticisms and new theoretical departures. A major flaw with S–C–P is that it is too simplistic, ignoring many of the linkages which can be argued to exist between the elements. A general theme is that conduct is very often not wholly determined by structure; firms have a wide degree of discretion over their conduct, and the decisions they make affect the structure of the industry and indeed the basic conditions. Rather than passively responding to outside influences, many firms actively seek to control their environments. Merger decisions are a clear example of firms changing structure, while advertising and branding, by changing consumer attitudes, act upon the elasticity of demand: one of the basic conditions. At the very least such expenditure affects barriers to entry and so affects structure. Similarly, research into new products serves to build entry barriers. Even technological factors such as economies of scale can be argued not to be simple givens but rather to be the fruit of deliberate research efforts. One response of industrial economists has been to rewrite S–C–P to accommodate these complex links between structure, conduct and performance (Fig. 1.2).

Another response of industrial economists has been to revamp the theory to include many of these effects. Whereas S–C–P was essentially a short-run theory which took industrial structure as given, the new approach involves a longer-run time horizon which encompasses entry (sometimes exit) and investment. The framework for these new theories is *game theory*. Typically in such games, players make moves to which their rivals then react. It is essential, of course, to specify what information players have, and the range of permissible moves has to be laid down. Other important considerations are the possibilities that players have for learning and the number of times a game is to be played: once, a known and finite number of times or indefinitely. One example of the way that games can be used pertains to the analysis of the decisions of an incumbent monopolist without entry barriers facing the threat of entry by one or more other firms (Vickers, 1988). The body of theory which has grown up around this core is sometimes termed the 'New Industrial Economics'.

Finally, because it stems from mainstream economics, S–C–P employs the assumption that firms are able to adjust swiftly to changes by unerringly selecting the course of action that will maximize profits (Parker and Stead, 1991). Many economists have questioned this assumption arguing that the processes of decision making in business are worthy of study in their own right. Economists deserving mention here include Edith Penrose (1959) and Nobel prizewinner Herbert Simon (1979), who in their respective ways analysed the effects of decision-makers'

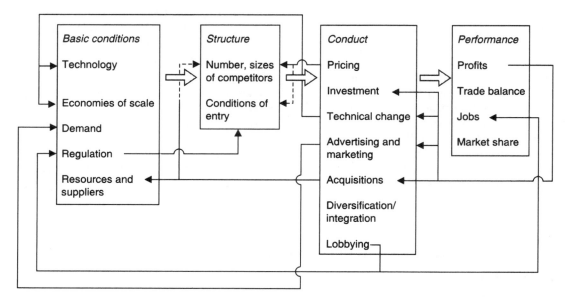

**Figure 1.2**   Structure, conduct and performance: new complexities

limited abilities to process information. The implication of this line of analysis is that firms will not react in a deterministic fashion to changes in the environment because decision makers will in all probability not be fully aware of changes in that environment. From this perspective, the conduct of firms cannot be predicted with confidence. Rather, economists should analyse decision making as a topic in its own right and include it in their analytical work.

## 1.4   Ideological presumptions: interventionists vs. *laissez-faire*

One of the major controversies in IE relates to the real extent of competition. Some economists argue in the Bain tradition that concentrated structures mean that competition is often restrained, implying that the State should intervene to recreate it. For others of the liberal tradition, such as Harold Demsetz and George Stigler of Chicago University, competition, like gravity, is an ever-present reality, however concentrated industries may appear to be. From this perspective, the implication is that governments should leave well alone (unless competition is inhibited by government itself). At an extreme in this spectrum are economists who place themselves in the so-called neo-Austrian tradition, for whom government intervention is also anathema. These economists (Kirzner, 1973; Littlechild, 1981; Schumpeter, 1953) take the view that markets are rarely if ever in equilibrium because underlying conditions of technology and tastes are in constant flux, and because business people are continually striving to find out what these tastes and technological possibilities are. Thus business people continually monitor the environment for new opportunities and experiment with new products, new forms of organization and new sources of supply. Some of these work but some do not and are discontinued. For neo-Austrian economists, central importance attaches to the flexibility of economic systems and to the incentives which agents have to adapt to new conditions and to try out new ideas. From this perspective, government intervention is wrong not simply because it may lead to an inefficient allocation of resources but because it inhibits the processes of experimentation and change. To give an overdrawn example, when a railway is in private hands, neo-Austrians would argue, its owners would constantly try out new timetables, standards of comfort in trains, catering systems, fares and so on. The managers of publicly-owned systems by contrast can continue to provide the same service despite changing consumer demands, technological opportunities and costs, because they know that the government will pay their salaries regardless of the railway's performance. For neo-Austrians, a main prescription is that governments should consequently refrain from taking industries into public hands and should sell off those which, through accident or misplaced philanthropy, they have acquired in the past.

## 1.5  Where do we go from here?

The first six chapters develop the theory of industrial economics. We begin by looking at the basic building blocks of the industrial system: firms and their decision-making processes (Chapter 2) and then at industries and their structure (Chapter 3). In Chapter 4 we move on to theories of the interaction between oligopolists. We then (Chapter 5) examine empirical research on the link, if any, between structure and profits before taking in the theory of competitive entry (Chapter 6), that is, competition between established firms and potential entrants.

In Part II we apply these ideas concerning the nature of competition to, successively, advertising (Chapter 7), the measurement of the welfare losses associated with restrained competition (Chapter 8), mergers (Chapter 9), technical innovation (Chapter 10) and the industrial economics of international trade (Chapter 10). In Part III attention turns to policy: competition policy (Chapter 11), privatization and deregulation (Chapter 12) and industrial policy (Chapter 13).

## Guide to further reading

Scherer (1980) explains the elements of the Structure, Conduct and Performance Paradigm in detail; Caves (1989) and Pickering and Cockerill (1984) apply it to American and British industries respectively.

# 2 Firms, decision making and entrepreneurs

## 2.1 Introduction

Much of the time, industrial economists take firms for granted. Pride of place goes to industries; the firms which populate them are assumed to act in a stable, predictable fashion so that attention rests upon the way that alternative structures or other conditions influence outcomes. Firms, however, are important institutions. This is especially true of the larger ones, for economic activity is heavily concentrated. Although there are nearly 128 000 firms in the UK's manufacturing sector, the largest 5000, that is, those with over 100 workers, employ three-quarters of the sector's workforce and produce 80 per cent of its net output. A substantial proportion of international trade moreover consists of internal transfers between the subsidiaries of multinationals.

Many industrial economists have attempted to analyse the activities of firms, by examining their forms of organization and methods of decision making and indeed the reasons for their very existence.

## 2.2 The legitimacy of studying firms

The view that firms should be out of bounds to economists was put by, among others, Professors Fritz Machlup (1967) and Milton Friedman (1953). Their propositions may be summarized in the following way. It is that the concern of economists should be to formulate theories that make clear conditional predictions about the world. Conditional predictions are statements such as 'if the wages of bank staff rise relative to other workers, then, *ceteris paribus*, (i) banks will tend to substitute capital for labour at a more rapid rate and (ii) banks will tend to lose business so that fewer bank workers will be employed'. A conditional prediction is thus one which links conditions (e.g. relatively higher pay for bankworkers) with a prediction (e.g. fewer jobs in banking), it is not simply a prediction about how many bankers there will be in the year 2001. To make such conditional predictions, argue Friedman and Machlup, it is not necessary to examine the inner constitution of firms. It is thus in order to assume, as most economists do, that firms seek to maximize profits and to ignore their inner processes, that is, to treat the firm as a 'black box'. The purpose of this assumption is not to describe actual firms but simply to generate predictions; to provide a link between hypothesized changes in conditions and changes in the patterns of output or prices. Friedman thus argues that the realism of the assumption that firms maximize profit can be safely ignored, arguing that theories should be judged solely on the accuracy of their predictions. In similar vein, Machlup justifies this procedure by reference to the natural sciences, where, he asserts, it is common for scientists to posit the existence of phenomena whose existence has not been accepted as a way of explaining results. For example, to make certain equations describing nuclear reactions 'work', scientists 'invented' a new particle, the neutrino, which had almost no mass or energy. The existence of neutrinos was accepted among physicists (even though none had been detected) simply because of their theoretical necessity. (The example could be replicated by referring to 'cold, dark matter' and anti-particles.) Such creations Machlup termed 'theoretical constructs', and his argument essentially was that firms were to industrial economics as neutrinos were to physics: a theoretical construct which was necessary to make the theories complete but which had no necessity to exist.

It is with trepidation that any writer would take issue with someone of such august stature as Professor Machlup, but the situation demands no other course. The flaw in Professor Machlup's argument is that while it is true that the existence of neutrinos was accepted *pro tem*, some scientists set out to discover whether such things actually existed or not. In the event, their search for neutrinos was successful and the particle thus moved from the status of imaginary 'theoretical construct' to that of real particle. In other words, in natural science it is legitimate both to accept the existence of theoretical constructs and to find out if they are real or not. This standpoint has been accepted by a substantial body of industrial economists, who have attempted to investigate the inner processes of firms. This chapter reviews their work. As a preliminary, we look briefly at the legal and organizational constitution of firms and at their economic importance.

## 2.3   The economic importance and constitution of firms

A landmark in the development of the modern firm was the adoption in the UK of limited liability in 1845. Up to this point, firms had essentially been family concerns, run by an entrepreneur-founder or his or her family, or partnerships in which several such entrepreneurs joined forces. Such firms, however, had unlimited liability: That is, creditors could call upon both the business itself and the personal wealth of the family for the settlement of debts. The disadvantage of this arrangement was that people going into business (even by merely putting capital into a partnership) were putting their family's wealth and position at risk. Limited liability changed that: henceforth, businesses became legal personalities in their own right, separate from the affairs of their owners. Firms could fail, but this would not ruin their owners, whose liabilities were limited to the capital which they had subscribed. This legal change permitted the development of so-called joint-stock firms; that is, firms which issued shares to people whose only interest was that of an investor; they sought no part in the management of the company. By issuing shares, entrepreneurs were thereby permitted to raise relatively large sums of money, with one predictable result: (some) firms grew larger. Indeed, by the late 1960s, some 40 per cent of UK manufacturing output was accounted for by the top 100 firms. During the late 1980s, however, many firms began to 'disintegrate' in the technical sense of the term by selling subsidiaries to local management, and by putting work such as running the staff restaurant (and even R&D: *Financial Times,* 6 January, 1995, p.7) out to contract.

A corollary of the appearance of large joint-stock limited liability firms was the development of a relatively sophisticated division of labour between the parties concerned. At one end are the shareholders, who require, in return for their capital regular and audited information on the conduct of the firm. At the other end are the managers of the firm, whose role is the supervision of its business with a view to the maximization of the wealth of the shareholders. Between the two is the board of directors, whose role is to supervise management. Normally directors are themselves shareholders. The division between directors and management is not sharp in that senior managers normally sit on company boards, so that in some firms, boards of directors may be composed wholly of managers. When managers are promoted to board status, they normally either have to buy shares in the company (often at a discount price), thus becoming share-holders. It is also conventional to include as board members directors who are not managers, so-called non-executive directors, whose role is to represent shareholders. The rights and duties of directors and shareholders (including those that concern the disclosure of information) are set out in law (Company Law) and the codes of the Stock Exchange.

Besides the division of roles between shareholder, director and manager, it is also possible to distinguish between the roles of different employees. First, firms are divided into departments of functional specialisms: finance, marketing, production, distribution, personnel and so on. Each department is typically hierarchical, that is, it is structured like a pyramid with layers of decreasing size. Staff on each layer supervise the workers below them and are in turn responsible to their superiors on the level above. Coordination between departments is the responsibility of the higher levels of management. Modern management theorists (Handy, 1993) argue that relationships at work are becoming more equal, that is, firms are frequently designed to be like teams of equals, but many remain quite authoritarian in style. As well as full-time workers, many firms today have networks of semi-permanent sub-contractors, consultants and part-timers whom they call upon as and when required. In some cases the policy of eliminating all but a central core of full-time workers has been carried so far as to give rise to the term the 'hollow corporation', implying that (in extreme cases) almost no one is left!

It should be emphasized that the model above is essentially Anglo-Saxon (i.e. it applies to the UK, the USA and other English-speaking countries). In other countries the powers of share-holders are limited in various ways so that management and in some cases other workers and even politicians have a greater voice. In Germany, all large firms ( > 2000 workers) are obliged to have a *Betreibsrat* or works council which managers must consult. Large firms also have an *Aufsichtsrat* or supervisory board made up of representatives of the workforce, management, shareholders and often local politicians, which oversees strategic matters. In France, there are often legal restrictions on the ability to buy and sell shares and upon the voting rights that shares may carry; again, limiting the rights of shareholders (Franks and Mayer, 1989). In Italy, even large firms are often owned and run by families, so that the distinction between owners, directors and managers does not have so much importance.

Besides the functional specialisms described above, it is possible to make distinctions between the decisions which are made within firms. At the lowest level are 'operational' decisions which are made by workers and their immediate superiors (so-called line managers) every day. Such decisions should relate to small-scale problems such as staff absenteeism, late delivery of supplies or the recruitment of new junior employees. In making such decisions, line managers are normally required to follow company policies which may be written down or which may be more informal 'rules of thumb'. These policies or practices are the basis of the firm's efficiency. They embody those past decisions that have been successful. They are thus in some sense the firm's collective wisdom or memory, and we shall return to them later in this chapter. Low-level managers normally report to a manager with wider responsibility (perhaps an area manager) who may well report to another and so on up an organizational pyramid or hierarchy. In contradistinction from operational decisions are strategic decisions which govern the longer-run development of the firm. These concern the range of markets which a firm should be present in, the array of products which it should be selling and the essential technologies in which it should seek to be competent. Strategic decisions thus relate to the extent and direction of R&D, to the raising of capital, to mergers and joint ventures with other firms, moves into other countries (multinationalization) and to divestiture of unwanted businesses. Some writers (Ansoff, 1965) argue that the organizational structure of the firm (how many layers of management there should be, for example, or how subsidiary companies should be integrated into the larger structure) form a third ('structural') category of decisions, while others hold that decisions on structure are in fact strategic. Whatever the merits of this last debate, it is clear that junior management has responsibility for operational decisions, while senior management including the board of directors, is responsible for strategic and structural issues as well as having oversight of the firm's operational matters.

These categories (operational, strategic and structural) were not created out of the blue by management theorists but were derived from analyses of the histories of real firms. Foremost in the field in this context is Chandler (1992), whose work commences with American business in the mid-nineteenth century when most firms were small and supplied local markets. Where firms served wider markets, they did so through wholesalers who sold in turn to retailers. For Chandler, a key role was then played by the railroads. First, the railroads were examples to other businesses because they pioneered new forms of organization. While 'local' railroads clearly had some value, the true scope of rail lay in serving regional and national markets, connecting destinations separated by thousands of miles. Organization on such a scale, involving thousands of employees and the coordination in real time of distant operations was clearly something of a challenge. Borrowing perhaps from the armed forces, the railroads developed a new form of organization, the 'line and staff' model, in which everyday decisions were delegated to local ('line') managers, each responsible for a given area. Certain matters were, however, outside the remit of the local manager, such as finance, the maintenance of the permanent way and choices relating to locomotives. Such matters were reserved for head office, which had a series of specialists (the 'staff') in these fields.

Railroads influenced other businesses in a second way by offering regular delivery service of potentially large quantities of both supplies and finished products. Operators of other manufacturing businesses could therefore afford to install specialist machinery to process other materials, secure in the knowledge that the plant would be able to operate semi-continually. Railways thus opened the door to the creation of large steel plants, oil refineries, chemical works and similar operations. This, however, created its own problems in that firms producing on a large scale needed to guarantee, to some degree, a regular rate of consumption. They were thus induced to integrate forward to varying extents. For some, this meant the creation of a body of sales personnel together with a wholesale network, while for others it meant the development of a retail network and the creation of a brand image through advertising. Some had to invest in specialist distribution facilities like refrigerated railcars, warehouses and retail display cabinets. By the early decades of the twentieth century, therefore, the American economy was already characterized by large manufacturing concerns with their own integrated distribution or supply networks, usually dealing in a wide range of products.

The next important change came in the 1920s. The paradigm was General Motors, already a large manufacturer of railway locomotives and other products as well as motor vehicles. Its chief executive, Alfred P. Sloan, found the senior management of the company to be struggling under the weight of decision making arising from the sheer range of products and markets in which the company had an interest. The production manager was thus responsible for production across the board, while the marketing department had to deal with the marketing of consumer products as well as products which were sold to industrial buyers. His contribution seems obvious in retrospect: Sloan divided the firm into several quasi-independent units, each headed by a senior manager who reported to a relatively small head office team of top managers. Each division, of course, was a miniature firm in that each had a production department, a marketing department, a purchasing and supply department and so on, although each could focus on its own product or narrow range of products. Head office meanwhile could concentrate on monitoring the performance of the subordinate units while delegating relatively large powers to the divisions. Chandler termed this innovation the 'M-form' firm, with M standing for multidivisional, as contrasted with the 'U-form' firm, U denoting unitary. This form was copied across

America and, largely after the Second World War, in Europe. In its classic form, it delegates operational decisions to divisions and reserves strategic decisions for head office. Head office is able to channel funds from currently profitable businesses within the group to units which have better long-term prospects but which require investment in the present. This, of course, is a role normally played by the capital market, and head offices of M-form firms have been likened to miniature capital markets.

The importance of the M-form principle was that it set the firm free to grow beyond the limits set by the U-form, just as limited liability had permitted growth a century before. Head offices could buy or sell businesses, for example, even those in industries in which they had no previous experience. Thus quite disparate sets of businesses could be grouped together under one head office as a conglomerate. M-form firms could also add foreign subsidiaries to their holdings, thus becoming multinationals. This potential is, of course, still being exploited.

These considerations have induced industrial economists to investigate several themes. One relates to the relative sizes of the markets and firms: firms appear to have been growing relative to the market, so that more economic activity is conducted within firms. Why should this be so? Indeed, given that markets are generally deemed to be capable of great feats of resource allocation, why is it that firms exist in the first place? More generally, what forces govern the choices between internal organization and marketplace? A second but related issue pertains to the conflict, or perhaps merely the contrast, between firms and markets. Markets are characterized by 'spot' contracting, short-term relationships and by the freedom of either party to come and go, whereas firms are, to varying degrees, characterized by authoritarianism: supervisors instruct workers what to do. (Karl Marx went so far as to term this the 'hidden abode of capital'.) Moreover resources within the firm are controlled by administrative instruction: shelf-space in supermarkets is swapped from tinned fish to catfood not through a market process of bidding but simply by the manager deciding that this shall be so and instructing the staff accordingly. How can this contrast be explained? The third issue relates to whether decision making within firms is different from individual decision making in the market. While the individual consumer or entrepreneur acting on her or his own behalf can be taken to be maximizing his or her utility, decisions within the firm, by contrast are typically taken by committees; the obvious question is: do committees maximize? The following sections examine these issues.

## 2.4   Why do firms exist?

The first explanation for the existence of firms was offered by Ronald Coase (1937).

### 2.4.1   Transaction costs

Coase's answer, in sum, is that using the market to conduct transactions is in fact costly; firms exist to save such costs. Firms are thus a device for economizing, that is, raising efficiency. What are these costs of using the market: these so-called transaction costs? After all, what are the costs of buying a newspaper beyond those of carrying cash and of walking down to the newsagent's? The answer is more easily seen if one bears in mind a different transaction, say, finding a firm to undertake maintenance work. Coase identifies four costs of using the market.

First, the would-be buyer has to survey or search the market. In our example, this may mean sifting through trade directories, compiling a shortlist and going out to tender; all time-consuming processes. The second is negotiation. For a standard product or service this may be negligible but for complex ones it could be more demanding. The results of the negotiation would, of course, have to be encoded in a contract—more work! The third cost is that of monitoring the contract to ensure that the undertakings given are being fulfilled. The last cost is that of enforcing the contract; if and when monitoring reveals a problem, the aggrieved party needs some recourse but this typically will involve some time and effort on his or her part.

Coase argues that for these reasons, it would be costly to buy in resources every time they were needed: firms thus do not hire maintenance people every time another lightbulb is to be changed. Rather, it makes sense to recruit resources on long-term (incomplete) contracts: maintenance staff will be hired on contracts of indefinite length to change bulbs as and when required, for example. Thus by establishing the contract, the firm saves on search and negotiation costs which are conducted only once, it can monitor the worker's performance more easily, and has the worker's consent to submit to the firm's internal adjudication procedures over the enforcement of the contract so there is less likelihood of costly resort to law. The question which clearly arises is why, if firms are such an efficient institution, do they not expand without limit? As noted, the answer is partly that firms are indeed expanding relative to world trade (although at national level firms appear to be diminishing in size). The process of growth is restrained by the fact that the internal control of resources brings its own costs. Typically there are limits to how many subordinates a manager can supervise, a concept termed the 'span of control'. As the number of workers in a firm rises, so the number of managers rises, requiring the creation of another tier of management to control them. This process progressively raises the costs of expansion—internal adminstration of resources runs into classical diminishing returns. Even M-form firms are presumably subject to analogous forces.

Coase's theory offers an explanation of the *boundaries* of firms. It tells us why firms may rationally choose to employ workers rather than perpetually recontract with staff agencies or why firms will integrate with suppliers or distributors. In particular, it has been used by Buckley and Casson (1976) to explain the growth of multinational companies. In brief, their view is that firms with a valuable product face in principle a choice between setting up an overseas subsidiary (i.e. becoming multinational) and licensing the idea to a local firm. The latter option means transacting in an 'information market'. Here, however, transaction costs are high. The greatest difficulty is that of displaying the product (the idea) without giving away so much that the prospective buyer has no need to pay. Yet without some disclosure, prospective buyers would not be convinced of the value of the project. Hence, argue Buckley and Casson, firms opt for multinationalization. This, however, is an *ex post* explanation. The theory does not offer falsifiable predictions by which it may be tested. It is moreover of interest to note that both firms and public bodies have turned increasingly to contracting out as opposed to integrating, on the grounds that competition in the market brings more efficiency to at least some transactions than does internal control.

## 2.4.2  Contracts

Coase's original notion of long-term or indefinite contracts as instruments for saving transaction costs can be extended into a second argument relating to the gains which are to be obtained from investment in equipment which is specific to a particular line of business; for example, a press for stamping body-panels for a car. At first glance, it may appear that a specialist supplier could invest in the press and sell stamped body-panels to the car-maker. The problem is that we have here a two-stage process (in the terminology of Chapter 4, a 'super-game') involving choices about investment followed by choices over the prices and volumes of body-panels. A company investing in a press would then find itself in a bilateral monopoly with the car-maker. The outcome of bargaining in such situations is inherently uncertain, so the press firm would have no guarantee of a return on its investment. Since the press is, by assumption, highly specific, it would have no other uses and the money spent would be lost, thus the investment would not take place and the efficiency gains therefrom would be foregone. This suggests that a contract should be established in stage 1 of the game to govern outcomes at stage 2: contracts for the purchase and sale of stamped panels should be signed before investment takes place (and should cover the life of the press). Again, however, there is a problem of bilateral monopoly in that the cost of the panels will be known only to the press firm while their value will be known only to the car-maker. It is thus not clear at the outset how the gains will be divided between the two firms. Open competition for the right to set up a press may be an answer, but clearly a possibility (probability!) is that the car-maker will invest in the press itself—integrating the processes and extending the car-making organization. These ideas could be easily extended to cover investment by workers in firm-specific training. Firms can thus be seen as a solution to the asset–specificity/bilateral–monopoly problem (Tirole, 1988).

The notion of firms as centres of contracts was developed in a seminal paper by Alchian and Demsetz (1972). The argument here is again that there are gains in efficiency to be had from the joint employment of several resources—not from just a particular machine but from the collective efforts of a work-team. The problem with this system, of course, is that shirking becomes relatively attractive for any individual: if the efficiency gains are to realized, the work has to be metered and monitored. It is thus in the collective interests of workers to have a monitor (or series of monitors, each of which is monitored by an super-monitor. We neglect this elaboration and imagine there to be just one monitor). Who then monitors the monitor? Alchian and Demsetz argue that the only effective device here is self-monitoring, that is, the monitor should have a personal interest in efficient monitoring. This is created by giving the monitor the rights to establish contracts with team members, to terminate contracts (that is, rights to hire and fire and to set conditions of employment) and, crucially, to keep the residual value left after the products have been sold and the contracted workers have been paid as well as to sell his or her interest in the firm. The right to the residual ensures that the monitor will keep the team members working efficiently. The residual is, of course, profit, and the Alchian and Demsetz argument provides a justification for the typical, hierarchical capitalist firm. To caricature, the greed of the capitalist and the petty tyrannies imposed upon the workers are the price of efficiency in the workplace.

### 2.4.3 Firms' internal labour markets

Alchian and Demsetz end their analysis with a speculative remark to the effect that the firm, because the central contractor or monitor holds contracts simultaneously with many owners of similar resources (i.e. with many workers), may be seen as a specialized or even as a *privately-owned market*. Indeed, many labour economists speak of firms as having 'internal labour markets' and we have noted above the role of head offices of conglomerates as miniature capital markets. Large firms also have the possibility of comparing productivity levels across their many units, allowing them to experiment and to propagate best practice. This system is known as 'benchmarking' or 'yardstick competition'. Large firms, of course, can run real competitions between their units for, for example, the best/most productive hamburger bar in the company, at once motivating staff and raising output. Although Coase originally argued that firms replace market transactions with administrative coordination of resources, it is clear that firms in formal terms replace spot contracts with indefinite, longer-run contracts. From this perspective, the distinction between firm and market does not appear to be quite as sharp.

## 2.5  Why are firms organized hierarchically?.

Oliver Williamson of the University of Pennsylvania, working in the 1970s and 1980s, used the ideas of Coase, in part supplemented with ideas taken from the work of other theorists such as the Austrian Friedrich Hayek and MIT's Herbert Simon to explain the fact that firms have not only edges but an internal structure; typically, one that resembles the Civil Service in having a pyramidal or hierarchical nature. In particular, Williamson (1981) stressed two ideas from these sources: ideas to which we shall return later in this chapter. One is that human beings, while wishing to act rationally in the traditional sense of reviewing all alternatives before choosing the best, are constrained by their own limited abilities to gather and to process information. They thus make decisions which are only 'boundedly rational', that is, they are the best which can be made given the information that decision makers have. A second feature which he stressed was the tendency for people to engage in 'opportunism', that is, to act in accordance with their own interests at the expense of others if circumstances allow. Williamson argues that a hierarchy is a rational, efficient response to these problems. First, it allows people to specialize in roles. This makes sense because people's limited capacities for information processing means that it is more efficient to specialize, that is, to remain in one role rather than taking on a new role every day. Taking this further, it is also arguably efficient for people to specialize 'vertically', that is, for some individuals or groups to specialize in making the strategic decisions while others concentrate on operational decisions.

(Williamson also uses Coase's ideas to explain vertical integration. Without integration, individual retailers who sell a nationally-known brand may be tempted to refrain from promoting the product because they feel that other retailers will do enough to maintain demand. For the manufacturer, the problem is that if all retailers take this view, no one may do any promotion at all. Under these circumstances, it would be rational for the manufacturer to integrate forward into retailing.)

Williamson (1981) and Alchian and Demsetz (1972) stress the voluntary nature of contracts and thus of hierarchies in firms: although workers may be subjected to authoritarian rule in working hours, it is a regime which they have agreed to voluntarily in taking up employment. Conversely, if they find conditions too irksome, they are free to leave. Economists of radical views, for example Bowles (1985) and Marglin (1974) by contrast tend to stress the control which capitalists enjoy over their workforce, the opposition which this engenders among workers and the resultant need for monitoring which is both oppressive to workers and costly. Costs arise from both the alienation which workers feel towards their work, which leads them to expend less effort than they might, and from the need for specialist monitoring equipment and staff. Capitalists indeed may well use suboptimal equipment if it generates information about workers' performance or permits their work to be controlled. For such a line of argument, the obvious problem is why these alienating, inefficient capitalist hierarchies are not beaten in fair competition by workers' cooperatives which bear no such impediments. Marglin argues that there would be no returns for any workers taking on the capitalist's role of integrating production and thus no incentive so to do. It is not easy to see the logic of this, since presumably an efficient non-capitalist producer surrounded by inefficient, capitalist competitors would be able to enjoy super-normal profit. Moreover, the economic success of Japan and Germany compared to the performance of the Anglo-Saxon economies may be in part associated with the fact that the former countries have more egalitarian, team-based approaches to work organization (see below) whereas the latter tend to be more hierarchical and authoritarian.

The 'cooperative' system of work organization in Japan is described by Aoki (1990). He affirms that coordination between departments in Japanese companies is effected not through senior management but by direct ('horizontal') contact between workers. Thus scheduling of work in a car factory is undertaken by its on-site engineering office in response to customer orders coming in on a daily basis. Again, production engineers constantly suggest modifications to design in the light of experience in production. While these may seem mundane, they represent entirely different principles of organizing work; so much so that Aoki terms the system 'J-mode' (J for Japan) in contradistinction to H-mode (H for hierarchy). The contrast is most clearly seen in the second example, design. In H-mode, one set of engineers, the design team, designs a product and then consigns it to another to manufacture. This may present the second group with problems if the design is demanding. It also deprives the designers of the ingenuity and creativity of the production engineers. The constant cross-fertilization between departments, Aoki argues, allows Japanese firms to be both responsive to market demands and constantly innovative.

## 2.6   The principal–agent problem

Coase, followed by Williamson and by Alchian and Demsetz, argues that semi-permanent organizations are efficient because they save transactions costs. As everyone who has ever employed a worker (or 'agent') knows, however, the matter is rather more complex, primarily because the employer normally has some difficulty in ensuring that the worker always works to best effect. When workers have no discretion over their work (such as, perhaps, someone fitting brake shoes at a car assembly-line) then it is clear whether the employee has been working or not simply by looking at the cars at the end of the shift. When, however, a job is not so well-defined, agents have to react to circumstances, for example, a tenant farmer who can produce large crops by working hard when rainfall is high but whose efforts are wasted when there is little rain. Table 2.1 shows the details. The numbers in the cells show the crop. The landlord thus has no way of telling (from the crop) whether a low crop is attributable to low rainfall or to laziness.

The principal–agent (P–A) problem is simply this: how can the principal (the employer) ensure that the agent works with the appropriate degree of effort (or, more generally, furthers the interests of the principal)? The P–A problem arises in many contexts, the one illustrated above concerns employers and employees, but another important instance is the relationship between managers and investors, in that shareholders expect managers to maximize the value of the firm, yet most shareholders do not in fact personally participate in the business: managers are the agents for shareholders. This situation is, of course, more complex than the example of the tenant farmer in that (senior) managers do not simply make quantitative decisions between more or less effort: they typically face complex, qualitative decisions about which projects to take forward, how to modify their products, what new training procedures to introduce and so on. While shareholders are interested in maximizing profits, they have little information on how, concretely, this is to be done and thus rely on managers to do it for them. The P–A problem can be seen as the converse of Coase's idea of transaction costs. Using the market has costs but

TABLE 2.1   Principal–agent problem

|  |  | Rainfall | |
|---|---|---|---|
|  |  | High | Low |
| Farmer's effort | Conscientious | 200 | 20 |
|  | Shirks | 20 | 0 |

employing workers (including managers) likewise brings costs in terms of inefficiency or of monitoring their efforts.

The resolution to the problem in principle is to give the agent incentives which encourage the agent to expend effort appropriately. This consideration rules out simplistic salary systems: a salary paid regardless of circumstances, for example, gives the employee no (immediate) incentive to expend effort. Likewise a salary based on effort, however, is wrong for two reasons. First, the principal cannot monitor effort: it is impractical. Second, it is inappropriate since high effort is simply a waste when the situation does not require it. The key is to relate the income of the agent to the success (that is, the profits) of the business; to pay the agent a proportion of the profits. In practice, of course, other considerations enter the situation. Employees (even top managers) are often averse to risk and thus seek payment systems which have a significant basic (i.e. unconditional) element which can then be augmented by a bonus which is related to performance. For many workers, intermediate targets can be used such as clients interviewed or in the case of a computer maintenance team the length of time for which the computers are available for use. Again, it would make little sense to pay bonuses based on the performance of the whole firm when the worker–agent has only responsibility for a small part of it. It is better to relate pay to the performance of a section or department. At more senior levels, however, payments systems based on profitability are more appropriate.

The P–A problem leads in two directions. The first is toward the empirical question of whether, in large companies, the problem actually exists. That is, are managers and shareholders separate groups so that ownership is divorced from control? The second issue is the effects of such separation, assuming it to exist in the first place. We take these in order.

### 2.6.1    Are ownership and control separate?

In PLCs, it is clear that the typical shareholder does not participate in running the business. Shareholders treat their involvement in the company simply as a financial investment. Company annual general meetings (the formal means by which shareholders could influence company policies) are generally characterized by low attendances, short debates and the acceptance of ideas proposed by the board of directors. Most owners do not manage. But is it true that top decision makers are *not* owners? One approach has been to examine patterns of shareholding to see if there is a block of shares large enough to control the firm. When shareholdings are dispersed, many conclude that the board of directors, who may have a small proportion of the shares, effectively subvert shareholder power (Marris and Mueller, 1980). Berle and Means (1932), the progenitors of this research programme, used a threshold of 20 per cent; that is, they argued that if no shareholder (or inter-related group) had more than 20 per cent of the voting stock, the firm was under the control of management. Larner (1966) used the figure of 10 per cent—naturally the number of firms deemed to be under control of management varied accordingly (44 per cent for Berle and Means; 75 per cent for Larner). By contrast, boards of directors have small shareholdings. Prais (1976) found that in 1972 among the largest 100 British manufacturing firms, boards' holdings amounted to over 10 per cent in only 11 cases and in 73 cases were less than 2 per cent. Hay and Morris (1991) conclude from this and similar evidence that the 'separation of ownership and control remains a significant if far from universal characteristic of large modern corporations'.

As Sugden and Pitelis (1986) point out, however, the evidence on shareholdings is not in fact relevant. The question is not 'does the typical owner control the firm?' but 'how are top decision makers remunerated?'. If their pay is related to the firm's profitability or if they own valuable shareholdings, then they may be taken to be interested in profit maximization and the principal–agent problem has been overcome, but if they receive simply a salary, the problem clearly exists.

Data to address the problem is not easy to find. The remuneration of an executive director or senior manager is often a complex package including a salary, a pension scheme, health insurance, and a company car as well as bonus elements related to company performance and share options, that is, the right to buy shares at discount prices. The value of this last element is clearly higher when the share price goes up; as it would if the company were profitable. Beyond this, top decision makers usually are, of course, shareholders in their own right; and while their holdings may be relatively small, they may be a significant source of income and wealth for those concerned. Two per cent of one of the UK's largest 100 firms is a lot of money even when divided among several board members.

### 2.6.2  Managerial theories of the firm

Several analysts have tackled the issue of the likely effects of the hypothesized separation of ownership from control in large firms. Here we look at the work of Robin Marris (1964), although it should be stressed that this is but one of a family of such analyses created by among others Baumol (1959) and Williamson (1965). A good overview is found in Wildsmith (1973). Marris began from the premiss that management and ownership were separate, and that managers' rewards were linked to growth rather than to profits. He argued that managers' desire for growth would, however, be restrained by two factors. The first had its origins in the capabilities of management itself. Moderate growth, Marris argued, would stimulate or dynamize management and could thus bring higher profits. Growth beyond this point, however, would entail the firm taking on more projects than could be looked after, and thus bring lower profits. The second factor limiting growth was the cost of finance. Banks and other investors generally perceive higher and higher risks as companies borrow more (relative to their own capital) and thus charge higher rates of interest. Another constraint is that management, while motivated by growth, is obliged to achieve some minimum level of profit to avoid criticism (or worse) from shareholders.

These three forces, shown in Fig. 2.1, or more precisely the growth/profit function together with one of the other two, determine an equilibrium rate of growth for any given firm.

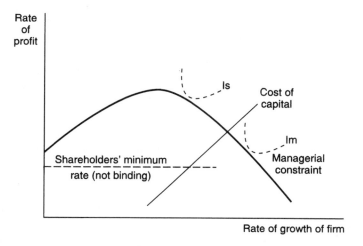

**Figure 2.1**  Growth-path of the manager-controlled firm

These principles may be made more plausible by arguing that growth and profits are both of interest to managers and to shareholders, that is, that they can be looked upon as substitutes. This would allow us to draw indifference curves upon the diagram. The difference between managers and owners can then be shown by the indifference curves, Im (for managers, with a relatively high emphasis on growth) and Is (for shareholders, emphasizing profits). The prediction from such a theory is that firms with different ownership structures would show distinct combinations of profitability and growth: owner-controlled firms having relatively higher profits than manager-controlled firms. Two studies looked for such differences in performance: Radice (1971) and Holl (1975). Both used samples of British firms which they divided into owner-controlled and manager-controlled groups before comparing profits and growth. In neither case were the differences between the groups large; in both cases the two groups showed extensive overlaps. The managerial-control thesis remains without extensive support.

## 2.7   Firms' networks: industrial districts

Kay (1993), in a lively application of the principles of industrial economics to business strategy, describes the internal and external linkages as a firm's 'architecture'. Internal links, H-versus J-mode, we have already discussed. External relationships are important because any product like a car or a pair of trousers is made not by one firm or even one design team but is (whether this is recognized or not) the fruits of the efforts of many contributing parties, that is, the subcontractors and suppliers as well as the main producer. Although economists tend to think of such relationships as simply those of purchase and sale, in reality relationships are often very long-term and 'intimate' in the sense that the companies concerned exchange quite sensitive information. Thus when a clothing retailer orders new garments, it will specify to its manufacturer the colours and textures of fabrics to be used; information which could be useful to competitors. In such a context, trust is essential. Japanese firms have developed these kinds of relationship to a high level, with their well-known 'just-in-time' system of continuous delivery of components. Behind this lies a willingness of the main company and its suppliers to cooperate fully, exchanging ideas and often personnel. In a similar fashion, Michael Best (1990), drawing on the work of others like Hirst and Zeitlin (1989) and Piore and Sabel (1984) develop the idea of the 'industrial district' (a phrase originally used by Alfred Marshall) that is, a geographically-concentrated network of inter-related firms who prosper by undertaking short production runs of specialist products by virtue of the ability to cooperate by subcontracting. The paradigm here is Emilia-Romagna, the so-called 'Third Italy'. Best optimistically refers to such districts as the 'New Competition' seeing great advantages in the flexibility which he argues is ideally suited to modern informatics: computer-aided design, numerically-controlled machine tools and robotics. Critics like Murray (1987) draw attention to low pay and insecure jobs of these areas while Cowling and Sugden (1987) argue that the reality is usually that one large firm dominates and exploits the rest. In this context it is, of course, not entirely clear where the boundary of the firm(s) lie(s).

## 2.8   Who hires whom?

We have noted above the idea that the firm is a web of contracts. In common parlance, firms hire labour. For neo-classical economics, there is no obvious justification for this; why is it that capital hires workers and not the other way about? The cause of this puzzlement is not difficult to see, mainstream economics focuses on transactions which are assumed to be made voluntarily by both parties. Thus it cannot be clear who is hiring whom; in a sense, they hire each other. It could alternatively be argued that management hires both labour and capital, with the proviso that top management generally have some capital of its own. From a neo-Austrian perspective, of course, there is no issue here; entrepreneurs, who are generally constrained by the capital market to provide some capital of their own, hire all other factors of production, and a firm is simply a semi-permanent (transaction cost-saving) device which entrepreneurs create in order to implement their ideas efficiently (Parker and Stead, 1991).

It is of some interest to observe that a similar concept of the inner nature of the firm is proposed by Cowling and Sugden (1987), who write from a radical perspective which is otherwise quite at odds with Austrian economics. For Cowling and Sugden, the essence of the firm is control and initiative by top management and the boundary of the firm is the range of events or people which those managers can control. They may well thus have complete control over a subcontractor, even though for Williamson and Coase, the latter would be outside the firm.

## 2.9   Decision making

Mainstream economists (including many working in industrial economics) generally assume that firms, seeking maximum profits, are able quickly and effectively to select the best course of action. For economists in this tradition, the process(es) whereby decisions are made is simply ignored. Researchers in the field, however, report that decision making is a complex and flawed process. The account given by MIT's Herbert Simon, economics Nobel prizewinner in 1978 (Newel and Simon, 1972; Cyert and Simon, 1971) shows that people are far from the omniscient rationalists portrayed in neoclassical economics. The crucial points are (i) that no mortal ever, anywhere possesses 'all relevant information' and (ii) we mortals have limited capacities for processing new information. These are simply inescapable aspects of the human condition. It is thus false to assume that people are fully informed when making decisions. It follows that people are very unlikely indeed to make optimum decisions: finding the best outcome is, according to Simon, not so much like finding a needle in a haystack but like finding the sharpest needle in a haystack containing an unknown number of sharp needles.

How do people react to these limitations? Generally, they have 'rules of thumb', that is, standard operating procedures (SOPs) for particular circumstances. Thus instead of making a new decision about which garage to use every time the van needs servicing, a firm will have its regular garage. These SOPs, of course, represent past decisions, that is, solutions to previous problems. In a sense they are the organization's collective memory or wisdom. The second reaction to limited information processing is, when faced with a decision, to gather information but only to a limited extent. What is clear is that people do not assemble a comprehensive list of options, and then research and evaluate each one. Two factors limit the search. The first is that people tend to search for solutions to problems in familiar areas; only rarely are radical options examined. Second, search tends to stop when a satisfactory (rather than an optimum) solution is found. 'Satisfactory' means something which meets expectations. (Indeed, the notion of what is satisfactory determines which events are perceived as problems in that first place.) Two key phrases summarize Simon's interpretation of decision making: 'bounded rationality', meaning decision making with limited information, and 'satisficing' meaning the adoption of satisfactory (as opposed to optimum) solutions.

Simon's analysis of decision making was taken forward into economics by Simon himself and by colleagues including Cyert, March and Cohen. Cyert and March (1967) used the analysis to develop the behavioural theory of the firm. They argue that the goal of maximizing profits is too vague to be used, so that firms or more precisely the senior managers, set more tangible targets for each department: the sales department should increases sales by x per cent, the production department should reduce costs by y per cent and so on. Such targets will be generally set with respect to past achievements or industry norms and may therefore not be the best attainable. Firms typically therefore have an unquantified measure of 'slack' in the sense that performance could be raised with more effort or more information. The notion of slack was comprehensively investigated also by Harvey Leibenstein (1966), who termed it 'X-inefficiency'. Such slack is generally only reduced when the firm faces problems such as increasing competitive pressure or when there are other incentives to reduce costs.

Adherents of the behavioural theory have generated testable predictions by finding the SOPs of particular companies and tracing their reactions to events (Cyert and March, 1967) For economists in general, however, the implications of Simon's work are somewhat unsettling because without a comprehensive account of every firm's SOPs there is no longer a deterministic relationship between the firm and its environment. (SOPs, furthermore are modified in the light of experience.) The appearance of new competition, for example, would be predicted to evoke some response; but if profits and turnover, although reduced, remain satisfactory in the sub-jective view of the firm, it is possible that no action would be taken. Models which thus relate environmental changes to changes in performance (the S–C–P tradition, for example) would lose their abilities to make firm predictions. The mainstream riposte to behaviourism is the argument that while firms may not always maximize, those which fail so to do will in time die out, leaving only maximizers. The strength of this point remains unproven. In recent years, many economists (for example, Thaler, 1994) have begun to experiment to see just how people do in fact make decisions. For the most part, however, work from this programme remains unintegrated into industrial economics.

## 2.9.1   Decision making and the growth of the firm

These considerations have not deterred all analysts, some of whom have in effect translated Simon's account into a dynamic version of the way in which decision-making capacities can increase over time. An early writer here was Edith Penrose (1959) whose starting point was the proposition that the firm is a collection of resources: human and material. These resources have multiple potential uses, but are at any point in time committed to a given set of activities. Typically, however, some resources are under-employed in the sense that workers have many abilities not all of which are being tapped at any given time. Generally then the managers devise new projects to undertake; these may, of course, be mere modifications to existing lines of business, which exploit the untapped potential of the firm. The new projects then go through a process: at first they require much managerial attention because of their novelty, but as the firm gains experience the need for close supervision diminishes. Thus decisions about the new project can be taken more rapidly (SOPs develop) and the decisions themselves can be delegated to staff at more junior levels. This frees the time of senior managers who can then devote themselves to further projects. Thus the firm's portfolio of activities expands: the firm grows.

David Teece (1980, 1982) goes even further, defining a firm precisely as a reservoir of expertise or knowledge. That is, a firm is not a collection of resources as much as a body of knowledge about how resources may be used productively and profitably. This knowledge or expertise has several features. First, much of it is tacit, that is, it is not (and possibly cannot be made) explicit. This perspective clearly contrasts with the mainstream view that technology or expertise lies primarily in the public domain as a set of blueprints or patents which anyone with the desire can pick up and use. For Penrose and Teece and others in this tradition, blueprints and patents from public sources can only be used by those who already have experience in the relevant field. Second, expertise is collective, to a large extent being embodied in firms' SOPs. Third, it is fungible, that is, it is capable of being applied to different markets. Finally through the mechanism described by Penrose, it grows. Teece then attempts to explode the argument that growth could take the form of the creation of new, independent firms with the original firm leasing its assets to a franchisee. Drawing on the ideas of Coase and Williamson, Teece argues that such arrangements would be difficult to establish because of the transactions costs entailed. The argument here is reminiscent of that advanced by Buckley and Casson (1976) to explain multinationalization.

## 2.10   Conclusion

We have reviewed a number of theories about the nature of the firm and a synthesis would be difficult. Most of the work in this field is long on *ex post* explanation but difficult to falsify. Research relevant to managerial theories and P–A theory is taken up in Chapter 9. Potentially the most damaging ideas come from Simon and the behavioural school, whose work remains unintegrated into mainstream industrial economics.

## Guide to further reading

Chandler (1992) gives an excellent résumé of transaction costs and associated arguments; Buckley and Casson (1976) apply the discussion to multinational firms. Wildsmith (1973) provides a good review of managerial theories of the firm, while Penrose (1959) is a thought-provoking contribution in an Austrian vein. Kay (1993) attempts to bridge the gap between economics and more traditional management texts.

# 3 Determinants of industrial structure

## 3.1 Introduction

This chapter looks first at the structure of industries, beginning with the problems of defining markets and assessing the changing degrees of competition within them. We then look at attempts to find the determinants of structure before examining research on the effects of concentrated structures.

## 3.2 Measuring industrial structure

Before measuring the structure of an industry, one must first define it, that is, set its boundaries.

### 3.2.1 Defining a market

Auerbach (1988) lists three approaches. The first is to define industries in terms of the firms which are conscious of each other's actions. The virtue of this approach is that it captures something of the spirit of oligopolistic markets where, as we shall see later, firms make decisions in part on the basis of their assessments of their rivals' action. On the other hand, it is unsatisfactory since it rests upon purely subjective considerations: Auerbach, citing the British motorcycle industry of the 1960s as an example, notes firms can be quite unaware of competitors who are in reality poised to mount a strong competitive challenge. The next approach, attributed to Cournot (1838) and Marshall (1920), is to observe the area in which a product sells for a single price. The logic here is that products can be clearly allocated to different classes or groups and that the rule of one price can be used to distinguish geographical submarkets. This approach plainly pre-dates widespread product differentiation: it is now commonplace for nigh-identical products to sell at different prices, as a perusal of the shelves of any supermarket will reveal. The Marshall-Cournot approach would thus require us to define separate markets for own-brand cornflakes and Kellogg's cornflakes (or even Kellogg's cornflakes from supermarkets A and B, cornflakes from the corner shop and so on). It is clear that a problem with this approach is that it lacks a method for establishing whether and when products which are not identical can realistically be counted as constituting a single market. The third approach addresses this problem by advocating the use of cross-elasticities of demand to define groups of products: high cross-elasticities would indicate that consumers see items as close substitutes and thus part of one market while low values would suggest they were in separate markets. Since data on cross-elasticities is not generally available, this approach is rarely put into operation.

In the absence of ideal data to define industries, researchers in the UK and the rest of the EU often resort to the Standard Industrial Classification (SIC). This categorizes industries on the basis of production technology or product characteristics. Issued in 1992, the present SIC applies the EU's 'NACE' system of classification which is, in turn, broadly, consistent with the United Nations' International Standard Industrial Classification (ISIC). The SIC uses a combination of alphabetical and decimal structures, dividing economic activities first into 17 Sections (each denoted by a single letter of the alphabet from A to Q) and then into Subsections (denoted by two digits). Subsections divide into Divisions (denoted by two letters) which in their turn are divided into Groups (three digits—letters now being ignored) and then into Classes (four digits). In some cases there are five-digit subclasses. To illustrate, Class 22.31: Reproduction of sound recording is part of Group 22.3: Reproduction of recorded media which in turn is a component of Divison 22: Publishing, Printing and Reproduction of recorded media, itself a constituent of Subsection DE: Manufacture of Pulp and Paper; Publishing and Printing. This last is a part of Section D: Manufacturing. Besides showing the technological basis for the SIC, this example illustrates its chief problem from an economist's point of view, namely that it is rather broad. For example, Class 22.31 lumps together the quite distinct markets for jazz, orchestral music and other kinds, making any analysis of, say, the rock music industry somewhat difficult. Another weakness of classification systems is their tendency to be overtaken by technology; the 1980 SIC, for instance, made no mention of CDs and it is curious to see in the 1992 SIC publishing classed with paper manufacturing as publishing moves steadily toward greater reliance on electronic media. A third problem is their implication that the national economy constitutes a single entity: one might read, for example, that 34 000 workers were employed in Subclass 15.51/1: Liquid Milk and Cream Production in the UK, whereas in reality, liquid milk at least is likely to be sold through a number of distinct regional or local markets. Finally, the SIC allocates a plant to an industry on the basis of its principal activity. The problem here is that most industrial establishments produce several outputs simultaneously. Breweries, for example, sell their spent hops to makers of cattle cake, while the old yeast goes to make spreads. Because of this rule, the cattle feed industry is shown as being smaller than it ought to be. As we shall see in Chapter 12, competition authorities, who have a clear need to define markets, use a variety of methods.

### 3.2.2 Statistical indicators

Compared with the dearth of methods for delineating markets, economists are faced with a superabundance of statistical methods for measuring the structure of an industry. All, of course, use some measure of company size, and as a preliminary step a choice must be made between such indicators as employment, assets, sales or value added. The indicator selected can then be used to assess two dimensions of industrial structure, namely, the degree of concentration and the level of inequality between sellers. (In principle, the same measures can be applied to the buyers' side of a market, but since concentration among buyers is usually low this is not usually undertaken.) The principal measures are discussed below.

Inequality can be illustrated by the Lorenz curve (Fig. 3.1) in which producers are counted cumulatively in percentages along the horizontal axis, while market share (if sales are used as the selected indicator) is counted, again cumulatively, up the vertical axis. If all firms are of equal size, the situation can be described by the line AB. If, however, 90 per cent of the firms account for only 5 per cent of sales, while a few very large companies account for the bulk of sales, the curve would run through point D. Clearly situation ADB is more unequal than, say, AFB, which lies closer to the diagonal. AFB and ADB can be compared quantitatively by means of the Gini Coefficient, which expresses the area between the line and the diagonal as a proportion of the entire triangle ABC—plainly, the Gini Coefficient for ADB exceeds that for AFB. All statistical measures, however, have weaknesses, and inequality measures are no exception. One is the paradox that while the loss of market share by a small firm to a medium-sized one would

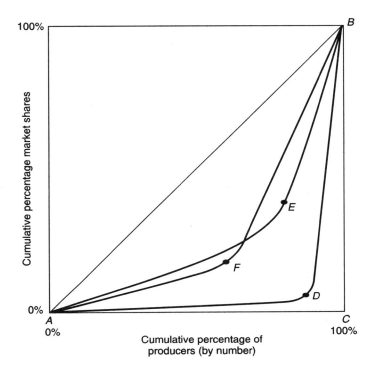

**Figure 3.1**  Illustrative Lorenz curve

raise the Gini Coefficient (more inequality), the absolute extinction of a small firm (with its sales either disappearing or being distributed evenly among the survivors) would in fact reduce the Gini Coefficient (because there is now less inequality among those who remain). Another weakness is evident from a comparison of AEB and AFB: while they might well have the same Gini Coefficient, the distribution of market shares differs in that in AFB the smallest firms have rather less of the market than they do in AEB.

Another dimension of market structure is the degree of concentration. One of the most common methods of representing this is the concentration ratio (CR), which expresses the total sales (assuming sales to be the chosen indicator) of the largest $n$ firms as a percentage of the industry's aggregate sales. Normally, to calculate concentration ratios, data such as those in Table 3.1, showing market shares in the EU car market in 1994, are needed. In this instance, a four-firm concentration ratio (CR4) would have been 54 per cent, while a CR5 would have been 66 per cent.

An alternative measure is the Herschman–Hirfindahl index (often called the H-index) which is the sum of the squared market shares of all firms in the industry.

$$H = \sum s^2 \qquad (3.1)$$

Thus in the case of the European car industry, the H-index would be 1077. If Volkswagen and General Motors were to merge, the score would rise to 1457, whereas a merger between Fiat and Renault would only raise the score to 1305. At the extremes, were the industry to fall into the hands of a monopolist, the index would be 10 000, while if it had 100 firms each with one per cent of the market, the index would be just 100. In effect, while the H-index uses the market

**TABLE 3.1   Shares of West European car market 1994 (first half)** (*Source*: adapted from *Financial Times*, 14 July, 1994)

| Company | Market share (%) |
|---|---|
| Volkswagen | 16 |
| General Motors | 13 |
| Peugeot Group | 13 |
| Ford | 12 |
| Fiat | 12 |
| Renault | 11 |
| BMW | 6 |
| Mercedes | 4 |
| Nissan | 3 |
| Toyota | 3 |
| Volvo | 2 |

shares of all firms, it allocates a greater weight to those of the larger firms. Thus, in Fig. 3.1, it would be able to distinguish between cases AEB and AFB: because it gives greater weight to data on larger firms, the H-index would give a higher score to AEB than it would to AFB.

A problem with the H-index is that it makes heavy demands for data; strictly, the size of every firm in the market must be known. By contrast, a CR4 may be calculated on the basis of the sales of the largest four firms together with information on total sales. In practice, any problems over missing data for smaller firms can be minimized by assuming that all sales (or value added, etc.) which are unaccounted for originate with either one firm or many. This would permit the calculation of an upper and a lower limit respectively for the true H-index.

Setting aside its data demands, the H-index can be shown to be superior to CRs on most important counts (as set out in Hannah and Kay, 1977). It would, first, rank ADB > AEB > AFB unambiguously while a CR measure would be unable to distinguish between two market concentration curves which fortuitously intersected at the vital point. Second, if (say) the sixth largest company were to raise its sales by taking custom from a smaller one, the H-index would necessarily rise whereas a CR would only change if $n \geq 6$. Similarly, a merger would raise the H-index but, again, would only affect a CR if one of the largest $n$ firms were involved. More analytically, as Sleuwaegen and Dehandschutter (1986) point out, any given CR$n$ is consistent with a range of values for the H-index. This range, moreover, widens as the CR$n$ value rises. For example, a CR4 of 0.4 is compatible with H-scores of between 500 and 1800, while a CR4 of 0.9 is compatible with H-scores ranging from 20 000 to 85 000! These analysts argue that any conclusion founded upon CR$n$s may be purely fortuitous. On the other hand, it must be appreciated that H-indices can also be ambiguous, in that the same value can be generated by different levels of concentration. For example, an industry dominated by one firm taking 30 per cent of sales, the others being infinitely small, would have an H-score of 900, but so would an industry with nine firms each taking 10 per cent of sales, the rest again being accounted for by extremely small firms.

Finally, Kwoka (1981) damns the CR technique by showing that the statistical significance of regression between concentration and profits can be greatly affected by the chosen $n$. Using data for US manufacturing for 1972, he demonstrates that when $n$ lies between 1 and 4, a significant and positive relationship emerges, but when $n$ exceeds 4, concentration ceases to be a significant influence. Although the critical $n$ is contingent on the data used, the substantive point remains that an essentially arbitrary selection of $n$ can make a fundamental difference to empirical findings. In general, it must be remembered that all measures of inequality and of concentration must, therefore, be used with an appreciation of their respective limitations.

## 3.3 Trends in concentration

In the UK, the most easily available data on concentration is provided in the annual Census of Production which is restricted to the manufacturing sector and which also omits foreign trade in manufactures. Analysis by the Department of Trade and Industry (1988) showed that during the 1970s, CR5s averaged just below 50 per cent and were, moreover, tending to rise. Direct comparisons of absolute levels of concentration with later years cannot, unfortunately, be made because of the adoption of a new SIC. What is clear, however, is that CR5s fell perceptibly from 1979 to 1984 on average, with most two-digit industries recording falls. The analysis proceeds to adjust for foreign trade by recalculating CR5s after adding imports to, and subtracting exports from, domestic production to establish the volume of domestic sales. There are, of course, problems with this procedure, notably its supposition that imports compete with domestic shipments; in reality, many imports are sold by domestic producers who simply have access to overseas plants as well as those in the UK. The adjustment may thus overstate the degree of competitiveness of markets. Nevertheless, the adjusted data show a fall in CR5s during the 1970s (as opposed to the rise shown in the unadjusted figures) and a second, steeper, fall in the early 1980s.

In the USA, Shepherd (1982) compares the position in 1980 with the eve of the Second World War and in the late 1950s by classifying industries into four categories: pure monopolies, dominant-firm industries (in which one company accounted for between 50 and 90 per cent of sales), tight oligopolies (in which CR4 exceeded 60 per cent, combined with medium-to-high barriers to entry, stable market shares and rigid prices or which were subject to regulation) and the rest – the last being the competitive sectors of the economy. Plainly, Shepherd sought other

TABLE 3.2  Trends in concentration in the UK (*Source*: DTI, 1988, Annex D)

| Series | Change in mean CR5 | |
|---|---|---|
| | 1970–79 | 1979–84 |
| Mean output-weighted CR5 | +0.5 | −1.6 |
| Adjusted for overseas trade | −4.8 | −5.5 |

TABLE 3.3  Trends in competition, USA 1939–80 (*Source*: Shepherd, 1982)

| Category | Share of marketed output (%) | | |
|---|---|---|---|
| | 1939 | 1958 | 1980 |
| Pure monopoly | 6.2 | 3.1 | 2.5 |
| Dominant firm | 5.0 | 5.0 | 2.8 |
| Tight oligopoly | 36.4 | 35.6 | 18.0 |
| Competitive sector | 52.4 | 56.3 | 76.7 |

evidence besides simple CRs: deregulation, import penetration and company behaviour were also used. His conclusion was that the competitive sector of the economy had increased its share dramatically during the 1960s and 1970s, with all the other three sectors losing ground.

## 3.4   Theories of industrial structure

Having attempted to quantify levels of concentration, the next task for economists is to explain them. The S–C–P approach starts from the position that structure is exogenous to economic behaviour. This does not imply that it is without a cause; rather the cause is sought in technological factors and their effects on economies of scale in the context of market demand. Briefly, the argument is that long-run average cost (LAC) curves are assumed to be L-shaped. This shape first reflects fixed costs which push up the average costs of small levels of output. As output rises, average costs fall but at a diminishing rate; eventually the savings in costs become imperceptibly small and the cost curve flattens out, with the least-cost level of output reflecting the importance of indivisible costs. The point at which the LAC curve effectively flattens out is termed the 'Minimum Efficient Scale' (MES) of production. If there are relatively large indivisibilities, average costs will be lowest at larger levels of output, that is, there will be economies of scale. Firms which operate at an uneconomically small level of output will have cost penalties and be forced to set prices above minimum levels and will then be undercut by rivals who operate at MES. In equilibrium, the market will be evenly divided between companies operating at MES, and thus the level of concentration will be determined, with industries which are characterized by economies of scale having higher concentration.

Corroborative evidence of the exogeneity of structural factors was supplied by Pryor (1972) who examined concentration levels (CR4) at both aggregate and industry level in manufacturing industries in 12 large industrial countries. He found that there was a strong correspondence between the ranking of industries by concentration levels in all 12 countries. A strong implication appears to be that similar forces (arguably technological ones) were at work. As an example, in Chapter 8 we shall see how rising plant costs have led to concentration in the semiconductor industry.

To test the theory more directly, economists have attempted to identify the MES for arrays of industries. How is this done? One method, the 'engineering approach', involved interviewing design engineers to obtain cost estimates for plant of different capacities (Scherer et al., 1975; Pratten, 1971; Haldi and Whitcomb, 1967). Scherer interviewed engineers in 12 'fairly representative major industries' while Pratten's UK questionnaire was directed toward capital-intensive industries. Several things became evident. First, as anticipated, economies of scale were available at the level of production plants, because of both construction and operating costs. The idea of L-shaped cost-curves was moreover confirmed, as was an association between economies of scale and concentration. The studies also found that sub-optimum production often involved cost penalties, though these were usually slight. Thus in motor vehicles, a volume of output of 500 000 units per year raises costs, as against an MES flow of 2 million units, by only 12 per cent (Pratten (1971) quoted in Johnson, 1993, p.127). The problem with this approach is that the costs are hypothetical rather than actual. The other broad approach (of which there are many variations) is to examine the sizes of plant at work in an industry and to pick one capacity arbitrarily (often that producing the median unit of output) to be the MES. A variant is to perform this examination on two separate occasions and to note which size-bands

TABLE 3.4  **Minimum Efficient Scale and concentration, UK 1970** (*Source*: Utton, 1982)

| (a)<br>Selected industries | (b)<br>MES as % of<br>UK market | (c)<br>CR5 implied by (b) | (d)<br>Actual CR5 |
|---|---|---|---|
| Motor cars | 50 | 100 | 98 |
| Cement | 10 | 50 | 89 |
| Petroleum refining | 10 | 50 | 95 |
| Beer | 3 | 15 | 64 |
| Bread | 1 | 5 | 77 |
| Shoes | 0.2 | 1 | 32 |

of plants are expanding their share of the industry's production. This size would then be the MES.

Having derived MES for each industry, the next step is to compare it with actual concentration. Theory might predict that an MES of 100 units when total sales of a product are 600 units should warrant a CR5 of 80 per cent, for example. As Table 3.4 shows, however, this is not often the case. In some industries, concentration levels are often far higher than would be warranted by production costs alone; the large players in many industries are far larger than is needed to reap plant-level economies of scale. At the same time, many industries contain firms and indeed plants which are below MES. In short, those who had hoped to find a simple and determinate relationship between MES, costs and concentration have been disappointed. Indeed, econometric studies of the determinants of structure (Levy, 1985; Weiss, 1974; Hart and Clarke, 1980), while often finding statistically significant relationships between MES and concentration, found the influence to be slight; as Levy notes, 'There is still substantial variation to be explained'.

Several ideas can be used to explain these data. Economists of the Austrian tradition would argue that the figures testify to the fact that markets are rarely in equilibrium, so that, for example, people buying from below-MES suppliers had yet to become aware of the existence of lower-cost producers. Economists whose interest centres upon the internal operations of firms have also pointed to the problems of attaining the hypothetical benefits of large-scale plant. Prais (1980), for example, notes the tendency for labour relations in large plants to be worse, while Leibenstein (1966) and Cyert and March (1967) have pointed to the tendency for costs to exceed theoretical minima under a range of conditions but particularly when competitive pressures are weak. Moreover a series of studies by the National Institute for Economic and Social Research (Steedman and Wagner, 1988) of plants of comparable size and age in Britain and Germany found great differences in productivity. These were explained by the skill-levels of the workforce, and their flexibility in moving between tasks. An implication is that a sub-MES plant could be more productive than an MES-plant, given the right organization of work. Such considerations could nullify the advantages of larger-scale operations, permitting sub-optimum plants to survive. Smaller companies may alternatively enjoy certain advantages on the demand side in terms of reputation or customer loyalty.

On the other hand, the notion that costs determine the scale of firms and thus concentration can be resuscitated by drawing attention to costs other than production costs; in finance, marketing and product development, for example. Thus, Utton (1982) reports that larger firms can borrow more cheaply than smaller ones for the same purposes. Again, Chapter 11 tells how design costs in aircraft manufacture produce economies of scale which dictate that only one or two companies can remain in the industry. Schmalensee (in Schmalensee and Willig, 1989, p.993) reports that almost no work has been done to determine the optimum size of firms.

## 3.5    Structure: endogenous or exogenous—or both

More recently John Sutton (1991) has put forward a rather simpler model which purports to explain market structure. He begins by disputing the traditional theory which predicts that low levels of concentration will occur when either sunk costs are low or the market is large. Sutton argues that this deterministic conclusion follows under conditions which hold only rarely. These are that the product should be homogeneous and unable to be differentiated, e.g. salt. In this case, sunk costs are determined exogenously by technology. As economies of scale arise, the industry will be forced to concentrate by either merger or exit. This is indeed the course which salt industries have pursued in all the countries which Sutton examines; the UK, USA, Germany and Japan. Where products can be differentiated or more precisely where advertising can be used to raise the product's value to consumers, an industry may become more concentrated than technology (MES) suggests. In other words some producers may advertise heavily and successfully, raise their market shares and make the industry more concentrated than an MES-based view would expect. Sutton organizes this process as a two-stage process or game (we examine games in Chapter 4) in which firms initially enter the industry, incurring exogenously-determined sunk costs to establish production facilities. In stage two of the game, they may elect to compete through advertising, incurring a second tranche of sunk costs. Where successful, these make the industry more concentrated. In markets where products may be differentiated and where any firm may offer more than one product, another route to concentration is opened up. This is product proliferation, whereby incumbents can offer greater and greater arrays of products. While markets may appear to have numerous competing brands, the number of companies involved may be quite small. Examples include detergents and breakfast cereals; to which we return in Chapter 5. The substantive prediction from this work is that concentration may be much higher than the Cournot-style logic of the equations above suggests. Specifically, concentration in Sutton's theory has only a lower bound (determined by exogenous sunk costs) but it has no *upper* limit. Sutton stresses that each industry has specfic factors which can modify the level of concentration. One is the strength of price competition, which may in turn be influenced by the authorities. For example, competition in sugar is often restrained for political reasons, governments frequently supporting both domestic beet-growers and former colonial producers. This leads to the persistence of structures that are rather less concentrated than are found in the salt industry.

Another factor is the actual history of the industry, that is, the order of the events by which the discoveries are made and the identities of the people who make them. Thus the first companies to make advertising work, sometimes through pioneering advertising on TV, established positions of leadership which endure decades later. Classic examples here are frozen food and mineral waters, where the leading brands (respectively Bird's Eye and Perrier) continue to command a premium prices. Relative positions in the frozen food market emerged after years of intense competitive struggle in the USA and UK. Markets which developed later such as Germany and Italy moved swiftly to equilibria similar to those seen in the USA and UK, bypassing the intermediate phase in which firms jockeyed for position. Sutton like Schmalensee (1989) stresses that each industry requires careful individual examination, rather than being subjected to uniform statistical analysis, and Sutton's work (which is restricted to the food and drink industries) is an outstanding example of this approach.

## 3.6  Conclusion

In this chapter we have looked at the determinants of industrial structure and the methods whereby concentration can be measured. Behind this lies the notion that structure influences the conduct and thus the performance of firms within those industries and hence determines their efficiency from the standpoint of the national economy. It is necessary now to look in more detail at competition between firms in concentrated industries, and Chapter 4 is accordingly devoted to this topic.

### Guide to further reading

Hay and Morris (1991) review past analysis of the determinants of structure well; Levy (1985) is an interesting application of a newer mathematical approach using lagged adjustment.

# 4 Oligopoly theory and games

## 4.1 Introduction

In Chapter 1 we looked briefly at the theory that the structure of an industry influences the conduct of the firms within it and thus its economic performance. This chapter examines that relationship in more detail. Structure, we recall, has two dimensions: internally, the number and size distribution of producers, and externally, the existence or height of barriers to entry. This chapter ignores entry. We are therefore assuming implicitly that the industries under analysis are 'blockaded'. This chapter is thus devoted to competition between incumbents. We know from elementary theory the economic performance to expect from two market structures: perfect competition leads to an optimum performance while monopoly leads to distortions. Most observed industrial structures, however, are oligopolistic, and here conduct and performance are not so self-evident. Industrial economists have accordingly tried to model such competition. We begin this chapter by looking at static, so-called 'reaction-curve' models before going on to look at game theory.

## 4.2 Reaction-curve models of oligopoly

The following models relate to situations in which firms produce homogeneous goods, are sheltered behind insurmountable entry barriers and are forbidden from explicit collusion. The models are set out as duopolies, but the conclusions hold for larger numbers of firms.

### 4.2.1 Cournot duopoly

Cournot's innovation was to specify the rules of behaviour of the two rivals. First, each is assumed to be a quantity-maker, that is, each firm is deemed to select its output volume. Second, each believes that its rival will not change its output: each thus discounts the possibility that the other will react to its own decisions. This belief about rivals' responses is termed a 'conjectural variation'; in principle it could be positive (A could believe that B will raise output as A raises its own) or negative (A might believe that B would respond to A's raising its output by cutting its output). Cournot opts for a conjectural variation of zero: A believes B will not respond at all.

How does this market structure and its conjectural variations generate equilibrium? Figure 4.1 shows output by two firms along the axes, so that any point represents their respective production volumes. It is possible to draw a curve which shows how much Firm A would produce, given an output decision from Firm B. Such a curve is called A's 'reaction curve'. Similarly we could draw B's reaction curve for given levels of production by A. For ease of exposition, we assume costs are constant and identical for A and B and that demand curves are linear. Firm A's reaction curve shows that at one extreme if B were to produce to the point where price equals marginal cost, B would take all the market and A would not find it worth

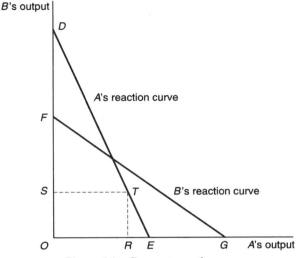

**Figure 4.1**  Cournot reaction curves

while to produce anything at all (OD). At the other extreme, if B were to stop production, A would be a monopolist and would produce half the competitive output (OE). These two points define A's reaction curve. Thus at intermediate points such as T, firm B produces OS, allowing A to select OR. In similar fashion, B's reaction curve can be similarly defined. Of course, a firm's profits vary along its reaction curve. A's profits are at maximum at OE, when A is the only producer.

At the intersection of the two curves, the market is in equilibrium; each is making maximum profit, given the output of the other. Such an equilibrium is termed a Nash equilibrium, after Nobel Laureate John Nash who analysed games and their equilibria. The characteristics of a Nash equilibrium are that (1) each firm is following its best course of action, given its expectation about its rival's actions while (2) those expectations are indeed fulfilled. Firms' expectations about each other thus interlock and neither has an incentive to change.

At this equilibrium, with a linear demand curve, output amounts to two-thirds of competitive output with the market being shared equally. (Equal shares reflect the assumption that costs are identical for the two firms; differing costs would lead to unequal shares.) Output thus lies between the extremes of competition and monopoly. More generally, the Cournot model shows that when there are $n$ identical firms, each has a market share of $1/n+1$ and that as $n$ rises, prices, profit and output move closer to the levels that would occur under perfect competition.

Cournot's model has two principal strengths. First, it is in principle falsifiable; it makes concrete predictions about output, profits and prices. Importantly, the Cournot model suggests that oligopoly shares in the sins of monopoly, to some (variable) degree: buyers are overcharged and undersupplied to an extent determined by the level of concentration in the industry. This prediction provided a basis for much early work in industrial economics, that is, the testing of relationships between structure and profits.

Second, Cournot can be interpreted as having asked the right questions in his attempt to model oligopolist's behaviour. He saw the need to specify their range of options (changing output), their beliefs about other firms and their strategies for reacting to action by others. Cournot's model does, however, have weaknesses. One is that while one player reacts to the moves of its rival, it discounts the possibility that its rival will react to its own moves. This is inconsistent; it is also erroneous since in the model other firms actually do react. The second weakness is that players have no capacity for learning; they do not change their ideas in the light of events. If the firms were able to 'play' the Cournot model several times, it is possible that they could learn how to collude, a scenario that we investigate later in the chapter. The third weakness is the anomalous implication that, in any situation except equilibrium, the firms' products sell for different prices, yet they are by assumption homogeneous. This point was taken up by Bertrand.

## 4.2.2   Bertrand's model

Appearing in 1883 as a critique of Cournot, Bertrand's model of oligopoly differs in only one respect from Cournot's: the firms are deemed to be price-takers rather than quantity-makers. The effects of this modification are drastic: all similarities with monopoly are erased as the incumbents engage in ferocious price warfare. The result is that the industry has prices, output and profits which are the same as under perfect competition. To see this, consider the options open to firm B when firm A has selected its profit-maximizing output and price. Since the products are homogeneous, the best tactic for B is to undercut A by a small margin and take all its customers. A's best option is to reply in kind, undercutting B. This process ends, logically, when neither can go any lower, that is, when economic profits are zero (assuming once again identical costs). If oligopolists behave like those in Bertrand's model, Cournot's alarmist predictions can be dismissed as baseless.

Bertrand equilibrium can be depicted by means of a reaction-curve graph as that shown in Fig. 4.2. Unlike the previous graph, this diagram is drawn in price-space: showing the prices of the two firms. For any price by A, B will opt for one just lower. Consequently, B's reaction curve lies below and is slightly flatter than the 45 degree line. A's lies, conversely, just above that line. The reaction curves intersect (the model comes to equilibrium, ON) where prices equal marginal and average costs and profits are just normal.

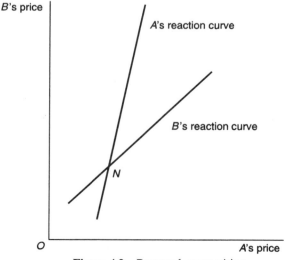

**Figure 4.2**   Bertrand competition

### 4.2.3   von Stackelberg: leadership and followership

The German economist Heinrich von Stackelberg (1934) used the principle of reaction functions to develop a model in which oligopolists are not identical; rather, one plays the role of leader while the others are the followers. In this model, conjectural variations thus vary across firms. While most firms (or in a duopoly, one firm) have Cournot conjectural variations, that is, operating with the assumption that rivals will remain inactive, one firm, the leader, say, firm A, perceives that its rival follows a Cournot rule but is not itself bound by such a rule. Thus firm A can select its profit-maximizing output in the knowledge that B will simply acquiesce. Firm A can in effect place firm B anywhere along the latter's (Cournot) reaction curve.

To examine this, we introduce the principle of iso-profit curves. In a Cournot diagram which is quantity-space, such curves show the combinations of output by the two duopolists which would generate a given level of profit. Like consumers' indifference curves, they resemble contour lines. The peak of firm A's profit hill lies at the point where it produces as a monopolist, with zero output coming from B. Greater or lesser output from A, even with no output from B, would diminish A's profit, generating iso-profit lines of lower value. Similarly, movements by B along its reaction curve away from the horizontal axis imply less output by A and increasing output from B, leading to lower profit for A. A's iso-profit contours thus reach a peak at M. (Analogous contours could naturally be drawn for B.) In the von Stackelberg model (Fig. 4.3), A selects the point on B's reaction curve that gives A the highest profit, that is, which is tangent to the best iso-profit curve: point M. Thus A selects output level OP (off its own reaction curve) knowing that B will sill select OQ.

### 4.2.4   An integration: Cowling and Waterston

It is possible to formulate the principle underlying the above models in a more general way. We assume there are *n* firms in a blockaded industry producing a homogeneous good with a given level of fixed cost *F* (per production period) and a constant marginal (and thus average variable)

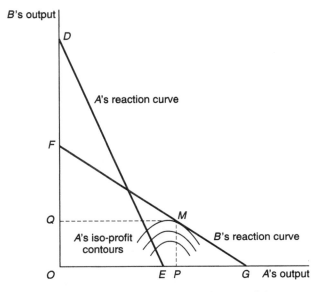

**Figure 4.3**   von Stackelberg model

cost of $c$. We start with a Cournot model (Lukacs, 1995) in which firms select their output levels rather than prices. The demand curve may be written in inverse form as $P = p(Q)$ where price is $P$ and industry output is $Q$. (The inverse form is consistent with the graphic representation in that price is the dependent variable.) Each firm's output is denoted $q$. Thus each firm's profit $!$ is

$$! = pq - cq - F \qquad (4.1)$$

To maximize profit, each firm sets Equation (4.1) at its maximum value

$$\frac{d!}{dq} = \frac{dp}{dQ}\frac{dQ}{dq}q - c = 0 \qquad (4.2)$$

The terms in Equation (4.2) require explanation. This describes the perceived marginal revenue of a change in output. The first element, $dp/dQ$, relates the price change experienced by the industry as a whole when output changes by one unit. The second, $dQ/dq$, is the relationship between a change in the industry's total output and a change in the output of the firm. This is no more or less than the firm's conjectural variation (CV). Indeed this can be decomposed:

$$\frac{dQ}{dq} = \frac{dq}{dq} + \frac{d(Q - q)}{dq} \qquad (4.3)$$

That is, the change in the industry's output is equal to the change in the first firm's output plus the change by the rest of the industry. The Cournot CV is that the second element is zero; $dQ/dq = 1$. Thus, in a Cournot market, we can derive from Equation (4.2):

$$p - c = \frac{dp}{dQ}q \qquad (4.4)$$

Divide through by $p$ and multiply the top and bottom of the right-hand side by $Q$:

$$\frac{p - c}{p} = \frac{-dp}{dQ}\frac{Q}{p}\frac{q}{Q} \qquad (4.5)$$

The first two terms on the right-hand side are, of course, the (inverse of the) industry's elasticity of demand, while the third term, $q/Q$, is the market share of the firm in question. Equation (4.5) thus says that a firm's profit margin $(p-c/p)$ will be related to its market share and (negatively) to the elasticity of demand. (This equation is not a causal relationship: a higher market share will not, from these equations, lead to a higher profit margin.) Concisely:

$$\frac{p - c}{p} = \frac{s}{e} \qquad (4.6)$$

If all the firms are the same size, each one's market share will be $1/n$, giving us:

$$\frac{p - c}{p} = \frac{1}{ne} \qquad (4.7)$$

Thus when firms have Cournot conjectures, price-cost margins are negatively-related to the number of firms in the industry and the elasticity of demand.

Other conjectures can be included by rewriting Equation (4.3) as $dQ/dq = \lambda$ where $\lambda = d(Q - q)/dq$ that is, the response of the rest of the industry to a quantity change by the first firm. This could go into Equation (4.6) so that:

$$\frac{p - c}{p} = \frac{s(1 + \lambda)}{e} \qquad (4.8)$$

In Bertrand competition, $\lambda$ is $-1$ because price cuts by one firm lead to the temporary but total replacement of its rival's production. $p - c/p$ is thus zero because there are no excess returns in

Bertrand competition. Price–cost margins, it may be noted, are also termed the Lerner index of market power, since they can be used as indicators of such power.


## 4.3   Structure and profit: initial findings

The reaction-curve models discussed generate differing predictions. In particular, Cournot suggests a 'concentration effect': that as concentration rises, price–cost margins will widen. By this logic, monopoly is not an isolated case but is rather one end of a spectrum, with inefficiency rising incrementally with concentration. This idea provided a basis for the research programme into the links between concentration and profitability initiated by Professor Joe Bain (1951). Bain examined 42 industries for differences in profit rates. The sample was determined by data availability, since information on the two variables was not obtainable for the entire sector. Some industries were rejected on the grounds that they served local rather than national markets, a factor which would render concentration indicators calculated on a national basis inaccurate. The indicators used were after-tax company income over net worth (companies' capital employed minus net borrowing) while the concentration measure was CR8. Entry barriers were ignored. The principal results are shown in Table 4.1.

The principal results were a more or less U-shaped relationship between the CR8 and profits: both high and low rates of concentration produced higher rates of profit than rates between 30 and 70 per cent. Bain and subsequent researchers ignored the lower peak (which was, in truth, based on evidence from only a few industries) and focused upon the top end of the data, where higher concentration was associated with higher profit.

Regressing CR8 on average profit, Bain found a non-significant relationship with $r = 0.33$ (implying an r-squared of 0.11). He nevertheless argued that a threshold could be seen at $CR8 = 70$ per cent. The hypothesis that the two groups had different rates of profits could not be rejected at the 99 per cent confidence level: Cournot's concentration effect appeared.

This research can clearly be criticized for its naivety: for example, it ignores barriers to entry, it assumes that reported profits correspond to economic profits and it uses CR8 to measure concentration. During the 1960s, moreover, economists were beginning both to see greater complexity in the relationships between structure, conduct and performance and to appreciate the limitations of reaction-curve models. They began to make use of a new approach: game theory.

TABLE 4.1   **Concentration and profit rates in US manufacturing 1936–40** (*Source*: Bain, 1951)

| CR8 (%) | No. of industries | Average net profit rate (%) |
|---|---|---|
| 90–100 | 8 | 12.7 |
| 80–89 | 11 | 10.3 |
| 70–79 | 3 | 16.3 |
| 60–69 | 5 | 5.8 |
| 50–59 | 4 | 5.8 |
| 40–49 | 2 | 6.3 |
| 30–39 | 5 | 6.3 |
| 20–29 | 2 | 10.4 |
| 10–19 | 1 | 17.0 |
| 0–9 | 1 | 9.1 |

## 4.4  Game theory in industrial economics

Bertrand's logic leads to a conundrum: oligopolists will compete fiercely until all economic profit is gone, despite the intuitive plausibility of cooperation. Tirole (1988) calls this the Bertrand Paradox: oligopolists are sitting on a powder-keg of a potential price war; how can they prevent it going off? It is indeed persuasive to argue that Bertrand duopolists would quickly realize the opportunities which they were throwing away and learn to collude. Indeed, there are many situations which seem to require economists to model not one decision or rounds of decisions but a long sequence of decisions. The tool for this task is game theory, an approach that gained in importance in many branches of economics, including industrial economics, in the 1970s and 1980s.

In game theory, 'players' are given a range of possible 'moves' (such as choosing a volume of output). Depending on the moves of other players, and perhaps the general environment (such as the state of the economic cycle), each player receives a payoff (profit). A game should specify the sequencing of moves; players may move sequentially as in chess or simultaneously. A game must also specify the information which players have at all stages. In some games, such as chess, it is quite clear what one's opponent has done, while in many business situations, moves such as giving discounts to certain customers or the development of new products may be kept secret. Another aspect of information is the payoffs that players receive, because if you know your opponents' incentives you will be able to predict their decisions. In principle, games divide into those in which players can make explicit and enforceable agreements to cooperate and those in which such cooperation is impossible. Since cooperation between competing firms in the real world is a criminal offence, industrial economists focus on non-cooperative games. It is also conventional to ignore the possibility of altering other players' payoffs by offering a 'side-payment' or bribe, since this is also not common business practice. Communication thus goes only through the play itself.

As an introduction, let us represent a duopoly as a game in which the rivals choose between two prices: high and low. (One drawback of game theory is that choices are easiest to represent in terms of discrete choices (High or Low) rather than continuous choices over a range.) A high price will yield big profits as long as the rival also charges high prices, since the pair will then act as a cartel. On the other hand, charging a high price when your rival sets a low one leaves you with no sales at all, resulting in a loss. A low price which is matched by the rival leaves both firms earning just normal profit, that is, zero excess returns. The best result, however, comes from a choice of a low price while the rival selects a high price, thus pricing itself out of the market and leaving the first player with large profits. This can be shown in a payoff matrix as in Table 4.2. Firm A's choices are in the columns, firm B's in the rows, so resulting in a four-cell matrix. In each cell, A's payoff is top right while B's is bottom left.

TABLE 4.2   Payoff matrix for a duopoly

|  |  | Firm A's price | |
|---|---|---|---|
|  |  | Low | High |
| Firm B's price | Low | 0    0 | −10    140 |
|  | High | 140    −10 | 100    100 |

Consider A's choices. If A selects Low, its payoffs (reading down the column) are zero or 140 depending on what B does. A's payoffs from High are analogously minus 10 or 100. It is plain that Low is better than High whatever B's selection. The word to describe these choices is 'dominated': Low dominates High. Now consider B's position. It is in fact the same: if B goes for Low, its payoffs are zero or 140 while High yields minus 10 or 100. For B also, Low dominates High. The outcome is easily seen: both players select Low and opportunities for excess profits are thrown away. In effect, we have a Bertrand-style outcome. This outcome is, of course, a Nash equilibrium and in contexts like the above is often termed 'Bertrand–Nash'.

(The above is an industrial economics version of a game often described in non-economic literature as the 'Prisoners' Dilemma'. This imaginary situation involves two people, say, Bonnie and Clyde, being held on suspicion by police who have no concrete evidence against them. The police can only secure conviction by means of confession(s) and their only tactic is plea-bargaining: if a suspect confesses and thus denounces his or her partner, he or she will get a light sentence. If one remains silent while the other confesses, that suspect receives a heavy sentence. Collaboration is prevented by the pair being held in different cells. If, however, both remain silent, they will be released. As in the duopoly case, confessing dominates remaining silent; both confess and receive medium sentences.)

A little reflection suggests a host of modifications which could be made to the above game which could permit the participants to collaborate or at least to generate outcomes other than Bertrand. One would be to allow the players to move in sequence rather than simultaneously. This would permit a Stackelberg solution to emerge, with the leader selecting its output and the follower accepting that as a datum and selecting its own output volume accordingly.

A sequential game can be set out in the form of a tree, as in Fig. 4.4. Here player 1 makes the first decision, moving from the top 'node' which thus bears a 1 in a circle. The two options are labelled A1 and B1. Each leads to another node where player 2 makes a decision having observed A's decision. B's choices are also labelled; while B's choices are the same at the two lower nodes (in each case, A2 and B2), the results or payoffs differ, depending on A's prior action. The payoffs are shown in the two rows of figures along the bottom, player 1's above player 2's.

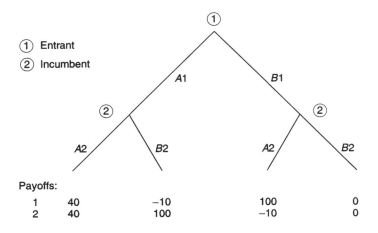

**Figure 4.4**   Game tree

### 4.4.1  Multi-stage games or 'supergames'

Another possibility would be to consider the duopoly as a two-stage game in which players first choose a level of capacity and then compete on price; that is, they 'dump' their output on the market, relying on competition between buyers to establish the price. Such second-stage competition resembles Bertrand behaviour but the two stages of the game together are more similar to Cournot (Kreps and Scheinkman, 1983). In such a game, rivals commit themselves to a certain capacity before engaging in Bertrand price warfare. Certainly, if players can foresee the exact implications of decisions at the start of stage one, then the game in effect reduces or 'folds back' to a one-stage game. Nevertheless, this two-stage perspective suggests one insight, namely that firms may deliberately take steps to mitigate price competition in the second stage by limiting capacity in stage one. This insight is rather more illuminating if we interpret 'capacity' more generously to include other options. Thus firms may take other steps to moderate second-stage price competition by differentiating their product through R&D or advertising, for example.

Another way in which the Prisoners' Dilemma/Duopoly game may be modified to permit collaboration is to allow the players to play many 'rounds' or stages, making a 'supergame'. Such a development would allow firms to learn about each other and thus, perhaps, to engage in tacit collusion. Industrial economists have expended much effort researching precisely this possibility, and their work uses another tranche of specialist terminology. Thus whereas players in a 'one-shot' game have a choice, a player in a supergame has a 'strategy'. In supergames, players have to make a series of choices (normally one in each stage). Even when the choice relates to the same variable (for example, price) in every stage, choice may vary between high and low. The choices will reflect the player's payoffs, information and (often) the record of the game to date. In principle it is possible to specify in advance what a player will do in given circumstances, that is, to compile a list of 'if ... then ...' statements describing the player's action under all circumstances. Such a compilation is a strategy.

The principal innovation which a supergame brings is dynamism: the ability of players to make decisions during the game rather than just one at the outset. This in turn permits players to explore their rivals' behaviour and to build relationships of cooperation with rivals even when explicit cooperation is forbidden, and indeed the only form of communication permitted is that which uses the game itself. Intuitively, it is perhaps easy to imagine that with sufficient rounds, players could develop an understanding of their opponents to such a degree that they trust one another. Trust is important because in the Prisoners' Dilemma, if Bonnie remains silent she risks long imprisonment if Clyde falls to temptation and confesses. Likewise in the duopoly game, trust is required before either firm deviates from its dominant strategy and opts for High, because it then risks being driven into loss by a self-seeking opponent. Trust is nevertheless a possibility in that all players can conceive that opponents may wish to cooperate, that is, a strategy of going invariably for a Bertrand–Nash choice (Low) is only one of many conceivable strategies. The alternative is clearly to begin with the expectation of cooperation by playing High in round 1 to see if your opponent will respond with a cooperative High. This raises the question of what move our first player should make if and when the opponent 'cheats' and plays a Low. Clearly it would be naive to continue with High since the opponent could just carry on exploiting the situation. A better idea would be to 'punish' the opponent, by, for example, playing a 'trigger strategy' in which our player reverts to Low in the next round and plays Low for the rest of the supergame. Thus with a trigger strategy, players give their opponents one chance to cooperate; the first defection by the rival leads to unrelenting, destructive price-cutting for ever more. Another, less extreme, possibility is to play 'Tit for Tat' (TFT) whereby 'punishment' is confined to one round: the strategy is to play High if the rival played High in the previous round but to play Low if the rival defected and played Low in the previous round. The intention of a TFT player is to let the opponent know that defection will bring negative consequences but that the TFT player is always willing to rebuild the relationship and return to cooperating. It is important to stress that cooperation and trust (however much they appeal to our intuitive understanding of everyday life in which cooperation is a common feature) run entirely contrary to the spirit of competition and egoism upon which both economics and the theory of non-cooperative games are based. The possibility of its emergence is thus due to the rather special circumstances of supergames.

More rigorous analysis (Kreps *et al.*, 1982; Tirole, 1988) of supergames shows that the possibility of collaboration between duopolists (or prisoners) in a supergame is not so easily attained. Indeed, when the game is repeated a finite (*and known*) number of times, cooperation fails to emerge altogether. To see this, consider a duopoly as shown in Table 4.2 played 26 times. After playing for 25 times, the players evaluate their tactics for the last round. Now the game is reduced simply to the one-shot game set out in Table 4.2, so A has to choose between Low (which would bring 0 or 140) and High which brings −10 or 100. A is moreover aware that B has the same payoffs. A thus knows that B's rational choice is to cheat. In such circumstances it is foolish for A to play High and be driven into loss. The only defensible choice is to go for Low. B, employing the same logic, also plays Low. Thus both cheat in the last stage. The logic is clear enough: strategies like TFT and Trigger are designed both to punish past defection and to threaten to punish further acts of defection with a view to rebuilding cooperation in the future. However, in the last game there is no future: punishments and threats have no effect, and players play Bertrand–Nash price warfare. The problem is, however, rather greater than in the last stage. If the play in the last stage is a foregone conclusion, how should one play in round 25, the penultimate stage? Haplessly, the same arguments apply again: if 26 is unalterable, then round 25 in effect has no future which can be influenced, so neither player has reason to offer cooperation in 25. This argument moves remorselessly through the stages by a process known as 'backwards induction': if 25 is a foregone conclusion, there is no reason in 24 either to offer cooperation or to respond positively to the other's offer of cooperation, and so on. Thus in a repeated but finite game, cooperation cannot arise.

Naturally the alternative to a finite game is an infinitely-repeated game. This raises one immediate difficulty: all positive payoffs become equal! In Table 4.2, 140 gained an infinite number of times is equal to 100 gained an infinite number of times: both have infinite value. To restore differences between payoffs (as well as to add realism), we introduce a discount factor which reduces the value of payoffs from later stages. This can reflect either time preference or the possibility that the game will end. The significant consequence of having a game with an infinite number of stages is that backwards induction fails to work, allowing threats-and-punishment strategies like TFT to operate without hindrance. This finally permits tacit collusion to emerge.

The conclusion that infinitely repeated games permit collusion is subject to a proviso about the discount factor. If a player is playing a trigger strategy (which is known to the opponent), this gives the opponent a choice between an infinitely long but discounted stream of payoffs of 100 against one round of lucrative cheating yielding 140, followed by an infinitely long (but discounted) stream of zeros. The second option might be the more attractive if the discount factor were sufficiently high, that is, when at least one of the players places a high premium on payments in the present and has relatively little interest in the future. For such a player, the instant gain of 140 might be more attractive than gains in future rounds. Whether the rival retaliates or not, such a player would go for Low: the Nash equilibrium.

In one sense, the thesis that infinitely long supergames permit cooperation is too successful. With one-shot and finitely repeated games, there was only one equilibrium: ruthless competition. In infinitely repeated supergames, this is no longer so. Many equilibria are possible, depending on the strategies played. If one player plays TFT while the other has a random strategy of playing High and Low unpredictably, the pair could win virtually any set of total payoffs. At one extreme, if the non-TFT player were to cooperate all the time, the two could behave like a joint monopolist, while at the other, the non-TFT player could play Low continually, resulting in a Bertrand–Nash outcome. Thus the infinitely repeated supergame does not predict any definite equilibrium but rather a multiplicity of possible equilibria. In other words, infinitely long supergames can have more or less any outcome, from monopoly profit for one player through shared profits of any level to monopoly profit for the other. This conclusion is known as the 'folk theorem' since no individual model-builder claims credit for it.

### 4.4.2 Credible and non-credible threats

It is important to understand how cooperation develops in supergames. The key idea is that players signal or communicate through their moves: they tell their opponents how ready they are to cooperate and how seriously they view defection. These signals, of course, come in the form of actions. Players do not explain how seriously they view defection, and they inflict punishment in the form of retaliatory defection. Moves in the game are at once responses to past action by a rival and threats and promises about the future. Players use these threats and promises to mould the behaviour of their rivals. As we shall see later in this book, there are situations in which players may wish not so much to build cooperation in which benefits are shared (as in the Prisoners' Dilemma) but to have rivals desist from Bertrand-style aggression largely if not wholly to the benefit of one party. An example is entry: a firm which has a market to itself may wish to deter potential competitors from entering. Success is an absence of competition, but could not really be described as cooperation. In such circumstances, an important role is played by threats; the incumbent has no rewards to offer for cooperation as would be the case in a Prisoners' Dilemma: the player can only suggest that failure to cooperate at stage one (i.e. entering) will be costly to the entrant. Typically, an incumbent could threaten price war in the event of entry. Such a policy would, of course, be damaging to the incumbent as well. In game theory, however, it is normal to assume that all players know each others' payoffs, so the potential entrant would know how damaging price war would be to the incumbent (as well as to the potential entrant). Figure 4.5 shows the data.

In Fig. 4.5, player 1, the potential entrant, chooses (first node) between entry and staying out. In the light of this choice, player 2, the incumbent, chooses between accommodating to entry, i.e. maintaining prices, reducing quantity produced and accepting a lower profit, or starting a price war. The payoffs at the bottom show that an entrant who stays out, earns nothing while the incumbent earns 400 from keeping prices high, that is, conducting business as usual, and 0 from price warfare (which would, of course, make little sense if player 1 had stayed out). If player 1 enters, player 1's returns (and those of player 2) depend on the response of player 2: both earn 200 if player 2 accommodates to entry but nothing if player 2 initiates price warfare. From a first glance, it seems that player 2 threatens player 1 with price war in retaliation for entry; 'entry will achieve nothing', player 2 seems to say, 'because I shall fight'. Closer examination shows a different picture. If player 1 chooses to enter, player 2 has no incentive to retaliate, player 2's best tactic is to accommodate. Price war does not pay, quite simply, once player 1 has entered. Thus player 2's apparent threat is empty. Carrying it out is more damaging to player 2 than is accommodation. Moreover, this fact is known to player 1, because by assumption all players know all payoffs and strategies, so player 1 can so to speak examine player 2's books. Thus 2's threat is described as 'non-credible' and can hence not form part of an equilibrium for the supergame. The principle of credible and non-credible threats is one to

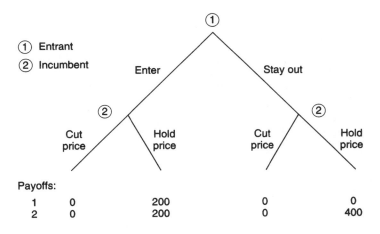

**Figure 4.5**  Game tree of entry and retaliation

which we shall return later in Chapter 6 when we examine entry and its deterrence. At this point, it may be useful to summarize the principal findings of game theory for models of oligopolistic competition. These are that oligopolists in a blockaded market may cooperate, that is restrain price-competition if:

- their interaction extends over an infinitely long period (or, more practically, its end cannot be seen)
- the players have a degree of time preference
- the players also have a degree of uncertainty about each other's likely actions.

## 4.5  Empirical tests of game theory

### 4.5.1  Experiments

To test the ideas of the model-builders, some researchers recruited subjects actually to play some games. One such experimenter was Robert Axelrod (1981) of the University of Michigan. He invited game theorists (experts in the field!) working in a variety of contexts such as political science as well as economics to submit strategies to him for use in a finitely repeated game of the Prisoners' Dilemma. To the 14 entries received, he added another, 'Random' (which played cooperation and confessing randomly) and then, using a computer, played each strategy against every other. 'The highest average score', he reports, 'was attained by the simplest of all strategies submitted, TIT FOR TAT.' A second invitation for strategies brought in 62 entries which were likewise played against each other; again, TFT gained the highest average score. What Axelrod's experiment demonstrates is that TFT is successful in eliciting cooperative behaviour from players with other strategies. Axelrod describes it as being 'nice' (that is, having a predisposition to cooperate), yet provocable (defection by a rival receives punishment), yet forgiving (TFT always permits cooperation to be re-established).

For model-builders, the success of TFT presented a problem because it is essentially a non-rational strategy. If one is playing against a TFT player, it is perfectly possible to predict that player's moves and thus to play Low when the TFT player plays High (so scooping the market and making high profits) and then to defend oneself against the ensuing punishment by playing Low in the next round. In effect, this means playing Low all the time, gaining a stream of payoffs of alternate 140s and zeros. The TFT player, however, does rather worse: collecting a string of alternate zeros (when both plays Low) and –10s (when TFT plays high and is attacked by a Low from the rival). TFT *offers* cooperation, so that both could get good payoffs (a stream of 100s for each), but there is no guarantee that opponents will take up this offer. It is rational for the other player to cooperate (a stream of $100 + 100 + 100$ > a stream of $140 + 0 + 140 + 0$, etc.) but without a guarantee of cooperation the TFT player runs the risk of ruin. In other words, when confronted with a TFT player, it is rational to play along with them, but it is not rational to be the TFT player oneself. Clearly it would be a successful strategy if played, but the logical problem was that no one would rationally adopt it.

Kreps *et al.* (1982) suggested an explanation. It is that a good strategy would be to *pretend* to be TFT. That is, one could behave in a TFT fashion, while reserving the possibility of playing another strategy; basically, that of playing a Nash Low at every move. Thus one would escape the problem of being entirely predictable (and thus exploitable) but at the same time one would go through the TFT motions of offering cooperation and punishing defection. The effect would be that one's rival could not be certain that one was truly TFT or not. More precisely, we build the model by inputing some distrust to the second player: who notes A's TFT behaviour but, we argue, is not convinced by it but entertains the suspicion that A may only be pretending and could revert to continual Low any moment. Kreps *et al.* showed that a small degree of uncertainty on the part of the second player would be enough to tempt the second player into cooperation with the suspected TFT player. In fact they modelled a finitely repeated game, and showed that B's best strategy depended on the discount factor, the number of stages yet to be played and the probability that player A was really a TFT player. Setting aside the first two (which relate to the finite nature of their supergame) the argument is that (i) cooperation by B is, for B, a strategy that pays, as we saw above while (ii) for A, Kreps and Wilson (1982) show that TFT is a dangerous strategy if and only if it is 'common knowledge' that A is a TFT-player (and is thus predictable and exploitable). 'Common knowledge' means that (in this context) (i) A is TFT with certainty, (ii) B knows A is TFT, (iii) A knows that B knows that A is TFT (and so on). In other words, something is common knowledge if it is 'in public domain': all players know this fact and all know that others know it. Kreps and Wilson show that in any other circumstances, that is, if there is any uncertainty about A's strategy, then the risks to A decline very substantially and it pays both A to pretend to be TFT and B to pretend to be deceived and thus to cooperate permanently with A. The introduction of doubt thus promotes TFT (or rather the appearance of TFT) to a rational (and successful) strategy. The importance of this idea is that such a situation is far more realistic in that usually firms' strategies are commercial secrets and thus not in the public domain, or indeed, that information about rivals (as about anything) is limited. The effect of uncertainty on decision making in the context of game-theoretic models is something to which we shall return in Chapter 6 on entry barriers.

### 4.5.2  Empirical tests of game theory: econometric evidence

In general, testing of game theory is hampered by the folk theorem: supergames can lead to an infinite range of payoffs. Supergames thus make such a wide range of predictions that it is almost impossible to reject it: any evidence will be compatible with the proposition that a given market resembles a supergame model. Nevertheless, results have been reported by Margaret Slade (1987). She analysed competition among petrol retailers in a part of the city of Vancouver during the summer of 1985. Daily data were obtained on retail and wholesale prices and volumes of three grades of petrol, for sales from 13 petrol stations owned by 10 firms. Gross margins could thus be computed from the price data. The firms were divided into 'majors' and 'independents', which were taken to operate in distinct markets. The price data showed periods of stability, interspersed with periods of turbulence in which prices fell rapidly and then recovered. From mere inspection of the data, however, it was not possible to tell whether turbulence reflected (a) changes in demand or (b) Bertrand-style price warfare. In (a), firms are reacting to stimuli from outside the market in the manner of perfect competitors; in (b) they are behaving more like players in a game-theory model. The implications are that if turbulence is (a), then periods of stability are periods of stable demand with price competition, but if turbulence is actually (b) then periods of stability are times of restrained Cournot-style competition. Slade concluded that the actual outcome of the Vancouver petrol game in terms of the price–cost margins that stations actually attained were well below perfect collusion (joint monopoly) levels but above Bertrand–Nash competitive levels. There was thus evidence for Cournot-style restrained competition. She also concluded that the process of price changes were broadly compatible with the proposition that firms were reacting to the price changes of rivals on an incremental basis (percentage point for percentage point) rather than merely all following the same environmental stimuli such as a fall in demand. Game theory thus seemed to emerge from the study with some support. Rees (1993) investigating price competition in the market for salt in the UK likewise found behaviour to resemble the predictions of game theory. Casual observation would suggest that the market for bulk electricity in which two major producers offer prices for every half-hour of the day should also provide a test-bed for game theory.

### 4.5.3    Other resolutions of the 'Bertrand Paradox'

An insight due to Tirole (1988) is the resemblance between Bertrand competition (out-and-out price war) and early models (Hotelling, 1929) of spatial location. Beginning from an assumption that demand was spread evenly along a straight line like a street or a beach stretching east-to-west, Hotelling modelled the location of producers, using the example of two ice-cream sellers on a beach, and came to the conclusion that the two ice-cream sellers would find themselves side by side in the middle of the beach, one in effect taking all western demand and the other all eastern. Their proximity, argued Tirole, was like the price proximity of Bertrand competitors. Tirole went on to review other models of spatial location, particularly that of d'Asprement et al. (1979). In Hotelling's model (1929), consumers suffered costs as they travelled to the seller, costs which were directly proportional to distance travelled. D'Asprement amended this to make costs rise with the square of the distance; the result was to make it optimal from the firms' point of view to separate and locate at points respectively one-quarter and three-quarters along the beach. Tirole went on to argue that spatial location could be considered as an allegory for quality or some form of differentiation, e.g. in terms of colour, weight or sweetness, with consumers' costs being the psychic costs of buying a less-than-ideal product rather than travel costs. If psychic costs were thus quadratic, firms would again tend to move away from the centre of the market, that is, to differentiate their products from those of their rivals. Moreover, differentiation can be 'vertical', that is, products may differ in terms simply of quality, some being better than others. Tirole (1988) concluded that differentiation was a plausible mechanism whereby the Bertrand Paradox could be resolved.

Our discussion in this chapter has centred on the Bertrand Paradox: that oligopolists are in a position to earn high profits but only if they can find ways of keeping price warfare in check. Game theory suggests that oligopolists can indeed learn (given enough opportunities) if not to collude explicitly, then at least to coordinate their actions and thus avoid a price war. This coordination may merely take the form of refraining from entering markets that are already occupied, with the incumbent taking steps to deter entry. A further route toward the moderation of price war is by turning to non-price forms of competition, for example, by differentiating their products from those of their rivals. These are themes which we take up in the three chapters which focus on advertising, entry barriers and the social costs of monopoly which follow our next topic: the economics of industrial structure.

## Guide to further reading

Tirole (1988) provides an easy introduction to game theory. His chapters 5, 6 and 11 are also comprehensive introductions to reaction-curve models as well as applications of game theory.

## Appendix A: the basic mathematics of game theory

### Expectations of duopolists: closed model no entry: homogeneous goods

Imagine that firm A has $m$ strategies and firm B has $n$ strategies; then the game is determined by the m × n matrix: $A = (a_{ij})$ where $a_{ij}$ is firm A's payoff if A uses its $i$th strategy and B uses its $j$th strategy. Assume that the payoff is from firm B to firm A, B's payoff is $-a_{ij}$. Firm A's objective is to make $a_{ij}$ as *large* as possible, whereas B wishes to make $a_{ij}$ as *small* as possible.

For any strategy that A may pick, A can be sure of getting at least

$$\text{MIN}_{a_{ij}}, \quad _{j<n}$$

whence this minimum is derived from *all* of B's strategies. Firm A is free to choose $i$; so A can define a choice in such a way that it gets at least:

$$\text{MAX MIN}_{a_{ij}} \quad _{j \le m \; j \le n}$$

likewise, for any strategy $j$ which B might pick, B can be sure of getting at least

$$\text{MIN}_{(-a_{ij})} = -\text{MAX}_{a_{ij}} \quad _{i \le m} \qquad _{i \le m}$$

So for any strategy $j$ which firm B might choose it can be sure that firm A gets no more than

$$\text{MAX}_{a_{ij}} \quad _{i \le m}$$

Since firm B is free to choose $j$, it can select it in such a way that firm A gets at most

$$\text{MIN MAX}_{a_{ij}} \quad _{j \le n} \qquad _{i \le m}$$

So there is a way for A to play so that A gets at least

$$\text{MAX MIN}_{a_{ij}} \quad _{i \le m} \qquad _{j \le n}$$

Similarly, firm B can play in such a way so that firm A gets no more than

$$\underset{j \leq n}{\text{MIN}} \; \underset{i \leq m}{\text{MAX}}_{a_{ij}}$$

Though these two amounts are different they satisfy the expectation

$$\underset{i \leq m}{\text{MAX}} \; \underset{j \leq n}{\text{MIN}}_{a_{ij}} \; \leq \; \underset{j \leq n}{\text{MIN}} \; \underset{i \leq m}{\text{MAX}}_{a_{ij}} \qquad \qquad ①$$

This can be proved as follows: suppose

$$\underset{i \leq m}{\text{MAX}} \; \underset{j \leq n}{\text{MIN}}_{a_{ij}} = a_{rs}$$

$$\text{MIN MAX}_{a_{ij}} = a_{ij} = a_{\alpha\beta}$$

Therefore, it is true that $a_{rs}$ is the minimum of the $r$th row or:

$$a_{rs} \leq a_{r\beta}$$

Also $a_{\alpha\beta}$ is the maximum of the $\beta$th column so:

$$a_{r\beta} \leq a_{\alpha\beta}$$

Hence,

$$a_{rs} \leq a_{r\beta} \leq a_{\alpha\beta}$$

and the inequality is proven.

For example, suppose the game between duopolists A and B is such that A's payoff matrix is given by:

$$A = \begin{array}{c} \\ ① \\ ② \\ ③ \end{array} \begin{array}{c} \begin{array}{cccc} ① & ② & ③ & ④ \end{array} \\ \begin{bmatrix} 20 & 30 & 40 & -10 \\ 50 & -20 & 20 & -30 \\ 40 & 10 & 30 & 20 \end{bmatrix} \end{array}$$

Then the MAX MIN$_{a_{ij}}$ = 10 and the MIN MAX$_{a_{ij}}$ = 20. So firm A can be sure of achieving at least 10. Firm A can guarantee this payoff by playing strategy ③. The most that firm B loses is 20. B can ensure this upper limit by playing B's strategy ④.

## Saddle points

If the inequality ① becomes an equality so that

$$\underset{i \leq m}{\text{MAX}} \; \underset{j \leq n}{\text{MIN}}_{a_{ij}} = \underset{j \leq n}{\text{MIN}} \; \underset{i \leq m}{\text{MAX}} = k \qquad \qquad ②$$

then firm A can pick a strategy so as to attain this common value $k$, and firm B can prevent firm A from getting more than $k$. In which case there are strategies $i*$ and $j*$ for both duopolists such that for all $i$ and $j$,

$$a_{ij}* \leq a_{i*j}* \leq a_{i*j}$$

$$\text{and } a_{i*j}* = k$$

So firm A can do no better than picking $i*$; similarly firm B cannot do better than to select $j*$.

Strategies i* and j* are called optimal strategies of A and B respectively. Optimal strategies have some interesting features for an oligopoly game:

- if A picks $i*$ then irrespective of what B plays A gets at least $k$
- if B plays $j*$, then no matter what strategy A picks, A cannot get more than $k$

If equation ② is satisfied, then $A = (a_{ij})$ is said to have a *saddle point* at $i*, j*$ and its value is: $a_i*_j = k$ where $k$ is the value of the game.

The necessary and sufficient condition for a saddle point to exist in a game is that there exists a member of the payoff matrix which is simultaneously the minimum of its row and the maximum of its column. Generally games with perfect information have saddle points. Examples of games with perfect information are chess and backgammon. So, if all the strategies for chess were known optimal strategies could be found by fixing saddle points in a payoff matrix whose entries consisted of $+1, 0, -1$. The existence of a saddle point in a chess game follows from the fact that it is a game with perfect information. The value of a game of chess is therefore $\frac{\text{win}}{+1} \frac{\text{draw}}{0} \frac{\text{lose}}{-1}$, however, because of the huge number of strategies for chess, the optimal strategies have not so far been computed.

## Games without saddle points

In many duopoly games the payoff matrices are

$$\underset{i \leq m}{\text{MAX}} \ \underset{j \leq n}{\text{MIN}_{a_{ij}}} \ < \ \underset{j \leq n}{\text{MIN}} \ \underset{i \leq m}{\text{MAX}_{a_{ij}}} \qquad ③$$

the LHS of ③ shows the minimum firm A can get and the RHS shows the most A can get. So duopolist A has a strategy which guarantees at least:

$$\underset{i \leq m}{\text{MAX}} \ \underset{j \leq n}{\text{MIN}_{a_{ij}}}$$

and firm B has a strategy that ensures firm A cannot get more than

$$\underset{j \leq n}{\text{MIN}} \ \underset{i \leq m}{\text{MAX}_{a_{ij}}}$$

Since the amounts are not equal this is not a solution to the game. The game defined by the payoff matrix A:

$$A \ \begin{array}{c} ❶ \\ ❷ \end{array} \begin{bmatrix} \overset{\boxed{1}}{50} & \overset{\boxed{2}}{10} \\ 30 & 40 \end{bmatrix}$$

does not have a saddle point. Since

$$\underset{j \leq 2}{\text{MIN}} \ \underset{i \leq 2}{\text{MAX}_{a_{ij}}} = 40$$

$$\underset{i \leq 2}{\text{MAX}} \ \underset{j \leq 2}{\text{MIN}_{a_{ij}}} = 30$$

and $\text{MAX MIN}_{a_{ij}} < \text{MIN MAX}_{a_{ij}}$.

In the above game firm A can guarantee itself a payoff of 30. However, firm B can ensure that the game will not cost it more than 40. Firm A in repeated plays will try to get more than 30 and B will try to cut its losses below 40. Firm A could win between 30 and 40 per play. Examine A's position: perhaps B could find A's optimal strategy. If this was A's first strategy B can cut A's winnings to 10; if the best strategy for A was the second strategy, A's winnings would be 30. So if A's strategy were discovered its winnings could be either 10 or 30 on each play. But A wants to get 30 or 40. Hence A is disadvantaged if B knows A's strategy.

So A could gain by focusing on concealing its strategy from B. Firm A could do this by choosing a strategy at random. Then B could not discover A's strategy. By similar logic B should also pick its strategies at random.

In this game the players instead of picking a single strategy each may leave the selection of strategy to chance. A random device, a Doomsday machine, selects strategies for both players at random over all possible strategies. A probability distribution over the whole set of strategies of a player is called a *mixed strategy*. This prevents the opponent discovering the strategy. Mixed strategies allow players in a game without a saddle point to conceal strategies from opponents. The opponent cannot know the strategy in advance since even the other player does not know it. The strategy is selected at the last moment by randomized methods.

The game above with no saddle point for a pure strategy now requires each player to select independently a mixed strategy. Let $P_i$ be the probability of selecting strategy $i$. The payoffs are now measured in terms of mathematical expectations. Having defined mixed strategies as probability distributions expected payoffs can be calculated. Suppose firm A picks strategy $i$ and B picks mixed strategy $Y_i$, the expected payoff to firm A is

$$h_i = \sum_{j=1}^{n} a_{ij} y_i$$

which is the $i$th component of the column matrix representing mixed strategies:

$$H = AY \begin{bmatrix} h_1 \\ h_2 \\ \vdots \\ h_m \end{bmatrix}$$

If B uses strategy $j$ and A uses mixed strategy $P$, the expected payoff to firm A is $t_j = \sum_{i=1}^{m} a_{ij} P_i$, which is the $j$th component of row matrix $T'$

$$T' = P'A = (t_1, t_2, \ldots, t_n)$$

If A and B use mixed strategies $P'Y$ respectively then the expected payoff to firm A is

$$E = P'AY = \sum_{j=1}^{n} \sum_{i=1}^{m} a_{ij} P_i y_i = T'Y = P'H$$

## Appendix B

In Chapter 3, we observed that mainstream S–C–P logic implies that there is a deterministic relationship between fixed costs, market size and the number of firms. To see this, we refer to Equation (4.6), which ran:

$$\frac{p - c}{P} = \frac{s}{e} \tag{4.6}$$

We also recall from Equation (4.1) that profit is defined as:

$$! = pq - cq - F \tag{4.1}$$

If the top and bottom of the lefhand side of Equation (4.6) are both multiplied by $q$, we have

$$\frac{pq - cq}{pq} = \frac{! + F}{R} = \frac{s}{e}$$

where $R$ is the revenue. Thus an increase in $F$ leads, *ceteris paribus*, to higher $s$, that is, greater market share. Thus higher fixed costs mean more concentration. Professor Sutton, certainly, would beg to differ.

# 5 Structure and profitability

## 5.1 Introduction

This chapter examines the basic structuralist proposition: that concentration raises profits. Tantalizing evidence for this was adduced, as we mentioned in Chapter 3, by Bain (1951, 1956) but we should also bear in mind the findings of Alberts (1984) and Salinger (1984) that variations in profit rates between firms in the USA is not large, regardless of industry. Subsequent industrial economists took up the challenge and this chapter reviews their work. We begin by looking at the usefulness (or otherwise) of reported company profits for such purposes.

## 5.2 Problems with reported profits

Profits play an important role in industrial economics. From the perspective of the researcher, however, profits as reported in company accounts are flawed. First, companies do not report a single figure for profit but employ a variety of definitions (see Table 5.1) between which the researcher must choose. Secondly, firms typically operate in several industries simultaneously yet normally produce only one set of accounts. The profits of any one subunit cannot therefore be established; nor, in consequence, can the profits of an industry which is made up of the subsidiaries of multidivisional firms. Researchers are forced to use other information. Thirdly, and most fundamentally, economists frequently object (Parker and Stead, 1991) to the way in which published accounts evaluate costs. In principle, economic profit is the residual which remains after the deduction from revenues of the opportunity costs of using resources ($P = R - C$ where $P$ is profit, $R$ is revenue and $C$ is opportunity costs). This can be expressed as a percentage of the capital employed ($P' = 100 \times (R - C)/K$ where $K$ is capital). In the case of fixed assets, the opportunity costs are the rental income which could have been earned by leasing them to another user. In practice, firms use either the purchase price (historic cost) or the 'replacement value', that is, the contemporary cost of a similar item. Neither may correspond to contemporary opportunity costs: in inflationary times, historic costs will progressively understate true value of assets, while in recessionary times, replacement values will overstate opportunity costs because there may be no one willing to rent or buy the asset.

Fixed assets give rise to a second problem when they are owned by companies rather than rented. Company accountants should, as noted, deduct opportunity costs from the gross profits made from using an asset. In fact they deduct a different sum: a depreciation charge which is a proportion of the historic or the replacement value which they use. The calculation is at the discretion of the firm; companies retain a substantial degree of discretion over their depreciation charges and hence over their reported profits (for example, Salamon (1985) reports that larger firms tend to make greater use of accelerated depreciation methods than do smaller, family firms). For this reason, economists fear that those depreciation methods used may bear little

**TABLE 5.1   Definitions of profit** (*Source*s: Annual Report, *Daily Mail* and General Trust, 1990)

| Item | £ million |
|---|---|
| Trading profit | 64 |
| Profit of related cost and investments | 17.9 |
| Less interest | (31.6) |
| Profit before exceptional items and tax | 50.3 |
| Exceptional items | (6.1) |
| Profit on ordinary activities before tax | 44.2 |
| Tax | (9.5) |
| Profit on ordinary activities after tax | 34.7 |
| Interest of minority shareholders | (1.8) |
| Profit on ordinary activities after tax but before extraordinary items | 32.9 |
| Extraordinary items | (6.1) |
| Group profit for financial year | 26.8 |
| Dividends | (10.9) |
| Retained profit | 15.9 |

resemblance to opportunity costs, so distorting profits. (Given the fact that declared profits attract tax, there is clearly some incentive to underdeclare profit.)

Given these problems with company profits, researchers have tended to make use of the 'price–cost margin' (PCM). This is derived from the Census of Production which gives data on gross output (sales revenue) and variable costs such as labour and materials, PCMs being the difference between the two. PCMs are accordingly the sum of profit, depreciation charges and overhead costs. (A slightly superior approach is to conduct the analysis in terms of value added (gross output less bought-in materials) in place of gross output.) From a theoretical perspective, the attraction of PCM lies in the estimates which can be derived from it. Thus dividing the revenue and cost figures by output volume yields estimates of, respectively, price and average cost; under conditions of constant returns to scale (as many believe to be the case at outputs above MES), the latter approximates to MC.

From a practical standpoint, the virtue of PCM is that it is collated as part of the Census of Production and is thus available for research purposes. It might appear that PCM provides a method of making inter-company comparisons while avoiding the problems of valuing $K$ which beset the task of calculating $P'$. Unfortunately, this is not the case. Companies (and industries) which use relatively large amounts of capital have, all else being equal, larger depreciation charges which will raise their PCMs. To control for this, tests of the determinants of PCMs are obliged to include a measure of the capital used in each industry. These caveats have to be remembered when reviewing work which uses data on profits.

## 5.3   Structure and profitability: some empirical results

The models described in Chapter 3 differ in their predictions. The Bertrand–Nash themes imply quite emphatically that oligopoly is equivalent in performance to perfect competition by virtue of price competition and that inefficiency is associated only with monopoly. Cournot and TFT strategies, by contrast, suggest the reverse: the evils of monopoly are shared (to varying degrees that depend upon the number of competitors) by oligopoly. Cournot thus implies a 'concentration effect'; the more concentrated a market is, the more price will diverge from marginal cost: inefficiency rises incrementally with concentration. This idea provided the basis for the research programme into links between concentration and profitability which was initiated by Joe Bain (1951) whose findings were reported in Chapter 3. To recap, Bain perceived a threshold at CR8 = 70 per cent, with those industries above that level having rates of return of 11.8 per cent as against a figure of 7.5 per cent for those below. The hypothesis that the two groups of industries had differing mean rates of profit could not be rejected at the 99 per cent confidence level: Cournot's 'concentration effect' appeared.

In the 1950s and 1960s, industrial economists retested the concentration effect by creating models which drew in barriers to entry as well as concentration. These models were often tested by means of multiple regression. In the USA, Collins and Preston (1969), to cite but one instance, analysed 243 US 4-digit manufacturing industries for 1963, using PCM as the measure of profit and CR4 as concentration. They used a dummy for geographical dispersion (GD) and a measure of capital intensity, $K/Q$ which affects the price–cost ratio and which is also a measure of scale economies and thus of one form of barrier to entry. They found that:

$$PCM = 20.23 + 0.095 \, CONC - 0.032 \, GD + 0.089 \, K/Q \qquad R^2 = 0.19$$

The coefficient on GD was not significant but those on CONC and $K/Q$ were significant at the 99 per cent confidence level. Surveying a bank of 46 similar studies (mainly but not exclusively American), Weiss (1974) was able to conclude that a concentration effect could generally be discerned.

In the 1970s, the growing appreciation of the complexities of the links between basic conditions, structure, conduct and performance led economists to use, not game theory directly, but models based on simultaneous equations. An example is Gupta (1983) who examines Canadian manufacturing at the level of 4-digit industries for 1968. The model employs five equations to determine, for each industry, concentration levels (measured by CR4), the extent of overseas ownership, the advertising-to-sales ratio, the extent of output deriving from sub-optimum sized plant and the profit margin. The interdependence is shown by the fact, for example, that ADS (the advertising ratio) is at once a dependent variable in its own right and enters into all the other four as an independent variable. In all, 17 variables are employed. (As ever, no attempt to include elasticity of demand is made.) Gupta solves the system of equations first using ordinary least squares (OLS) followed by two- and three-stage least squares (2SLS, 3SLS) and is thus able to compare the results from the different methods. For present purposes, the most important finding is that while OLS indicates a significant concentration effect, this disappears in 2SLS and 3SLS. (It should be noted as an aside that Schmalensee, reviewing this sector of industrial economics (1989) argues strongly that simultaneous equation systems usually have insufficient exogenous variables to identify the endogenous ones.)

Gupta's conclusion receives added significance because it echoes the finding of Martin (1979). This research built upon a model originally developed by Strickland and Weiss (1976) which used three equations to determine price–cost margins, the advertising-to-sales ratio and concentration measured by C4. Martin (1979) tested his version of the model on 209 manufacturing industries using data for 1967 from the US input-output tables. Most industries corresponded to 4-digit SIC industries, although 28 were in effect 3-digit industries; dummy variables were used to distinguish regional markets and producer-goods industries. Solving the equations by 2SLS, Martin found that PCM was described by the equation on page 56,

$$PCM = \begin{array}{l} 1.0905 + 2.333REG + 0.821CD/S - 0.4083IM/S + 0.09BCR + 0.128GR + 0.618A/S + \\ \quad (0.8252) \quad\quad (0.9232) \quad\quad (1.7055) \quad\quad (0.409) \quad (1.7047) \quad (2.515) \end{array}$$

$$\begin{array}{l} 0.0703K/S + 0.4824MES/S + 0.049CDR + 0.0782CR4 \\ (0.8351) \quad\quad (1.6801) \quad\quad (0.2663) \quad\quad (0.8959) \end{array}$$

where REG is a regional industry dummy, CD/S is the share of final consumers in total sales, IM/S is import penetration, BCR is buyer concentration, GR is growth, A/S is the advertising ratio, K/S is capital-intensivity, MES/S is the hypothetical maximum number of MES plants, CDR is the cost disadvantage ratio (the cost penalties of suboptimum plant size) and CR4 is concentration. Like Gupta, Martin finds no evidence for a concentration effect.

By the mid-1970s, studies showing a *negative* relationship began to appear. For the USA, Schmalensee (1988) lists Porter (1976), Grabowski and Mueller (1978), Connolly and Hirschey (1984) and Hirschey (1985). These negative links were statistically significant. Similar results were reported for Europe; for example Phlips (1971) who researched industries in France, Italy and Belgium, and Jacquemin, de Ghellinck and Huveneers (1980) who looked at Belgium alone.

Research in the UK has been far more limited. Reviewing the results, of eight studies between 1972 and 1978, Clarke *et al.* (1984) notes that six could be faulted on procedure, while the remaining two (Phillips, 1972 and Hart and Morgan, 1977) produce conflicting findings: a significant positive relationship and a non-significant one respectively. Schmalensee, echoing Clarke, summarizes research in the area thus: 'The relation, if any, between seller concentration and profitability is weak statistically and the estimated concentration effect is usually small. The estimated relation is unstable over time and space and vanishes in many multivariate studies.'

## 5.4  Structure and profit: causality or coincidence?

In 1973, just as evidence that high concentration led to higher profits was proving hard to find, an economist of the Chicago tradition, Harold Demsetz (1973, 1974) put forward the argument that an entirely different construction could be placed upon the data. High profits and high concentration, where they existed, Demsetz suggested, could be the simultaneous effects of higher efficiency on the part of a small group of firms. Figure 5.1 shows the position of a firm in an industry in which product differentiation is the norm, so that all face a downward-sloping demand curve with its associated marginal revenue curve. With constant costs, MC = AC at $OC_1$, leading to a profit-maximizing output at $OQ_1$. If all firms had access to the same cost curves and if demand conditions were identical, firms would be of equal size, all would earn profits of $P_1ABC_1$ and the industry would not appear concentrated. If, however, one firm were to become more efficient and reduce its costs to $OC_2$, it would raise output to $OQ_2$ and earn larger profits ($P_2SRC_2$). The industry would now be more concentrated and more profitable than before, that is, a concentration effect would appear. This, however, is not causation but a spurious correlation, according to the argument put forward by Demsetz, for both are the effects of differences in efficiency.

To test his approach, Demsetz used the novel idea of comparing the returns earned by large and small firms in the same industry. In unconcentrated industries, he argued, there is no particular reason to expect differences in profit between large firms and small firms. After all, in these industries, the range of differences between firms in terms of size is not great anyway. In concentrated industries, however, something is happening to elevate the profits of the larger firms, either superior efficiency or collusion. If the cause is collusion, Demsetz reasoned, the

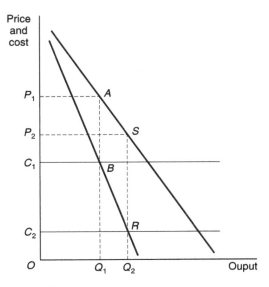

**Figure 5.1** Profit, market share and efficiency

returns to all firms, large and small, are raised, so again there is no real divergence between large and small firms' profits. But if superior efficiency is at work, then concentrated industries should show a difference in profit between large and small firms. Thus a divergence in profits between large and small firms in concentrated industries would substantiate the 'efficiency' hypothesis and falsify the collusion/restrained competition hypothesis. The evidence which he adduced, reproduced in Table 5.2, is broadly consistent with the 'efficiency' view.

Demsetz' intervention brought forth two kinds of response, one theoretical, the other empirical. The theoretical response was to deny Demsetz' initial proposition that the high profits of larger firms were caused either by collusion or by superior efficiency. Rather, it was argued (Martin, 1988), the two go hand in hand. The central role in this argument is played by the idea of economies of scale and MES, which economists of the S–C–P tradition have always seen as important determinants of industrial structure. One implication of economies of scale is that sub optimum-sized firms suffer cost penalties, which reduce their profits. Second, economies of scale promote concentration both of themselves and by virtue of acting as a barrier to entry. Thus

**TABLE 5.2  Industrial concentration and returns to groups of firms** (*Source*: Demsetz (1973), Table 2)

| Concentration | No of industries | Rates of return in each group | |
|---|---|---|---|
| | | R1 | R4 |
| 10–20 | 14 | 7.3 | 8.0 |
| 20–30 | 22 | 4.4 | 11.6 |
| 30–40 | 24 | 5.1 | 11.7 |
| 40–50 | 21 | 4.8 | 9.4 |
| 50–60 | 11 | 0.9 | 12.2 |
| 60 and above | 3 | 5.0 | 21.6 |

Concentration: CR4 in 1963
Returns: Profit plus interest over total assets as per cent
R1: Firms with assets below $500 000
R4: Firms with assets over $50 million

Demsetz' results could be explained simply as the result of economies of scale (Scherer, 1980, pp.280–281). (Such a view would, of course, deny that firms enjoying economies of scale could claim credit for creating those economies themselves.) The argument as presented by Martin (1988), Bain (1956) and Collins and Preston (1969), however, goes further and asserts that collusion and economies of scale are not alternatives but complements. Thus, Collins and Preston (1969, p.280), believe that 'Theory would suggest that when the largest firms possess distinct advantages, the potential competitive impact of the smaller firms would be reduced and the ability of leaders to pursue a shared monopoly behavior pattern would therefore be enhanced'. In other words, efficiency (in terms of economies of scale) and collusion, in this view, may be found operating simultaneously. In this formulation, larger firms could still be colluding or engaging in Cournot competition even if they were also more efficient than small firms. The effect is to render the idea that collusion gives rise to profit almost invulnerable to disproof; let Chicago economists marshal whatever evidence they may on the superior efficiency of large firms, followers of the S–C–P tradition can argue that collusion is still at work!

The second response to Demsetz' work was to engage in further empirical testing. A method of testing the Demsetz view, proposed by Weiss (1974), was to undertake multivariate analysis, including both concentration (the Bain perspective) and market share (the Demsetz view) as independent variables. When several industries are examined at once, concentration exerts no influence on profit whatever, while market share, however, appears to be linked to profits, which is in line with Demsetz' view. To make matters more complicated, however, this relationship is not found at the level of the single industry. It only holds when several industries are in the sample. This suggests that the relationship between profit and market share is limited to a few industries but is not uniform.

In the US, Martin (1988) and Ravenscraft (1983) attempted to assess the efficiency of large firms directly. Martin used data on 185 4-digit SIC industries to establish the determinants of profits. Profits were measured by price–cost margins and the model accordingly included a variable for capital-to-sales ratio to correct for bias induced by capital intensivity. An advertising-to-sales ratio was also included since advertising is known to be correlated with PCMs. Firms in each industry were divided into three groups according to size: the largest four (denoted 14 in the regression), numbers 5 to 8 (58) and the rest (9P). The efficiency of each group was assessed by finding the ratio of its value added per worker to the value added per worker for the industry as a whole. The PCM of each group was then regressed first against its own relative efficiency ratio (RP) (a direct test of the 'superior efficiency' hypothesis) and against the PCMs and market shares (CR) of other groups. The logic here was that if collusion were the main factor in determining profit, PCMs of all groups would be correlated with the PCM and the market share of the largest four firms. Conversely, profits would be negatively correlated with a large market share for the small firms. Martin's results were as follows (the advertising-to-sales ratio and the capital-to-sales ratio being omitted for brevity and because they were not, in the main, significant).

Large firms

$$
\begin{array}{ccccccc}
 & RP1 & PCM58 & PCM9P & CR14 & CR58 & CR9P \\
PCM14 = -0.316 & + 0.2241 & + 0.306 & + 0.692 & + 0.1933 & - 0.2071 & + 0.0138 \\
 (7.23) & (7.66) & (4.03) & (6.19) & (4.33) & (2.68) & (0.38)
\end{array}
$$

Medium-sized firms

$$
\begin{array}{ccccccc}
 & RP58 & PCM14 & PCM9P & CR14 & CR58 & CR9P \\
PCM58 = -0.3239 & + 0.2724 & + 0.55 & + 0.37 & + 0.11 & - 0.156 & + 0.05 \\
 (7.34) & (11.9) & (5.84) & (2.79) & (2.12) & (1.89) & (1.36)
\end{array}
$$

Small firms

$$\begin{array}{cccccc} & RP9P & PCM14 & PCM58 & CR14 & CR58 & CR9P \\ PCM9P = -0.2454 & + 0.35 & + 0.49 & + 0.21 & + 0.066 & - 0.03 & - 0.04 \\ (5.6) & (9.98) & (9.84) & (4.44) & (1.9177) & (0.48) & (1.78) \end{array}$$

First, the results support Demsetz' thesis that efficiency and profits are related. For every group, the correlation between PCM and its own relative efficiency is significant at the 99 per cent confidence level. On the other hand, each group's PCM is significantly correlated (again, at the 99 per cent confidence level) with the PCMs of other groups. This could be seen as the reverse of Demsetz' finding that *when an industry is concentrated* group PCMs would diverge. Finally, the PCMs of all three groups 1–4, 5–8 and 9–P are positively correlated (at the 99 per cent, 95 per cent and 90 per cent levels of confidence respectively) with the market share of the largest four; in other words, the higher the CR4, the higher are profits for all groups. This evidence is not inconsistent with the supposition that high concentration produces high profits by means of collusion. Recalling that Demsetz' hypothesis was that there would be a zero correlation between the PCMs of the smallest firms and the market share of the biggest four, the discovery of such a correlation could be taken as a refutation of his ideas. It should be noted that the correlation which Martin reports, at 0.066 with a t-statistic of 1.91, is rather weak, and the results cannot be taken as decisive.

In the UK, Clarke, Davies and Waterson (1984) attempted to replicate Demsetz' results on a larger sample of industries over two years (147 3-digit industries in 1971 and 155 in 1977). The research sought to establish (as Demsetz) whether differences between the returns of the top five firms and all other firms in an industry were related to the level of concentration. In the event, the pattern predicted by Demsetz failed to emerge. First, in both years, higher returns were found for both groups of firms in concentrated industries when compared with unconcentrated industries (where Demsetz predicted no elevation in profit for small firms). Second, again for both years for more and less concentrated industries, the profits of the two groups of firms were indistinguishable at the 95 per cent confidence level, so we return to the background fact: that variations in profit between firms are not large.

## 5.5  Competition, stability of profit and of market shares

Demsetz begins, like all true Chicagoans, from the proposition that markets are basically competitive. Some, however, have tried to assess the strength of the forces of competition by examining not structure but the speed of changes in profits and market shares over time. Thus Geroski and Jacquemin (1988) examined the speed with which the profits of larger firms in several western countries fell back to average level following a disturbance. The argument was that a swift return to normal would testify to low entry barriers and strong competition. Their findings were that in general across Europe and America returns in excess of the average fell away within the space of a year. The UK was an exception, for here differences in return were found to persist for indefinitely long periods. Utton took another approach, looking at the evolution of market shares in the UK: one sample of six industries ranged over most of the century, while another of 19 covered 30–40 years. In the first group, leaders in four of the six cases retained their position; in the second group leaders suffered 'significant' declines but retained pole position; in five cases leaders extended their dominance. Shaw and Simpson (1986), examining the stability of market shares of firms in UK industries investigated by the MMC and the (now defunct) National Board for Prices and Incomes in the late 1970s, likewise found considerable evidence of stability. Mueller's (1986) research on market shares in US manufacturing was limited to 350 industries for which data over the period 1950–72 was consistent, and found that the same firm held the largest share in the two years. Again, this suggests that the forces of competition operate ponderously.

## 5.6  Conclusion

This chapter has looked at the effects of structure on company profits. All work in the field, we noted, is dogged by measurement problems. Reviewing this aspect of industrial economics, Schmalensee (1989) is critical of the proxy indicators which are used in this work and the frequent insufficiency of exogenous variables, together with the deeper problem that many researchers seem to confuse structure with conduct, with advertising being a prime example. He recommends a return to a more descriptive approach directed towards discovering the regularities in the data as well as taking proper cognizance of factors specific to each industry. Sutton's efforts to distinguish exogenous from endogenous sunk costs and the precise nature of first-mover advantages is certainly persuasive. Attempts to test for the virulence of competition by looking at the volatility of profits and market shares have found conflicting evidence, though in the UK at least competition appears to be somewhat muted. We are left thus with the puzzle of how this relates to a generally uniform level of profits. One possibility is that excess profits are being earned and then dissipated. Evidence to suggest that when competition is restrained, profits are appropriated by other factors of production comes from the USA, where a study by Rose (1987) found that unionized workers in the then regulated trucking industry were receiving over 60 per cent of the monopoly rents that regulation had produced. In the UK it is clear that the privatized industries have been able to economize quite sharply on payments to labour. Beyond such over-payment, several possible routes remain for the absorption of profits which could have the effect of restraining Bertrand price war. These include the creation of market niches or entry barriers through advertising, brand proliferation or innovation. These topics form the agenda for the next chapters.

## Guide to further reading

An excellent review is to be found in Schmalensee's chapter in vol. 2 of the *Handbook of Economics* (1989) edited by himself and Willig (Schmalensee and Willig, 1989).

# 6 Entry barriers and limit pricing

## 6.1 Introduction

We continue the theme of mechanisms by which firms may dampen direct, profit-eliminating Bertrand-style price-based competition by examining the ways in which firms already trading profitably in a given market (incumbents) can deter would-be entrants. That is, it concerns barriers to entry.

## 6.2 Types of barriers to entry

Bain identified three types, all of which confer cost advantages on incumbents. The first category can be decisive, that is, it may blockade an industry against entry altogether. Examples include the exclusive control of a necessary resource as well as state-made devices such as licences and regulations or forms of intellectual property such as patents. Second is the preference, perhaps caused by reputation, image or sheer inertia, of buyers for established brands, perhaps buttressed by advertising. Third are economies of scale which compel a would-be entrant to enter either on a large scale or not at all (anyone entering on a small scale would face cost penalties). Economies of scale thus reduce the number of potential entrants to those with access to large amounts of capital; to finance entry and to bear the risks. Recent analysis draws attention to *exit costs* as well as to entry barriers. If there are ready buyers for the equipment which an entrant has bought, entry barriers are in effect zero. To the extent that costs are irrecoverable ('sunk'), entrants face barriers. It should be noted that entry barriers also vary (generally falling) as longer time-spans are considered: patents expire, economies of scale can be bypassed by new technologies and established brands can be replaced by new brands which find favour with consumers.

Neo-Austrian economists (Parker and Stead, 1991) have long argued that barriers should be ignored as they are of little importance. From an Austrian perspective, cost differences between firms, whether incumbents or potential entrants, are inevitable, as are efforts by new entrepreneurs to overcome obstacles. Thus neo-Austrians would not expect barriers to persist; if an entrepreneur invents a better product and mounts a more effective advertising campaign, that entrepreneur will be able to take on an entrenched incumbent. For neo-Austrians, the only true barriers are those deriving from governmental activity, because only state-created barriers cannot be overcome by enterprises.

Conversely, it is clear that incumbents can create barriers. Economies of scale, for example, are produced by decisions to develop new ways of production using specialized equipment, while consumer preferences can be strengthened by advertising and branding. Conduct which creates barriers deliberately is termed 'strategic' because it attempts to influence the strategic decisions of potential competitors. (The inadvertent creation of barriers is termed 'innocent'.) Its implication is that structure is to a large degree endogenous in all but the short run. Modern models of entry attempt to include strategic conduct: under-emphasized by the S–C–P tradition, it now takes centre stage.

The analysis begins with the basic entry model: the Bain–Sylos–Modigliani (BSM) model. We shall view this model through the lens of game theory, using the concepts of backward induction developed earlier. Later we have a mathematical treatment which examines rivalry between two firms in more than one rivalry. Two aspects of the models deserve attention. First is the concept of sunk costs or commitment. Incumbents wishing to deter entry face the problem of communicating their determination to resist entry (e.g. by means of price war) to outsiders. The appearance of a retaliatory temperament may in fact be more important than its reality. This has led economists to consider ways in which incumbents can commit themselves publicly to retaliation. Incurring sunk costs is one way of doing this. Money spent irretrievably on assets for which there is no second-hand market, for example, shows that a firm is in earnest about staying in a particular industry and by implication is ready to meet any entrant with price war. Sunk cost by an incumbent thus creates entry barriers.

A second aspect of the models is their welfare implications. Inefficiency, as noted, arises when competition is limited by concentration which in turn is bolstered by barriers. While barrier creation may be profitable for the firm, it may be a waste of resources for the system as a whole.

## 6.3   Price as an entry barrier: limit pricing

A market with no entry barriers is termed 'contestable'; we examined contestability briefly in Section 5.4. In the case of markets with insurmountable barriers, entry is impossible. Interest here focuses upon the intermediate case of moderate barriers, where incumbents can set prices above their marginal costs but below monopoly level. This is the situation modelled by the BSM model. Like other game-theoretic models, theories of entry specify the moves, beliefs, pay-offs and reactions of players. One assumption common to most models is that a potential entrant would need to know that it would be possible to charge a price at least equal to his LRAC (Long run average cost) in order to earn a normal profit before the potential entrant would enter. The distinguishing feature of the BSM model is the Sylos postulate, that is:

1 the incumbent intends to hold its output constant when entry occurs
2 the entrant is aware of this.

Any resemblance to Cournot is coincidental!

With these expectational rules the entrant's demand curve (see Fig. 6.1a) starts from the Y-axis (price at the pre-entry price) and is delineated so that all the increase in total industry demand for each price reduction accrues to the entrant. The potential entrant's demand curve is thus the industry demand curve minus the constant production of the incumbent(s). BSM models assume steeply-falling L-shaped cost functions, so this approach allows us to write an equation that defines the highest price (and thus lowest volume) which still deters entry by allowing any entrant too small a market share to be profitable:

$$PL \text{ (approx)} = P_c/(1 + X_m/X_c z) \tag{6.1}$$

where:   $PL$ = limit price
   $P_c$ = competitive price
   $X_m$ = minimum efficient scale
   $X_c$ = competitive output at $P_c$
   $z$   = elasticity of demand at $P_c$

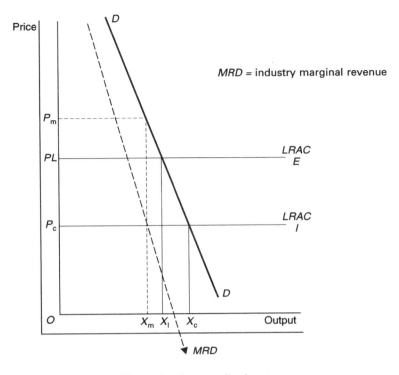

**Figure 6.1a**    Entry despite cost disadvantage

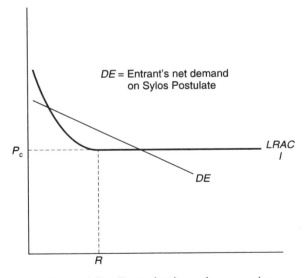

**Figure 6.1b**    Entry despite scale economies

This formulation yields the following testable hypothesis: *PL* varies directly with MES and indirectly with both the absolute market size and the price elasticity of industry demand. These propositions, of course, relate to variations in profit margins between industries and for an industry at different moments in time.

Under the Sylos postulate, entry can still occur if the entry price chosen by the incumbents implies that a potential entrant's demand curve is above its LRAC. Figure 6.1a shows that even in the face of absolute cost disadvantages, entry can be successful, implying Bain's case above.

Figure 6.1b shows the potential entrant's expected demand post entry is DE, which lies above the entrant's cost curve. Hence entry in this case, despite disadvantages, implies profits for the entrant. The entrant's expected demand curve lies to the right of D and its image is translated as DE.

## 6.4   Some extensions

Some economists have noted that the Sylos postulate generates a Stackelberg equilibrium, since the potential entrant thinks the existing colluders maintain constant outputs (Cournot assumption) and hence act like a Stackelberg follower. Dixit (1980) has used classical theory reaction functions to depict entry-forestalling behaviour for the limiting case of an established monopolist and a single potential entrant. The entrant's reaction function, DEF (see Fig. 6.2), describes the locus of the entrant's outputs expected by the established monopolist on the basis of the Sylos postulate. The existing monopolist's reaction function is DPE. Any one of these iso-profit contours is concave to the existing firm's x-axis and is a locus describing the potential entrant's maximum profits at alternative outputs. Iso-profit contours represent preferred positions for a potential entrant as they approach the monopolist's axis. The established firm's maximum profits is at point $M_1$, that is, where its reaction function intercepts the x-axis. However, given the entry threat and the Sylos postulate, the incumbent's maximum profit will be at the

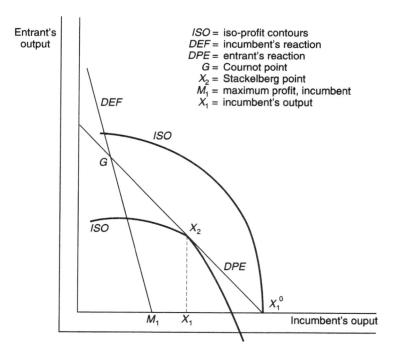

**Figure 6.2**   Entry with Stackelberg equilibrium

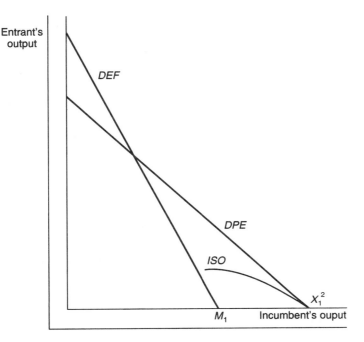

**Figure 6.3**  Blockaded entry: natural monopoly

point of tangency between its iso-profit system and DPE: a Stackelberg equilibrium. At this junction, the monopolist will select its output and corresponding price. The output at this Stackelberg equilibrium is $X_1$ and the entrant's output is $X_2$. So the unique Stackelberg equilibrium is $X_1, X_2$. Entry-blocking output associated with limit price is determined when DPE $= 0$ and possesses the largest positive root $X_1^0$; such that any output $X_1^0$ deters entry.

In Fig. 6.2 $X_1, X_2$ the Stackelberg equilibrium output allows entry, corresponding to moderately easy entry. So here to maximize long-run profits the monopolist will produce $X_1$ and permit entry by a single firm. However, $X_1$ need not be less that $X_1^0$; it could equal or exceed it. To illustrate this case where long-run profit maximization blocks entry consider Fig. 6.3.

At the block point, the potential entrant's reaction function is steeper than the iso-profit contour which intercepts the block point. Given that the loci are smooth then common tangency between them occurs at, or to the right of the entry deterring point $M_1$. So now Stackelberg equilibrium production blocks entry. This case is consistent with Bain's blockaded case. In short, the existing monopolist can stop entry provided that its iso-profit contour intercepting the block point is no steeper here than the potential entrant's reaction function.

Finally, when limit price is different from the Stackelberg price it could be argued that a situation where existing firms are uncertain about the exact number of likely entrants and limit pricing produces optimal results. Existing firms might presume that in maximizing against an $N$-reaction function, they might induce not $N$ but $N+2$ entrants. Colluder profits might then drop below those at $X_1^0$ leading them to regret their decision. So the lower profit at the entry block point might be preferred to the seemingly greater but uncertain profits at the Stackelberg equilibrium. Nevertheless, it should be noted that there is uncertainty about limit price. Expositions of the theory in terms of the Sylos postulate conceal this uncertainty.

The Sylos postulate presents difficulties. If the potential entrant does enter, then rational behaviour for the incumbents is to embrace the new producer in a loose cartelized arrangement and reduce output (Wender, 1971). This way higher profits are available compared with those maintaining a static output post entry. Realizing this, the entrant may not be put off by Sylos-type expectations. In this situation the only deterrent would be the threat of irrational retaliation by the incumbent(s).

Problems with the Sylos postulate initiated a rethink of the standard BSM model. There are two aspects to this reconsideration. One approach focuses on strategic factors (absent in traditional expositions of BSM) with which an incumbent must be concerned if it wishes to establish credible threats of losses for newcomers hence deterring or retarding entry. The second approach explains the rate of entry in cases where potential competitors are ineffectively impeded. Analysis here is focused on the former approach.

## 6.5    Gaskin's dynamic limit pricing case

With hindsight it is reasonable to argue that the approach of Bhagwati (1970) and Gaskins (1971) to dynamic limit pricing made an extraordinary impact on the development of thought about strategic entry deterrence. In this case a dominant firm oligopolist selects a price over time $(PL_t)$ to maximize profits from:

$$\pi(t_0) \int (PL_t)(Q_d(PL_t) - X_t)e^{-r(t-t_0)dt} \tag{6.2}$$

When $Q_d(PL_t)$ is industry demand at $(PL_t)$, $X_t$ represents rivals' (fringe competitors) supply, the dominant firm has constant average costs, and $(r)$ is the discount rate. It is presumed that rate of entry is an increasing function of price set by the dominant firm. Hence the dominant firm's position erodes as its market share over time approaches zero. The only feasible limit price in this case is the competitive price.

However, Gaskin's specification of dynamic limit pricing is flawed. For example, how does the price-setting dominant firm stay pre-eminent as its market share is whittled away? Moreover, the dynamics of the entry game are arbitrary, being unconnected with the optimizing conduct of actual entrants or strategic interactions between entrants and the dominant firm.

As noted the static BSM limit price model is open to the objection that the incumbents' threat to maintain a constant output pre- and post-entry is not credible. Normally an incumbent might be expected to cut output and accommodate entry. A glance at the game tree (Fig. 6.4) confirms

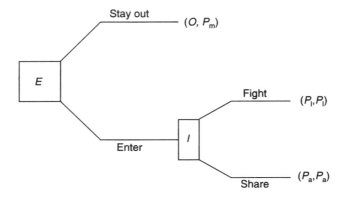

**Figure 6.4**   A non-credible threat

the view that the threat to fight does not offer a Nash equilibrium. This latter involves the condition: that the incumbent does the *best* it can given what entrants may do and the entrant does the best it can given the incumbent's behaviour. To elucidate these decisions, we turn go game theory (Norman and La Manna, 1992).

## 6.6    Game theory and entry

Figure 6.5 shows a game tree representing an incumbent and a potential entrant. The entrant moves first (E) and the incumbent (I) selects its output reaction in the light of the entrant's decision. Payoffs are shown on the right, entrant first, incumbent second. The entrant has two strategies: enter or stay out. The incumbent's strategy is of necessity more complex, consisting of 'if ... then ...' statements. Two sets of strategies yield Nash equilibria. One is: E stays out; if there is entry I expands and if there is no entry, I expands also. The second Nash equilibrium is: E enters; if there is entry, I holds output static and if there is no entry I expands. In both situations, each is maximizing given the other player's expected behaviour, and each is conforming to the other's expectation. On closer examination, however, the first case is not a perfect equilibrium because I would not expand if E were in fact to enter. After E had entered, the maximizing choice for I is to hold output static, i.e. to acquiesce. Since by assumption all payoffs are common knowledge, the entrant would be aware that fighting would be non-rational for I and would ignore the threat.

In a similar vein, economists have considered situations in which entrants may 'nibble away' at an incumbent's position. A notable example (Selten, 1978; Kreps and Wilson, 1982) is that of a retail chain which has, let us suppose, a monopoly in each of several cities. It also faces, in each city, a potential entrant. These entrants, we assume, make their decisions in sequence rather than simultaneously, and each does so in the light of the fate of previous entrants. In particular, therefore, each entrant knows whether previous entrants were met with retaliation from the multiple monopolist. It seems intuitively clear that the big firm should fight the first entrant whatever the cost, so as to deter the others and thus maintain its position. Selten (1978) demonstrated that this intuition is false. The logic is that set out in Chapter 4: this is a

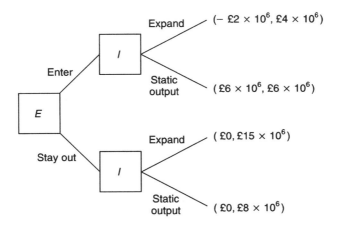

**Figure 6.5**    An entry game with one credible Nash outcome

finitely-repeated prisoners' dilemma. In the last game/city, the monopolist is better off if it acquiesces. Fighting would bring a loss and could not influence future rounds as there are none. In the last game but one, however, the same logic applies: the future (the last game) is already determined and fighting would again bring a loss to no advantage, so the rational policy is to acquiesce. At no stage in the supergame therefore is it rational to fight. Kreps and Wilson (1982), however, show that this conclusion holds only under very restrictive conditions. In particular, the serial monopolist's pay-offs have to be 'common knowledge': the entrants should know that the monopolist's highest-paying strategy is to acquiesce, and the monopolist should know that they know. If, however, there is only the slightest doubt on the part of an entrant, it pays to stay out because the monopolist might fight. Naturally it therefore pays the incumbent to foster such doubts among the entrants by fighting the first one (to warn off the others). In short it pays the incumbent to create and maintain a reputation as a fighter.

From the perspective above, building a large factory or incurring other sunk costs can be seen as only one of a variety of possible devices for *signalling* to entrants one's willingness to fight. In the real world, of course, information (for example, about an incumbent) is limited. In particular, entrants may use the prices charged by incumbents as an indication of their costs. So setting a low price may indicate low costs and high efficiency and thus a strong willingness to fight.

## 6.7   Entry deterrence, commitments and sunk costs

To deter entry the incumbent must convince any potential entrant that entry will be unprofitable. Credible threats involve commitments whereby a firm takes non-reversible action to change its outcomes prior to any entry so that it is in the incumbent's interest to execute threatened behaviour (Tirole, 1988).

Assume an incumbent decides to adopt the strategy of responding to entry by going for expansion of output. How can the incumbent commit itself in advance to such retaliation? One option is for the incumbent to incur sunk costs by building a large factory with low marginal costs, so that output expansion consequent upon entry represents profit maximizing conduct. Hence imagine Fig. 6.6 illustrates outcomes with a large factory. With a large factory and low marginal costs the incumbent's threat to expand output with entry is credible. If entry appears in Fig. 6.6 the incumbent responds with a large expansion of production yielding profits of $1.4 \times 10^6$ instead of choosing static output which yields only $1.3 \times 10^6$. Now there is a unique perfect equilibrium; the potential entrant does not enter and the incumbent goes for output expansion. Here no matter what the potential entrant may do the incumbent goes for output expansion, the entrant stays out and a Nash equilibrium condition exists (Dixit, 1980).

A military analogy may help. When the Vikings attacked Saxon England, the worst smell for the Saxons was that of woodsmoke. This smoke came not from Viking campfires, nor from burning Saxon villages. It came from burning longships, for it meant that the Vikings could not go home; if the Saxons attacked, the Vikings would fight to the death.

Generally in an entry game when an incumbent can choose plant size/scale it can use the strategic investment in an excess capacity to deter entry. Strategic investment effects are also present in industries where there are multiple incumbents, even if additional entry is not expected. Hence, when a firm goes for cost-cutting technologies the firm enjoys lower future costs. A fall in costs will normally raise profits. This is a natural occurrence whether the firm is competitive, monopolistic or an oligopolist (Norman and La Manna, 1992).

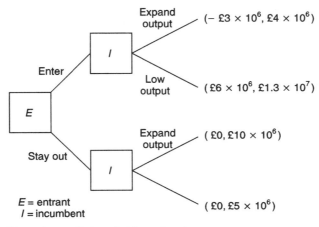

**Figure 6.6** A Nash equilibrium

In oligopoly a cut in marginal costs caused by investment in new technology causes a strong pressure to expand output. Rivals must recognize this and may reduce their own output in the face of an aggressive low-cost rival. A reduction in the rival's production may push up prices for the oligopolist with the new technology. Hence the oligopolist may count this 'strategic effect' as one benefit of new technology. Strategic investment in oligopoly and monopoly can commit a firm to behave more aggressively which makes rivals (actual and potential) retreat (Tirole, 1988).

## 6.8 Limit pricing as a game of asymmetric information

Limit pricing may be viewed as a game with incomplete information. Suppose an entrant is considering entering a monopolized industry but does not know if the incumbent has high or low marginal costs. The potential entrant needs this data since these affect the incumbent's payoffs and so the incumbent's optimal retaliation. Figure 6.7 depicts the case: there are different sets of outcomes for a low-cost and a high-cost incumbent, but the potential entrant does not know which tree to use. In Fig. 6.7 the entrant's uncertainty about all parameters in the game are given by CHANCE. So the entrant's uncertainty about the incumbent is captured by CHANCE selecting the incumbent's cost profile. The entrant must view the choice of the incumbent's marginal cost as a CHANCE event. CHANCE in this game represents a special player in a game with incomplete information. The dashed oval surrounding the entrants' two decision nodes represents the fact that the entrant cannot identify or isolate them when the decision is made.

In this game CHANCE is making the initial choice. Unlike the incumbent. CHANCE does not optimize strategy. CHANCE is merely a presentation of the oligopolist's beliefs about the possible states of the world.

Once more the entrant must form a view or prediction about post-entry equilibrium. This forecast depends on whether the incumbent has high or low marginal costs. If the incumbent has low costs and the entrant comes in then the incumbent selects the output-expansion option,

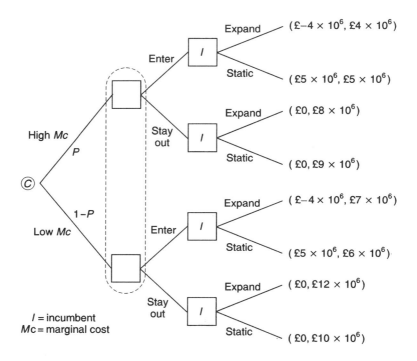

**Figure 6.7**   Limit pricing: asymmetric information

leaving the entrant with losses of £4 million. This conclusion is reached by backtracking through the tree. Hence confronted with entry, an incumbent with low marginal costs maximizes profits by expanding output. Or, if the incumbent is a high cost producer then its response is static output and the entrant obtains £5 million profits.

The attractiveness of entry for the potential competitor depends on its beliefs about CHANCE moves. In Fig. 6.7 $(P)$ denotes the entrant's belief about the probability that the incumbent has high marginal costs. Thus the entrant's belief about the probability that the incumbent has low costs is $(1-P)$. The entrant's expected profits are therefore:

$$P(£5 \times 10^6) + (1 - P) \times £-4 \times 10^6 \tag{6.3}$$

yielding:

$$(£9P - 4) \times 10^6$$

The expected profit from staying out is zero. Consequently, the potential entrant will come into the industry if $(P > \frac{4}{9})$ and steer clear of entry otherwise. Entry occurs if the potential entrant believes the incumbent probably to be a high-cost producer.

The limit price game can be extended over several periods so perhaps the entrant could ignore the incumbent's initial output choice. However, this would be dangerous since the initial output selection might give clues about the incumbent's cost profile.

## 6.9 Contestable markets

'Contestable markets' was a phrase used in the early 1980s to describe markets which, while concentrated, had negligible entry costs. It was argued (Baumol, Panzar and Willig, 1982) that such markets would approximate to perfect competition with prices equalling marginal costs, costs being minimized and firms earning only normal profit. Any deviation would invite entry by 'hit-and-run' raiders who would undercut the incumbent and cream off its 'monopoly' profit. A favoured example was air travel, whereby a route could be monopolized but remain vulnerable to competition from another airline which could fly a plane into the market at an instant's notice. The ensuing debate brought several issues to light (Shepherd, 1984), including the infrequency of real industries with zero entry/exit costs and the implausibility of assuming that raiders would continue to exist even when semi-perpetually under-employed. At a theoretical level, however, economists broadly endorsed Baumol's conclusions, if only because in hindsight they can be seen as a restatement of the conventional wisdom: the threat of competition can be as strong an incentive to be as efficient as the real thing.

## 6.10 Conclusion

Work on entry began with consideration of the perfect price: a price that would be high enough to maximize the incumbent's profit yet low enough to keep entrants at bay (given certain assumptions about the behaviour and expectations of incumbent and entrant). This approach was criticized as implausible because, it was argued, price was a poor vehicle for communicating to would-be entrants the willingness of an incumbent to meet entry with price war. In particular, price was felt to be too variable (too easily changed) to communicate an irrevocable decision. Attention then turned to other vehicles such as investment in excess capacity which would commit an incumbent to retaliation. Further consideration led to the appreciation that such investments were being undertaken largely for the effect that they would have upon would-be entrants, that is, as signals. This in turn led to a partial rehabilitation of prices: the prices that an incumbent sets are, among other things, signalling devices which convey information to would-be entrants. High prices encourage entry not only because they suggest that an entrant could set a high price itself. They also suggest that incumbent does not have its costs under control, has poor productivity and would not be able to retaliate. Low prices, conversely, are a public statement to the effect that the incumbent is lean, hungry and ready to meet fire with fire.

## Guide to further reading

As with other topics, Tirole's (1988) treatment is fairly comprehensive; see his Chapter 8. Shepherd's (1984) review of Baumol and Willig discusses many of the issues.

## Appendix: game theory and entry

### Optimal strategies for multi-product entry: a game theoretic approach

This section considers a zero sum game model where a single incumbent faces actual entry from an equal-sized entrant for both single- and multi-commodity cases. It focuses on optimal entry and defensive advertising strategies. The implications of the models described have wide real-world applications and accord with casual observations and rational economic calculations. A precise determination of optimal defensive and attacking advertising budgets are discussed. The conclusions reached for entry strategies are unusual mixed strategy allocations.

*Introduction*

The discussion focuses on opimal strategies for both a multi-product incumbent and a multi-product entrant. The incumbent must defend its market shares against significant attack from a single entrant (Friedman, 1977a). This entry market share game is played using advertising outlays as the strategic weapon on both sides. Hence this game theoretic model focuses on optimal advertising strategies for incumbent and entrant in an actual rather than a potential game (Bulow *et al.*, 1985). So whereas many modern treatments of entry and oligopoly focus on the decision to enter or not by entrants, or whether to fight or not for incumbents, this model focuses on the anatomy of the market share battle once the decision to enter has been made and the incumbent has decided to fight entry (Kreps, 1991).

## The game model

The objective of the entrant is to maximize market share in two product areas and the incumbent wishes to make these gains as small as possible. Hence this is familiar territory of the two-player zero sum game. Each rival knows the strategies open to it and its rival and focuses on these. In this case advertising outlays to attack and defend market share are the strategic weapons. Each firm behaves rationally and delivers a best response/counterplay to the other's actions. Initially the analysis concentrates on the two-good case: namely incumbent defence of two product areas against entry (Shubik, 1959).

Assume that the incumbent has two product groups $P_1$ and $P_2$ which yield profitability values/indices of $\pi_1$ and $\pi_2$, respectively. These product groups represent exclusive target areas for the entrant. Moreover, assume that the incumbent and the entrant possess equal economic strength and have equal advertising budgets 'A'. Neither firm is assumed to contemplate price competition so the optimal advertising outlays for both are the focus of analysis.

A strategy for the entrant is an advertising allocation of £$x$ aimed at product $P_1$ where:

$$0 \leq x \leq A$$

and the remainder, $A - x$, is earmarked for $P_2$. A strategy for the incumbent is an advertising outlay of $y$ to product $P_1$, where $0 \leq y \leq A$, and $A - y$ is allocated to $P_2$. These strategies are summarized as:

|  | Product $P_1$ | Product $P_2$ |
|---|---|---|
| Profitability index | $\pi_1$ | $\pi_2$ |
| Entrant's advertising outlay | $x$ | $A - x$ |
| Incumbent's advertising outlay | $y$ | $A - y$ |

Let the payoff to the entrant be proportional to the number of advertising messages delivered to the targeted product and that product's profitability. Thus if $x \geq y$, then $A - x \leq A - y$, in which case it can be assumed that $x - y$ units of messages are successful in product group $P_1$ and none are successful in product area $P_2$. In this case the payoff to entry is $\pi_1(x - y)$. If $x \leq y$ then $A - x \leq A - y$ and $y - x$ units of advertising messages are successful in target area $P_2$ while none are successful in product area $P_1$. The payoff can be summarized as follows:

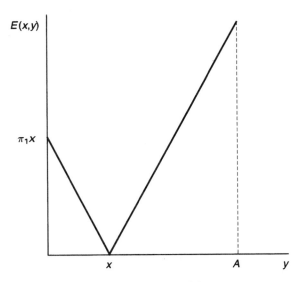

**Figure 6.A1** Optimal advertising strategy

$$E(x, y) \begin{cases} \pi_1(x - y) \text{ if } x \geq y \\ \pi_1(x - y) \text{ if } x \leq y \end{cases} \qquad (6A.1)$$

$\pi_1$ may be interpreted to be the average payoffs per advertising message that successfully penetrate the incumbent's defences in product area $P_1$. Clearly $E(x, y)$ is a convex function of $y$ for each of $x$. It consists of two curves shown in Fig. 6A.1.

So:

$$k = \min_{y} \max_{x} E(x, y) = \min_{y} \max[(\pi_2 y, \pi_1(A - y)] \qquad (6A.2)$$

The function max $[\pi_2 y, \pi_1(A - y)]$ achieves a minimum at the level of $y$ for which

$$\pi_2 y = \pi_1(A - y) \text{ or } y^* = \frac{\pi_1 A}{\pi_1 + \pi_2} \qquad (6A.3)$$

Thus the incumbent's optimal strategy is to allocate

$\dfrac{\pi_1}{\pi_1 + \pi_2} A$ advertising resources to product area $P_1$ and the rest, $\dfrac{\pi_2}{\pi_1 + \pi_2} A$ advertising

resources, to $P_2$

The value of the game is

$$k = \frac{\pi_1 \pi_2}{\pi_1 + \pi_2} A \qquad (6A.4)$$

The entrant's optimal strategy is derived as follows: set

$$E\left(x, \frac{\pi_1 A}{\pi_1 + \pi_2}\right) = k \qquad (6A.5)$$

This equation yields solutions of $x_1 = 0$ and $x_2 = A$.

However,

$$\frac{\delta E(0, y^*)}{\delta y} = \pi_2, \ \delta E \frac{(A, y^*)}{\delta y} = -\pi_1 \qquad (6A.6)$$

Use of STIELTES integral for a step function yields:

$$S^*(x) = \alpha I_0(x) + (1 - \alpha)I_s(x) \qquad (6A.7)$$

where

$$\alpha = \frac{\pi_1}{\pi_1 + \pi_2} \ \text{or,} \ \alpha\pi_2 + (1 - \alpha)(-\pi_1) = 0$$

The solution of the game can be summarized as follows. The incumbent splits its fighting advertising budget adopting a fixed deployment: allocate $\frac{\pi_1}{\pi_1 + \pi_2}$ to product area $P_1$ and $\frac{\pi_2}{\pi_1 + \pi_2}$ of total resources to product area $P_2$. The entrant's optimal strategy is mixed. The entrant targets its advertising outlay on either $P_1$ or $P_2$ selected at random. The entrant selects $P_1$ with a probability $\frac{\pi_2}{\pi_1 + \pi_2}$ and picks $P_2$ with a probability $\frac{\pi_1}{\pi_1 + \pi_2}$.

Hence if product $P_2$ is four times as valuable as product $P_1$, or $\pi_2 = 4\pi_1$, then the incumbent defends $P_2$ with 0.8 of its advertising allocation. The optimal strategy for the entrant is to target $P_1$ with its entire advertising budget with a probability of 0.8.

### N-product entry case

The foregoing results can be generalized for an $n$-product case. Once more the problem is viewed as a two-player zero sum game. The entrant aims for maximum market share gains whereas the incumbent wishes to minimize these. This game can be analysed in a very simplified form in which each player has to make a single choice. The entrant must select an optimal allocation of advertising resources among product targets and the incumbent chooses an allocation of defensive advertising resources for its product portfolio. Interesting questions arise when the game is stylized in this form. For example, should all products be defended by the incumbent? If the incumbent decides to defend some products how will these be chosen? How should the entrant select its product areas? Consider the following model: assume both the incumbent and entrant have equal resources and are of equal size. The incumbent has $Q$ units of advertising resources to allocate among $n$-products, which are $P_1, P_2, \ldots, P_n$. These products have relative profitability values of $\pi_1, \pi_2, \ldots, \pi_n$ respectively and are ordered as follows:

$$0 < \pi_1 < \pi_2 < \ldots < \pi_n$$

The entrant has $Z$ units of advertising resources to distribute among $n$ product targets, and $Z \geq Q$.

A strategy for the entrant is an advertising allocation of resources $Z$ among $n$ product targets, so the entrant's strategy is a set of numbers:

$$x_1, x_2, \ldots, x_n \text{ such that } x_i \geq 0 \text{ and } \sum_{i=1}^{n} x_i = Z$$

A strategy for the incumbent is the set of numbers $y_1, y_2, \ldots, y_n$ so that $y_i \geq 0$, $\sum_{i=1}^{n} y_i = Q$. Each $y_i$ gives the amount of advertising allocated to defend product $P_i$.

*Payoffs*

It is assumed that one unit of defensive advertising from the incumbent can counter one unit of aggressive advertising from the entrant. Moreover, assume that the market penetration to any given target area is proportional to the number of attacking messages which outnumber the defensive messages from the incumbent. Finally, assume that the payoff is the sum over the targeted products of market penetration to each product area. The entrant's payoff is:

$$E(x, y) = \sum_{i=1}^{n} \pi_i \max(0, x_i - y_i)$$

where

$$x_i \geq 0, y_i \geq 0, \sum_{i=1}^{n} x_i = Z \text{ and } \sum_{i=1}^{n} y_i = Q$$

Clearly $E(x,y)$ is convex in $y$ for each $x$ and vice versa. The incumbent has a pure strategy which is optimal and the entrant has a mixed strategy which is optimal.

It can be proved that it is optimal for the incumbent to allocate its defensive budget $Q$ to protect relatively high-profit products. Similarly it can be proved that it is optimal for the entrant to choose one high profit product at random, subject to a given probability distribution, then allocate its entire advertising budget to that target area. The entrant's optimal mixed strategy is never to enter low value product areas $P_1, P_2, \ldots, P_n$ and use the whole budget $Z$ on a product selected randomly. The incumbent's optimal pure strategy is: leave low-profit products undefended and always defend high-profit products. If the incumbent has allocated its budget optimally there will be no soft targets. An entrant would get less than the value of the game if it attacked an undefended product. Given values for $\pi_1, \ldots, \pi_3, \pi_n$ precise optimal strategies can be calculated for both players (Dixon, 1986).

## Conclusions

The model outlined above yield interesting configurations and insights into an incumbent's defence/entry attack game when advertising budgets are used as the single strategic weapon (Porter, 1976a). In recent years game theory has been used to explain entry-preventing strategies when the incumbent has a pre-commitment to fight entry and to explore the Bayesian–Nash features of the sub-game(s) (Friedman, 1991). Moreover, the theory of strategic behaviour (Tirole, 1988) has been used to examine circumstances where entrants may be discouraged. Few models recently have focused on the actual entry battle which will occur given a pre-commitment to fight entry and a determined unstoppable entrant (Schmalensee, 1988). The models here change focus of attention to an actual market share battle and optimal entry strategies (Milgrom and Roberts, 1987). The game models described here are one-shot consisent types but could be extended to supergame configurations without loss of generality (Friedman, 1977b). Moreover, the models used here are capable of understanding actual entry/defence strategies used recently in the European car market under threat from Japanese entry in single-product and/or multi-product areas (Piggott and Cook, 1993). The obvious limitations of the models concern the reliance on a two-player zero sum game which excludes cooperative behaviour between entrants and incumbents (Kreps, 1991). The advantage of the zero sum approach, however, is that it permits exact calculation of optimal strategies for both players when both are of equal economic strength. The conclusions are in line with fundamental economic reasoning: for example, enter high profit product areas. However, the entry strategy of selecting a target at random and concentrating all marketing resources on the single target product (though typical of many real world cases) has not received much attention by theorists using the sharper lens of game theory.

# Questions on Part I

1 Review your understanding of the following concepts:

structure–conduct–performance

U-form firm

standard operating procedures

Cournot competition

supergame strategy

common knowledge and reputation

deterrence

dissipation of monopoly profit

deadweight-loss

transaction costs

J-form firm

Bertrand competition

von Stackelberg's leader-follower model

prisoners' dilemma

minimum efficient scale

game tree

committed sunk cost

2 Explain the paradox that industrial markets are for the most part concentrated, implying that firms should, in the absence of ruthless price competition, be earning super-normal profits yet profits do not appear to be higher in such concentrated industries.

3 'A reputation for mindless, destructive retaliation may be a company's best asset, even its management may in reality be chicken-hearted cowards who would do anything rather than upset their opposite numbers in other firms.' Explain and comment on this statement.

4 What importance attaches to the fact that the directors of a company usually own only a small fraction of its shares?

5 Examine trends in corporate organizations by selecting a group of firms finding their annual reports for say ten years ago and a recent year. See how the numbers of employees have changed. Examine also changes in the numbers of subsidiaries and the degree to which the firm(s) operate as multinationals.

6 Use recent and previous reports on the Census of Production to trace changes in the structure of a given industry; for example, brewing and malting. Explain such changes.

# PART II   APPLICATIONS

# 7 Advertising

## 7.1 Introduction

Chapter 6 noted that product differentiation is one way whereby oligopolists can moderate or even avoid price-based competition or, to be more precise, to avoid competition which takes the form of a Bertrand-style price war. Since product differentiation is often associated with advertising, this chapter examines the industrial economics of advertising. Beginning with industry level analyses, the chapter moves towards the consideration of advertising as the strategy of the individual company, where strategies such as induced (spurious) differentiation and the creation of barriers to entry come into play.

We begin with some data and some stylized facts. Data is relatively poor; we know that in the UK, advertising expenditure on press and TV slots amounts to over £3.4 billion (1991 prices), that is, over one per cent of GDP and moving towards two per cent of consumer spending. Industries noted for heavy advertising include food, motor vehicles, retail and mail order, while the heaviest spending firms are household names such as Unilever, Procter & Gamble, Kellogg, Ford and BT, all of whom in 1991 spent over £50 million. One stylized economic fact is that advertising tends to be found in oligopolistic industries selling consumer goods, as opposed to more fragmented industries and to monopolies. A second is that advertising intensity (the advertising-to-sales ratio) tends to be greatest not for the largest firm in the industry but for those ranked second to fourth. A third is that such ratios tend to remain constant over long periods of time.

Perhaps the most troublesome fact for economists, however, is that advertising exists in the first place, since it appears to run counter to two traditional economic notions. One is the dated idea that products are homogeneous: industrial economics took some time to accommodate to the reality that products are normally differentiated. Although recognition of product differentiation can be traced back to the writings of Edward H. Chamberlin (1933), it is only since perhaps the mid-1970s that it has really become part of the normal discourse of industrial economics. Second and more importantly, economics traditionally deems consumers to be rational economic agents who know their own preferences. Advertising which seeks to persuade seems somehow to threaten all notions of economic welfare. Only more recently have economists begun to accept that consumers may have both established tastes and yet a degree of ignorance about new possibilities; ignorance which prompts them to search for new information.

Economists of the Austrian school reject totally the notion of 'selling costs' (of which advertising would be a sub-category) as separate from production costs (Kirzner, 1973). Such a distinction is artificial; for Austrian economists, products are not first made and then sold. Rather, products are designed and made only with a view to sale, so all costs are in some sense selling costs.

The result of these tensions has been to pull researchers in two directions. On the one hand there are those who focus on the observable world and thus ask questions like 'What is the optimal level of advertising? Is advertising a barrier to entry? How does it affect prices?'. On the other hand there is a continual tendency to seek the effects of advertising on consumers' perceptions; does it inform or persuade? Does it actually create differentiation out of nothing? Cutting across this we have as ever the rival schools of economics: Chicago *laissez-faire* economists argue that advertising promotes competition, while interventionists see it as an obstacle to competition, a means whereby barriers to entry can be erected.

Finally it is possible to observe a process of evolution from a fairly simplistic understanding of advertising toward a richer appreciation of the position of advertising both in the corporate strategy of companies and in the search behaviour of partially-informed consumers. Thus industrial economists have come to understand that from the point of view of the producer, advertising expenditure is but one element of the 'marketing mix' which also involves the design of the product, its pricing, the selection of a target group of consumers, decisions about how the product is to be displayed (for example, the kinds of sales outlet to be used), packaging and a host of other factors. Producers thus try to promote a brand image (a statement about the quality or qualities of the product) in the minds of consumers; advertising merely plays a supportive role in this strategy. From the viewpoint of buyers, advertising again is but one element in the larger task of gaining information about consumption possibilities. Other methods which they can use include word-of-mouth and reports by consumer groups or specialist magazines. With some goods ('experience', 'convenience' or 'fast-moving' goods) such as marmalade it is possible for consumers to obtain information about a good directly by buying a jar; when goods last longer, would-be buyers are more likely to search for advice or information from indirect sources including advertising (hence 'search' goods).

## 7.2   Optimum levels of advertising

Post-war economic theorists first approached advertising with the rather basic notion that it was merely publicity which had the effect of raising the volume of sales. On the basis of such a supposition, it was possible to ask questions about the determinants of levels of advertising expenditure in terms of demand and cost conditions. Analysis began by considering the case of a single firm in static conditions before extending to take account of time and of interaction with rival oligopolists.

### 7.2.1   A dominant firm static case

For a given level of sales revenue there is always one optimal level of advertising expenditure for profit maximization. The Dorfman–Steiner condition describes the optimal mix of inputs for profit maximization. In the static case, the firm can optimize the following variables:

1 The price of its product.
2 The level of advertising outlay.

The Dorfman–Steiner condition states:

A firm which can influence the demand for its product by advertising will, in order to maximize its profits, choose the advertising budget and price such that the increase in gross revenue resulting from a one dollar increase in advertising expenditure is equal to the ordinary elasticity of demand for the firm's product.

Assumptions of the condition are:

1 The impact of advertising on sales lasts one period.
2 The firm is a monopolist of the classic type.

An increase in advertising outlay will shift the demand curve to the right.
The demand function is:

$$X = X(P, A)$$

where: $X$ = output
$\quad\quad\ P$ = price
$\quad\quad\ A$ = advertising

The profit function ($\pi$) is equal to the total revenue ($TR$) minus production ($TC$) and advertising costs ($AT$):

$$(\pi) = PX(A, P) - CX(A, P) - AT$$

where: $A$ = the number of advertising messages
$\quad\quad\ T$ = cost of an advertising message per unit (fixed at unity)
$\quad\quad\ C$ = variable cost

The firm determines the levels of price and advertising that will give profit maximization as follows:
First order condition:
w.r.t. advertising

$$\frac{\delta\pi}{\delta A} = P\frac{\delta X}{\delta A} - \frac{\delta X}{\delta Q}\frac{\delta X}{\delta A} - T = 0 \tag{7.1}$$

w.r.t. price

$$\frac{\delta X}{\delta P} = P\frac{\delta X}{\delta P} + X\frac{\delta P}{\delta P}\frac{\delta X}{\delta X}\frac{\delta X}{\delta P} = 0 \tag{7.2}$$

Rearranging Equations (7.1) and (7.2) in terms of their respective elasticities yields:

$$\alpha = \frac{\delta X}{\delta A}\frac{A}{X} \tag{7.3}$$

The symbol $\alpha$ denotes the elasticity of demand with respect to advertising. Whence further manipulation yields:

$$\alpha = \frac{AT}{XP - \frac{\delta C}{\delta X}} \tag{7.4}$$

The first part of the equation describes the change in revenue brought about by the purchase of an additional advertising message. The latter half of the equation shows the increase in costs due to an extra advertising message.
Rearrange Equation (7.4) gives the firm's advertising decision:

$$\frac{AT}{PX} = \alpha\frac{P - \frac{\delta C}{\delta X}}{P} \tag{7.5}$$

This shows that for profit maximization the ration of advertising expenditure to total sales depends upon the price-cost margin and the elasticity of demand with respect to advertising messages.

Altering Equation (7.5) gives

$$\frac{\delta X}{\delta P}\frac{P}{X} = E \tag{7.6}$$

$$\frac{P - \frac{\delta C}{\delta X}}{P} = \frac{1}{E} \tag{7.7}$$

Equation (7.7) gives the normal conditions for monopoly pricing. The left-hand side of the equation is the Lerner index of monopoly power. This mark-up can increase as $E$, denoting the elasticity of demand with respect to price becomes smaller. Here $E$ must be greater than one at equilibrium with the monopolist operating on the elastic part of its demand curve. Thus the greater the market power of the firm, the more it can raise price above marginal costs and so the larger the advertising expenditure will be.

Substituting Equation (7.7) into Equation (7.5) gives the Dorfman–Steiner condition:

$$\frac{AT}{PX} = \frac{\alpha}{E} \tag{7.8}$$

This equation shows us that the monopolist will raise advertising until the advertising expenditure to sales ratio is equal to the ratio of the advertising elasticity of demand to the price elasticity of demand. If $\alpha > E$ the firm would benefit by raising price and advertising expenditure. The more inelastic the market demand curve the lower the price elasticity of demand and so the higher the level of advertising.

It is assumed that the effect of advertising initially leads to increasing returns, but then these diminish. Hence there is no justifiable case for advertising where interception of the marginal revenue product curve with the price line occurs. However, advertising is profitable with the lower price elasticities seen in oligopoly conditions. The smaller the price elasticity, the larger the optimal advertising outlay. In monopoly, advertising intensity is likely to be high because of the inelastic demand for the product. In perfect competition, however, advertising will not occur, since a firm can sell an indefinite amount at the going price. By contrast in oligopoly and monopoly advertising intensity will vary inversely with price elasticity of demand. Hence, on *a priori* grounds we expect advertising intensities and outlay to be large in markets with marked product differentiation characteristics.

The condition implies that as demand becomes more price-inelastic then it is optimal to increase the advertising-to-sales ratio. Doyle (1968) argues that for frequently-bought products, advertising is less effective because of buyer inertia. Moreover, the advertising-to-sales ratio will be fairly constant for mature products. Hence the advertising budget is likely to be a constant proportion of sales, as seen in practice.

Again, the advertising-to-sales ratio will usually be higher for a new rather than an old product. This is because a new product initially has:

1 A higher advertising elasticity of demand which gradually falls.
2 A lower price elasticity of demand which gradually rises.

Finally, if the elasticities stay constant, then as sales increase so will advertising outlay, but this could also be true for a drop in demand.

Obvious difficulties with the Dorfman–Steiner condition are:

1 Advertising outlay, price and quality inputs must be able to be changed quickly and smoothly. In reality such changes will occur in different amounts and may be indivisible.

2 Other elements in the 'marketing mix' may alter demand.
3 The relationship between price, advertising and quality is assumed to be known exactly which is never true in an uncertain world.
4 Oligopoly rivalry is ignored.
5 Actual advertising differs in effectiveness and appeal which is not reflected necessarily in outlays.

## 7.2.2  Dominant firm dynamic case

Unlike in the dominant firm static case, advertising might affect sales in an unknown number of future time periods. Here, continuous advertising activity, past incomes and prices will create a 'stock of goodwill'.

Advertising may therefore stimulate:

1 subsequent repeat purchases over time
2 interest enough to purchase the good
3 a lasting advertising effect over time
4 loyalty to a product.

The time period for points 1 and 2 depends upon the type of good. Luxury items are not purchased often and so years may pass before the product is tried.

Nerlove and Arrow (1962) extended the advertising decision to include this concept of time (a holdover rate). Products purchased frequently will have a greater holdover rate than durables. Thus advertising may be viewed as investment and so evaluated like other investments. This 'stock of goodwill' will erode and must be calculated via costs and future earnings.

If the internal rate of return is greater than the market rate of interest firms should advertise. Nerlove and Arrow used Equation 7.9 to show this notion where $S$ = the elasticity of demand with respect to goodwill, $ST$ =stock of goodwill, $r$ =the discount rate, $d$ = the rate of depreciation of the goodwill, $E$ = the price elasticity of demand, $PX$ = sales revenue.

$$\frac{ST}{PX} = \frac{S}{E} \frac{1}{(r+d)} \tag{7.9}$$

Moreover Schmalensee (1972) extended the Dorfman–Steiner condition to include time. This shows that along the optimal present value maximizing path, the optimal advertising-to-sales ratio, *ceteris paribus* is:

$$\frac{AT}{PX} = \frac{\alpha^*}{E^*} \tag{7.10}$$

This condition assumes:

1 The firm has market power and so ignores rivals.
2 Sales at a point of time will be influenced by past and present levels of advertising expenditure.
3 Previous prices, incomes and purchases can influence current purchases.
4 A dominant firm chooses the time-path of advertising and price to maximize the present rate of profits.
5 The stock of goodwill erodes exponentially.
6 Actual $X$ moves gradually to the long-run equilibrium demand $X^*$.

In Equation 7.10 $\alpha^*$ and $E^*$ are the long-run elasticities of demand with respect to advertising and sales.

If long-run elasticities are fixed then changes in the price of the advertising messages and interest rates will not have any effect on the advertising-to-sales ratio. Hence, the Dorfman–Steiner condition reappears but with long-run rather than short-run elasticities. Once again this may explain why advertising-to-sales ratios for different firms appear constant over time.

### 7.2.3  Advertising and oligopoly

The static advertising optimization condition was modified by Schmalensee (1972) to include the recognition of oligopolistic rivalry. Schmalensee argues that 'if an increase in a firm's advertising has any effect, it must permit the firm to increase its sales without lowering price or to raise price without lowering sales'. It is therefore permissible for there to be more than one price in an industry at a point of time. However, since there is no general model of advertising and price for industries with product differentiation, Schmalensee's oligopolistic model is for homogeneous products and not for oligopoly in general.

The assumptions of Schmalensee's oligopoly case are:

1  Businesses aim to maximize profit.
2  Oligopolies react to advertising by rivals.
3  Price ($P$) is exogenous and the same for all oligopolies.
4  Advertising expenditure is not directly linked to price.
5  The ith firm's sales ($X_i$), are a function of its advertising messages ($A_i$), advertising messages of its rivals, ($A_r$), and price.

The demand function of the ith firm is now:

$$X_i = f(A_i, A_r, P)$$

Giving a profit function of:

$$\pi = PX_i(A_i, A_r, P) - C[X_i(A_i, A_r, P)] - A_i T \tag{7.11}$$

The first order derivative of the profit function for profit maximization is:

$$(P\delta C/X_i)(\delta X_i/A_i + \delta X_i/\delta A_r \delta A_r/\delta A_i) = T \tag{7.12}$$

Two additional short-run elasticities needed are:

$$\alpha_r = \frac{\text{proportionate change in demand for ith firm's output}}{\text{proportionate change in rivals' advertising outlay}}$$

so:

$$\alpha_r = (\delta X/\delta A_r)(A_r/X)$$

$$\mu_i = \frac{\text{proportionate change in rivals' advertising outlay}}{\text{proportional change in firm's own advertising outlay}}$$

or:

$$\mu_i = (\delta A_r/\delta A)(A/A_r)$$

Substituting the above elasticities into Equation (7.12) yields Equation (7.13).

$$AT/PX_i = L(\alpha + \alpha_r \mu_i) \tag{7.13}$$

In this last equation, r will be positive and i will be negative in sign, *ceteris paribus*. This is the firm's optimal advertising-to-sales ratio. It is a function of the Lerner index of market power ($L$), where: $L = (P - \delta C / X_i)/P$, its own advertising elasticity of demand ($\alpha$), the elasticity of ($\alpha_r$) and also the elasticity ($\mu_i$), as defined. Thus the optimal advertising-to-sales ratio will be larger, the smaller the expected retaliation of rivals' advertising. This seems entirely reasonable.

Moreover, if:

$\alpha_r = 0$ then the firm i is a monopolist and we get the normal Dorfman–Steiner optimization case.

$\mu_i = 0$ there is a Cournot oligopolist model where rivals are not expected to retaliate to a change in firm i's output.

There are two reasons underlying the above:

1 There is a time lag before rivals may react.
2 Advertising impact depends upon the message as well as outlay. Hence a rival may not be able to achieve an equal campaign despite expenditure being the same.

Once more if some elasticities are thought to be constant then so too will be the advertising-to-sales ratio. The stock of goodwill can be included in this model, making it dynamic. If elasticities are constant and pricing reacts to dynamic considerations the ratio is again constant.

Oligopolies may advertise more than monopolies because they are competing for market shares, but not all costs are passed on to consumers. Alternatively it is argued that oligopolistic rivalry via advertising is wasteful. However, Comanor and Wilson (1974, pp.424–425) reason that oligopolistic advertising may help to stabilize informal collusive pricing agreements and so preclude price warfare.

### 7.2.4  Preliminary conclusions

The models above define optimal advertising-to-sales ratios, depending upon the sort of market. The Dorfman–Steiner condition is very important in deciding the optimum ratio under different market situations.

The advertising- and price-elasticities of demand play key roles in the models. This is obvious in the simple static model of advertising under monopoly. It is clear that the lower the price-elasticity of demand the higher the optimum level of advertising. However, it is not certain as to the direction advertising has on the elasticity of demand. This model is made dynamic by the incorporation of goodwill, but instead of the short-run elasticities being used in the Dorfman–Steiner condition, here the long-run elasticities are utilized.

Given oligopoly rivalry, the optimal advertising to sales ratio will be larger, the smaller the expected retaliation of rivals' advertising and so depends upon rival expectations of behaviour in the market. Again, including goodwill yields a dynamic model which is more realistic.

All the models explain why advertising-to-sales ratios may be seen to be constant. This is due to constant advertising and price elasticities whether they be long or short-run. Clearly the results of the different models reveal there is a simultaneous relationship between advertising and sales.

## 7.3   Effectiveness of advertising as a market weapon

Many theorists believe there to be chain reactions of advertising effects which arise from learning and attitude-change through the purchase and repurchase stages to the final impact on a firm's sales and profits. A simple way to envisage this process is to analyse some of the basic functions advertising performs in marketing a product to the consumer. These may be viewed as possessing the following attributes:

1 *Familiarize*: making a product well known to the consumer. This minimizes the fear of the unknown, by reducing uncertainty.
2 *Reminding*: re-announcing the brand's intrinsic values to consumers who already use it.
3 *Spreading news*: this is the stereotyped role of advertising, announcing new products, changes in the existing product, price reductions and new sizes or colours.
4 *Overcoming inertia*: for example, exercises where the rewards are remote and the costs are immediate. Advertising can provide a simulated experience of the reward, on the same principle as a virtual reality computer game.
5 *Adding a value not in the product*: it may be argued that advertising creates genuine and real values that are, nevertheless, purely subjective. This is not surprisingly the most controversial function of advertising. The persuasiveness of messages is difficult if not impossible to quantify.

This fifth aspect creates a difference of opinion between the two schools of thought which will be discussed later.

### 7.3.1   Advertising: informative or persuasive?

Traditionally, economists begin from the notion that consumers have pre-existing tastes. This implies that advertising can only be informative, that is, it can only serve the role of announcing prices and product features (including availabilities). It also follows normatively that persuasive advertising is somehow immoral in that it undermines consumer sovereignty; see, for example, J. K. Galbraith (1961) and Vance Packard (1957). It is more reasonable perhaps to accept that even informative advertising can persuade; thus the information that ski holidays are on special offer can induce someone who had never considered skiing to try it out. The debate about the nature of advertising nevertheless persists in industrial economics. Adherents of the S–C–P tradition (as seen in Chapter 5) have often included advertising expenditure in their compendia of structural features, that is, they consider it an aspect of structure. Implicit in this view is the theory that advertising persuades consumers that product B is a poor substitute for product A, and thus breaks otherwise competitive markets in a series of narrow sub-markets characterized by relatively high elasticity of demand which in turn permits firms to exercise a degree of market power, that is, to charge prices in excess of marginal cost.

The alternative (Chicagoan) view is based on information theory and maintains that advertising provides information to consumers. This will raise price elasticity and thus reduce both price and market power. The approach also stresses that the key function of advertising is to announce the attributes or existence of a product and thereby decrease the cost of information searching by consumers.

A useful model of the consumer and search for information was set out by Nelson (1964). Nelson assumed that the price elasticity of demand depends upon knowledge that consumers have about close brand substitutes and not upon the actual number of substitutes the consumer knows to exist. The central concern is the probability that consumers will obtain information about substitutes in any given category. As market power is usually believed to be based on the ignorance of the consumer, then knowledge of substitutes raises price elasticity in the industry and industry price falls.

Convincingly Nelson believes the greater number of searches or samples the consumer makes, the greater the price-elasticity of demand for the specific product. A search is defined as the ability to inspect product options prior to purchase. Clearly, this is impossible or irrational under some circumstances. Despite these problems the most obvious way to gain information is by a search. Nelson argued that advertising is higher for goods or products containing a higher percentage of experience qualities, that is goods that can be sampled or tested before purchase, cars for example.

Also, if other information costs are high, advertising again comes to the fore. Nelson develops this model by subdividing these experience goods into durables and non-durables to account for the differences in purchase.

But why would a firm advertise the Nelson way? Would it be altruism? To inform customers, raise price elasticity of demand and decrease both its own prices and market power?

In this model consumers are believed to have fixed tastes. Therefore, advertising cannot change these tastes, differentiate a product, or create any form of brand loyalty. Advertising affects the customer's perception about the product by signalling product characteristics. Although it cannot create attributes it can increase the value of the product by promoting lower prices for the product.

So what are the general implications of the model? Efficient firms with a high-value product find that it pays to advertise more than does the smaller or less efficient firm. In the case of the efficient firms, advertising increases sales and is more effective because high-value products have more inelastic demand curves.

The main criticisms of the model are: It first assumes that the consumer is a perfect judge of the merits of competing products and constantly knows what he or she wants. This is not always the case, and with complex durable goods it would be an impossibility. Secondly, it assumes that misinformation can affect an initial purchase but never a repeat purchase. In other words a consumer will never make the same mistake twice. Moreover, consumers are believed to have fixed preferences and tastes that cannot be altered by advertising. Surely this must be debatable.

However, despite its failings and the criticisms of the model, it cannot be denied that Nelson develops an influential view of how advertising works as a business strategy.

## 7.3.2 Advertising and product differentiation

The question of product differentiation seems to have evolved as a way of explaining why, when two brands have similar product attributes but different prices, some consumers prefer the more expensive. Obviously most competing producers do not manufacture identical products, because consumers differ, and so do consumers' preferences. It is therefore natural to assume that customers with given preferences will continue to buy the brand that best satisfies needs. Advertising may intensify product differentiation because it may make consumers see greater differences between products than actually exist. Enhanced product differentiation has been known as induced differentiation. In turn this induced differentiation may lead to increased prices for consumers.

Alternatively innate product differentiation may be far greater than consumers believe. For example, Steiner (1973) cites life insurance policies where people believe that there are only tiny differences in services provided between firms. For such circumstances induced product differentiation may be brought more into line with the innate differences between policies by advertising. A key feature may be induced product differentiation. How can this be defined and measured? How much is too much?

To define induced differentiation two other definitions are required. Innate product differentiation is the degree of difference in product performance among key product attributes that actually exist in the market; while perceived product differentiation is the degree of difference in product performance among key product attributes that the consumer believes exist. Having made these distinctions then induced differentiation is the difference between the two.

Having considered product differentiation the issue of measurement arises. Because of numerous definitions, product differentiation is very difficult to quantify. Some theorists state that product differentiation occurs if consumers see few close substitutes for a particular brand. Simply making a product a little different from its rivals whether in price or attributes does not ensure increases consumer demand as the goods may not contain the qualities required.

The issue of product differentiation becomes more acute when the impact of advertising is taken into consideration. Product differentiation arises from the lack of perceived substitutes for a certain brand. Brand loyalty may indicate the presence of product differentiation, but not necessarily advertising-induced product differentiation. Some types of advertising (increasing the number of substitutes) could induce less product differentiation for one brand. However, critics of advertising are disturbed by the fact that it may lead to excessive product differentiation (Scherer, 1979).

Because of the problems in measurement it seems impossible to quantify the amount of product differentiation actually due to advertising. What is real and what is an artificial basis for product differentiation remains indeterminable and any attempt to separate the two will inevitably involve some form of value judgement. But what kind of products and services are capable of being differentiated through advertising?

Much of the research in this area has centred around the concept of perceived risk. Cox (1958) concluded that products whose purchase had a high perceived risk were products for which the consumer relied heavily on sources other than advertising. Roselius (1971) concluded, following a survey of 500 consumers, that buying a major brand or a previously-purchased one was preferred to other methods of risk reduction, government reports, word of mouth, shopping activity, etc. Advertising is less potent when perceived risk is high.

Product differentiation plays a significant role in the theories of the economic effects of advertising; yet no operational definition exists. The type of risk involved, whether it be social or economic, is central to disentangling the concepts of advertising and product differentiation and making sense of the evidence. A closer examination of consumer behaviour is needed in order to formulate new measures of product differentiation.

Apparently product differentiation can have significant effects upon sales, and advertising can have varying effects on product differentiation. Brand loyalty is the tendency of consumers to purchase one brand on a regular basis. One of the major functions of advertising is to promote brand loyalty. So a number of issues arise:

1  How may brand loyalty be affected by advertising?
2  What is the effect of advertising in relation to other elements in the marketing package?
3  What is the impact of advertising on brand disloyalty?
4  Could new products be introduced into the market without advertising?

So what empirical evidence is available on the subject? Schmalensee (1972) argues that brand loyalty created by advertising can only be considered a barrier to entry if loyalty could not easily be changed. Evidence that brand loyalty does not necessarily stem from product differences supports Schmalensee's view. Lambin (1976) concludes that product quality is the key determinant of brand loyalty. The relationship between product quality and brand loyalty will hide any weaker relationship that may exist between brand loyalty and advertising intensity. There is actually very little evidence in market research to show a relationship between brand loyalty and advertising. Many researchers believe consumers have a shortlist of preferences which they choose from in an irregular and erratic way.

In conclusion therefore from the evidence available, there is no convincing evidence to suggest that advertising increases the amount of brand loyalty in an industry. Product quality is a much more important factor. However, the impact of advertising can vary considerably across various markets.

## 7.3.3 Advertising and prices

The argument that advertising reduces price in oligopoly is invalid unless the following conditions are satisfied: advertising must increase the quantity sold, and either unit profit must be reduced or unit production cost must decline with increases in output. So, if total industry demand for the advertised product remains unchanged, demand for one firm's products can only increase at the expense of another. Under these circumstances advertising can only cut the industry price if some sellers are driven out of the market allowing others to benefit from scale economies.

Alternatively, if one firm increases advertising outlays and competitors respond, then advertising has had the effect of raising costs. If firms cooperate and reduce advertising, costs are lowered and industry profits are increased. If price is increased due to advertising, then the costs of the product plus the cost of information may be lower to buyers than without advertising.

Few studies have examined explicitly the effect of advertising on price sensitivity. Some studies are summarized in Table 7.1.

When interpreting these studies it should be remembered that the impact of advertising on price will largely depend on the kind of advertising campaign. As seen in the table, some studies show that advertising decreases price sensitivity, while others show it increases it. It is interesting to note that those supporting the second view have studied consumer prices, while those supporting the first view focused on factory prices. This is consistent with the models put forward by Porter (1976a) and others. Most analyses attempt to subsume the many possible effects of advertising under one all-encompassing framework, ignoring the specific conditions of particular markets. Porter (1976b) and Steiner (1973) by contrast focus on the role of manufacturers' advertising and its impact on the relationship between manufacturer and retailer.

Porter (1976b) examines the structural determinants of profits in the industry. Although manufacturer advertising intensity is a major determinant of profitability, Porter believes no simple structural relationship exists between manufacturer advertising and market power (measured by manufacturer profits). Rather, for some products, consumers are likely to obtain information from manufacturer advertising, hence giving the advertiser the potential to increase profits. Similarly for different goods the consumer seeks different information from a different source, usually retail outlets. This weakens the manufacturer's ability to increase profits. The implications of the model are derived mostly from this bilateral market relationship between manufacturers and retailers. Porter's key focus is on the manufacturer's profits and how these are affected by the retailer's role in the market.

To strengthen the model, Porter defines two types of goods based on the product characteristics and the character of the consumer search: convenience and non-convenience goods. This delimits the goods outlets to characterize the distinction in types and product markets. This is the key to Porter's explanation of how and why manufacturers' advertising operates differently through various product markets.

**TABLE 7.1   Effect of advertising on price sensitivity**

| Study | Independent variable | Dependent variable | Relationship found | Conclusions |
|---|---|---|---|---|
| Camanor and Wilson (1974) | Industry price elasticity of 38 consumer goods industries | Industry advertising-to-sales ratios | Negative | Advertising decreases factory prices |
| Lambin (1976) | Brand advertising intensity (18 to 23 brands) | Price-elasticity of demand; cross-section of firms and industries studied | Negative | Advertising lowers factory sensitivity |
| Wittink (1977) | Share of advertising for a single brand in different sales areas | Sensitivity of market share to retail prices | Positive | Advertising raises retail price sensitivity in most areas |
| Shultz and Vantionacker (1979) | Shares of single brand's advertising expenditures | Sensitivity of market share to relative price | Negative | Advertising lowers retail price sensitivity |
| Eskin (1975) | Manufacturer advertising and retail price for a single brand in different locations | Retail sales per store adjusted for shop size | Negative | Advertising raises retail price sensitivity |
| Eskin and Baron (1977) | Manufacturer advertising and retail price for a single brand in different territories/ stores plus three additional cases | Retail sales per shop adjusted for outlet size | Negative | In two of the three extra cases, advertising increases retail price sensitivity |
| Prasad and Ring (1983) | Surrogates for advertising exposures achieved in various media interactions with relative retail price | Brand share of panel expenditures | Negative relation between relative prices and media exposure indices | Negative signs for two out of three interactions between relative price and different media types; inference made that high retail price reduces advertising impact |

Porter considers how the supply of and demand for information differs according to the type of market at issue. He argues that the consumer strategy for collecting information guides the seller in deciding what mix of sales promotions to employ. So, the buyer uses a mix of information, hard (for example, consumer reports) or soft (for example, television advertisements) determined by the attributes of the products and the utility risked by a right or wrong decision. Consumers naturally take care about decisions when purchasing goods of a high price or where a bad decision is not easily corrected. The manufacturer's advertising effectiveness differs between products with different attributes as does the consumer's information search.

Having classified goods into two types Porter does likewise with retail outlets to reflect the nature of the buyer's choice: convenience and non-convenience. In the convenience goods market the retailer has little power to differentiate goods and provides little more than display areas. Advertising, however, may be used by the manufacturer which may increase factory price to the retailer and decrease the retailer's trade margins. The retailers accept low margins in the case of convenience goods since the size of the purchases is small, but advertising outlay is high and this will lead to a higher turnover.

Researchers have observed that big advertisers or firms with large market share have lower advertising-to-sales ratios than smaller firms. The declining advertising intensity with a larger market share or larger sales volume could be the result of advertising carry-over effects from previous periods. Alternatively, it might be due to several factors: improved product quality, better distribution or lower prices which lead to increased sales without advertising. Moveover, some have concluded that advertising ratio data alone provides an *a priori* basis for examining the existence of scale economies in advertising. So a sound test for increasing returns would be controlled samples in various test areas. If economies of scale exist these would be revealed explicitly. A majority of such studies report results indicating that an S-shaped response curve best fits the data. This evidence is representative of the type of research needed to conclude whether scale economies in advertising do exist. However, far more evidence is required for this function to be generalized to all products and brands. Surely advertising economies are more likely to be connected with major strategic changes, for example, switching from regional to national markets than mere repetition of the same advertising messages?

In the case of non-convenience goods the retailer is needed to give information to consumers and thus to differentiate the product. Manufacturer advertising will be used primarily to strengthen the brand image. Advertising will, however, take a secondary role to other promotional devices and so factory prices will be higher and trade margins wider than for similarly-priced convenience goods.

Porter argues the level of alternative product differentiation therefore affects the potential profit margin for industry. Manufacturers of convenience goods follow a pull strategy with the reward of higher percentage industry profits. Manufacturers of non-convenience goods follow a push strategy which allows retailers a higher percentage of industry profits.

What are the major implications of Porter's model? There are two propositions based on a view of buyer behaviour for convenience and non-convenience goods. First, advertising is a more powerful determinant of sales and profit in the convenience goods sector. Secondly, advertising messages that influence buyer behaviour in convenience goods industries are less likely to be based on measurable product attributes.

Porter gives no verifiable evidence for either proposition, but he does cite the literature on the issues and tries to confirm the propositions. Thus some have showed that purchases characterized by high risk were those about which consumers sought most data, not given by the seller. Surveys of consumer information preferences for types of perceived risk situations, moreover, placed store image and comparison shopping ahead of advertising. Further research information supports the view that consumers are more likely to take greater care assessing product data when involved in the purchasing decision (Reekie, 1981). Porter offered insights into the relationship between the manufacturer and retailer and the retailer and consumer which affects the role of advertising in the strategy, and the type of economic impacts expected. The convenience/non-convenience (experience/search) divide is clearly a powerful one that deserves to be developed.

## 7.4 Advertising as a barrier to entry

The traditional model of industrial organization holds that advertising is a means of persuasion that changes consumer preferences, leading buyers to believe that there are fewer substitutes for a particular brand. Demand thus becomes less elastic. In this traditional view, advertising serves as a barrier to entry, allowing incumbents to raise prices and profits. The interpretation is supported by Bain and others from the structuralist school; in Chapter 5 we noted that research in the 1960s and 1970s frequently found profitability to be partially explained by advertising-to-sales ratios. An extension of this issue is whether brand proliferation, supported by advertising, directly prevents new firms from entering a market. Intuition suggests that it might in that, *ceteris paribus*, entrants would have to bear heavier costs in order to acquire market share. If, however, one begins from the proposition that tastes are a datum (that is, are not created *ab initio* by advertising) the question that arises is whether incumbents or entrants have the greater incentive to meet those tastes by offering new brands.

In a seminal article, Scherer (1979) critically reviewed the issue of brand proliferation in the ready-to-eat breakfast cereal industry. The industry had seen rapid growth (roughly 10 per cent per year) in the period 1950–65, and was dominated by four firms (CR4 = 90 per cent). It was also noted for a high profit mark-up over direct production costs, high returns and high advertising (the second highest advertising-to-sales ratio among over 300 industries). It was also noted for its rapid rate of product introduction: in the period 1957–70, the top six firms brought out 51 new brands and withdrew 38 so that the opening total of 38 brands grew to 67. The US Federal Trade Commission (FTC) reviewed the industry, seeking to establish whether brand proliferation was a barrier to entry, and Scherer assessed and extended their work.

Among Scherer's important contributions was his analysis of the incentives facing incumbents and entrants who considered offering new brands. As an investment decision, firms will clearly weigh expected profits against the costs, that is, price-cost margins against fixed costs. The key concept here is that of 'cannibalization': a new brand will take sales from a firm's existing brands as well as from competitors. Thus a monopolist sheltered by barriers has no incentive to offer new brands as the monopolist would suffer cannibalization. If, however, there is competition then cannibalization ceases to be an issue; the sales of existing brands are under threat from entrants or present rivals, so a firm may as well offer new brands so as to maximize revenue. The process of proliferation will only cease, Scherer concluded, when the gross profit of the additional brand is only just sufficient to cover fixed costs. Is brand proliferation a barrier to entry? The FTC concluded that it was not, in that any company could offer new brands. In practice, the experience of incumbents gave them a material advantage, but it remained true for example, that incumbents had not noticed the development of a market for muesli in the early 1970s, with the effect that new producers had occupied this niche. This instance aside, entry remained only a theoretical possibility.

A related topic is the issue of economies of scale in advertising. This would naturally give large incumbents an advantage over entrants. Furthermore, if a firm is small, the problem can be enhanced by an 'absolute cost' disadvantage when it comes to raising the necessary capital to advertise efficiently. Moreover, to capture a share an entrant would have to spend more per customer, compared with established firms, and at greater risk.

The presence of economies of scale in advertising or absolute cost barriers are by themselves insufficient to block entry or create a barrier. Entry occurs only if entrants anticipate demand conditions which allow them to make profits. Existing producers may deter entry only by charging a price that does not exceed average cost by more than the height of the entry barriers.

Whether incumbents attempt to deter entry depends upon the relative profitability of charging a short-run profit maximizing price and pricing to deter entry. This decision depends partly on the anticipated lapse of time before entry occurs in response to incumbents charging prices higher than the entry deterring level. This is seen clearly with the aid of Figs 7.1 and 7.2.

So although absolute cost advantage and economies of scale do provide some barriers to entry, the entrant's main focus is how incumbents set prices and outputs, and what form the potential entrants demand curve might assume. This cost advantage will rely partly on the level

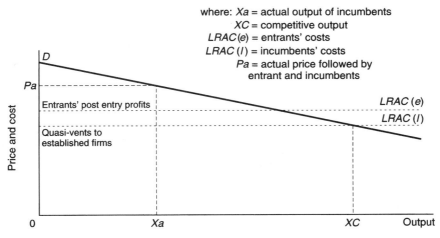

**Figure 7.1** Entry with barriers

of brand loyalty a firm possesses and this in turn depends partly on the effectiveness and level of its advertising budgets. Moreover, cost of advertising for a potential entrant to compete on equal terms with incumbents may constitute a barrier itself. The existence of a threshold level as a source of scale economies is more defensible than any proposition about increasing marginal revenues via the repetition of messages. However, the general conclusion remains that while product differentiation is a workable business strategy, poorly-designed tests, bad interpretations and above all varying definitions have clouded research efforts to analyse its costs and effectiveness.

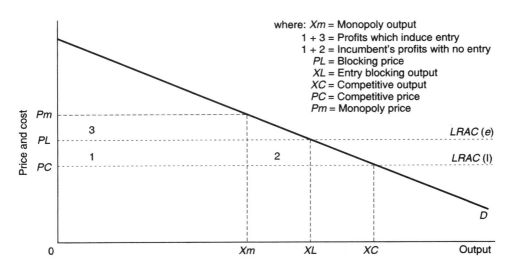

**Figure 7.2** Limit pricing

## 7.5   Conclusion

Findings in this area are even more tentative than in other aspects of industrial economics. Partly this reflects data problems. More important, however, is the relatively unrefined conceptual base. We have noted the objections of neo-Austrian economists to the idea of 'selling costs' (and thus selling resources) as separate categories, as well as the frequently poor match between economists' notions and the real-world practices of marketing. A gulf divides those who see advertising as reducing competition by creating barriers and those who see it as diffusing information and thus enhancing competition. What is clear is that the heritage of Marshallian microeconomics which presumes that an 'industry' produces a homogeneous product, with firms competing essentially on price, is a poor foundation for understanding a world of differentiated products, and the profession has been forced to innovate or to borrow ideas from business and management; the process of evolution and adaptation, in economics as in business, goes on.

## Guide to further reading

Martin (1993) and Hay and Morris (1991) have useful discussions of this topic from an economic perspective, while Kay (1993) views it more from a business standpoint.

# 8 The welfare losses of monopoly and oligopoly

## 8.1 Introduction

The last chapter reviewed work on the environments which stimulate firms to advertise the effects of advertising on industrial structure and profits. In this chapter the emphasis shifts to consider the welfare costs of monopoly and oligopoly from the standpoint of consumer welfare. The chapter follows convention insofar as the welfare impact is discussed in a partial equilibrium, as opposed to a general equilibrium framework. In this sense modern industrial economics pursues the Marshallian tradition of 'consumer surplus' losses bounded by a *ceteris paribus* methodology. This has not daunted attempts at calculating economy-wide welfare losses but readers should beware of the licence adopted by empiricists in moving from firm and/or industry sample-based estimations to views as to economy-wide calculations of aggregate potential losses.

The chapter first considers early attempts at welfare loss calculations and then moves to the modern approach. This latter approach is much wider in scope but simultaneously is more controversial especially from the standpoint of pure theory.

The controversial aspects of welfare loss estimation is seen clearly if consideration is given to the view offered by theoreticians who adopt an 'Austrian' methodology, a snapshot of which is offered. The reader should note that the 'Austrian' approach represents a vigorous challenge to the neo-classical mainstream methodology, and enjoys support from a small but illustrious minority of economists.

The chapter ends by discussing some current issues in the control of market power and considers these as new areas for research and further study. Current issues in the control of market power create the agenda for the future and look beyond narrow econometric estimates of what to include in the welfare loss calculus.

## 8.2 The basic model of monopoly welfare loss

The analysis starts with the basic deadweight loss model used by Harberger (1954) and presents the model both diagrammatically and mathematically, before commenting on results. Basic problems with this methodology are then discussed. Attention then focuses on other Harberger-type studies and the main extensions of the basic model, after which alternative arguments relating to relationships between market structure, conduct and performance are analysed. Finally, we consider some of the more recent issues which arise in this area. The discussion closes with an attempt to link issues raised in this chapter with the detailed analysis of policy issues considered in later chapters.

The traditional argument against monopoly is that it restricts output below competitive levels, implying a misallocation of resources in the economy. The problem arises from price being greater than marginal cost in the presence of market power, precluding a Pareto-optimal solution. The key question then is the magnitude of the potential gains to society obtainable in moving to Pareto equilibrium, given that distribution of real income is unchanged. Clearly, the answer to this issue is fundamental when formulating anti-trust policies, since the costs of enforcing such laws must be weighed against the size of the welfare gains which result. To provide a solution, theorists have formulated the 'welfare-loss concept', which measures the potential gain of a movement from monopoly to perfect competition.

### 8.2.1    Diagrammatical approach

Figure 8.1 illustrates the demand and cost conditions relating to the product of a particular industry. Under perfect competition, price and output would be at $OP_c$ and $OQ_c$ respectively. The demand curve shows that for units up to $OQ_c$, consumers would be willing to pay more than the price actually charged. The benefit to consumers is gauged by the vertical difference between the demand curve and the price line. Aggregate consumer surplus consists of areas 1, 2 and 3, while the total cost of producing $OQ_c$ is areas 4 and 5.

Faced with the same demand and cost conditions, a profit-maximizing monopolist would equate marginal cost with marginal revenue and charge $OP_m$ for an output of $OQ_m$. Consumer surplus is consequentially cut to area 1. With units $OQ_m$–$OQ_c$ no longer produced, the associated surplus, area 3, disappears. This gain is completely lost to society and as such is termed a deadweight or allocative loss. In contrast, area 2 represents a transfer of benefit from consumers to producers. What was formerly consumer surplus is now excess profit. In reducing production, resources have been released and production costs have fallen to area 4. Area 5 is not a loss to the economy since these resources are merely transferred to alternative uses. Monopolization thus results in a net loss of area 3.

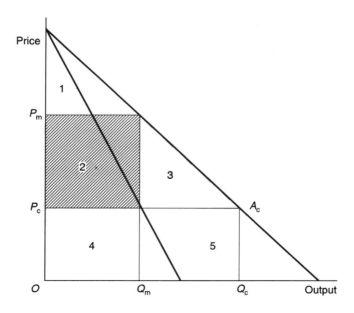

**Figure 8.1**   The simple welfare loss model

## 8.2.2  Algebraic approach

Clearly this diagrammatical relationship needs to be translated into an algebraic one so that welfare losses can be quantified. Since the area of a triangle is half its base multiplied by its height, then the deadweight loss, area 3, is given by;

$$WL = \frac{1}{2}\Delta P \Delta Q \tag{8.1}$$

where: WL = deadweight welfare loss
  $\Delta P$ = change in price between competitive and monopolistic levels
  $\Delta Q$ = change in output between competitive and monopolistic levels

Define the market price elasticity of demand as:

$$\mu = \frac{-\Delta Q}{\Delta P}\frac{P_m}{Q_m} \tag{8.2}$$

then rearranging the equation yields:

$$\Delta Q = \mu \frac{\Delta P}{P_m} Q_m \tag{8.3}$$

The relative price distortion under monopoly, that is the ratio by which monopoly price deviates from competitive price, is the price cost margin and may be defined as:

$$\Delta \frac{P_m - P_c}{P_c} = \frac{\Delta P}{P_m} = M \tag{8.4}$$

Clearly then:

$$\Delta P = M P_m \tag{8.5}$$

Substituting into Equation (8.3) gives:

$$\Delta Q = \mu M Q_m \tag{8.6}$$

Substituting for $\Delta P$ and $\Delta Q$ into Equation (8.1) gives:

$$WL = \frac{1}{2}(M P_m)(\mu M Q_m)$$

$$= \frac{1}{2}\mu M^2 (P_m Q_m) \tag{8.7}$$

Approximately therefore, one can estimate the deadweight loss to society by using the price-cost margin ($M$), the market price elasticity ($\mu$) and market sales revenue ($P_m Q_m$).

For many years these results rested in theoretical oblivion until, in 1954, Arnold Harberger utilized them to estimate in dollar terms the actual deadweight loss due to monopolistic resource misallocation in US industry.

Harberger proceeded by calculating the deviation of industry profit rates from the average for all manufacturing. These deviations were then translated into dollars of 'excess profits' and expressed as a proportion of sales to give the value of $M$. The market price elasticity of demand was assumed to have a value of unity, such that deadweight loss is given by half of $M$ multiplied by the value of sales ($P_m Q_m$). The sum of these losses across all sectors gave the welfare loss for the economy as a whole. Harberger's estimate of $59 million (0.08 per cent of GNP) at first sight appears to downgrade the importance of monopoly as a source of resource misallocation to insignificance. However, this estimate has been the subject of much debate and argument.

### 8.2.3   Other Harberger type studies

Methods similar to Harberger's have been employed by, among others, Schwartzman (1960), Bell (1968), Worcester (1973) and Siegfried and Tiemann (1974), finding broadly similar results. For example, Schwartzman based his measure of monopoly price distortions on a comparison of price-cost ratios for concentrated Canadian industries against unconcentrated US industries using 1954 data. Assuming the average price elasticity to be 2.0 or less, he concluded that the welfare loss did not exceed 0.06 per cent of GNP.

Worcester conducted a further estimate for the USA in 1958 and 1969, using data from the *Fortune 500* list of firms, rather than industry data as used in previous studies. Industry profit rates tend to bias the estimates of welfare loss downward since the high profits of dominant firms are offset by the low profits of followers. However, even assuming the degree of monopoly observed in the largest firms was typical of the whole manufacturing sector, Worcester was unable to obtain a deadweight loss much more than 0.3 per cent of GNP.

Using data for 1956–61 and statistically estimated industry price elasticities, Kamerschen (1966) estimated the economy-wide welfare loss for the US in an article published in 1966. His estimates range from 1 per cent to 8 per cent of GNP, the most realistic in his view being roughly 6 per cent, clearly much higher than that of most previous estimates.

Even if the total welfare loss is small, it may be high in particular industries. Siegfried and Tiemann (1974) found the total welfare loss in mining and manufacturing in the USA in 1963 to be very small, roughly similar to Harberger's figures. However, these results showed that the bulk of the loss was concentrated in five industries: plastic materials and synthetics, drugs, petroleum refining and extraction, office and computing equipment and motor vehicles, all of which together accounted for 67 per cent of the total estimated loss. The motor vehicle industry alone was responsible for almost one half of the aggregate loss.

### 8.2.4   Limitations of the basic model

By focusing attention on the price-fixing effects of monopoly rather than on other possible effects, Harberger's study considers only part of the story and may thus give a biased perception. Costs as well as prices may differ between competition and monopoly. In some industries, concentration of production is associated with the existence of economies of scale. In such cases a trade-off may exist between monopoly power and real cost savings which should also be considered. Conversely, if monopolization gives rise to slack and inefficiency, then welfare loss will clearly exceed the deadweight loss triangle. The issue of the inefficiency associated with monopoly was discussed by Comanor and Liebenstein (1969) under the generic name of 'X-efficiency'. Their argument proceeds by assuming that a shift from monopoly to competition not only lowers price but also lowers costs, that is decreases X-efficiency. Figure 8.2 depicts this approach.

Assume a shift from monopoly to competition will reduce monopoly profit per unit of output by $y$ units, and will reduce unit costs by $x$ units. Comanor and Liebenstein then distinguish the various components of welfare loss as follows. ABC is the potential welfare loss which results from allocative inefficiency associated with monopoly and is the standard deadweight loss triangle. Triangle ADE describes the full measure of allocative inefficiency which results from monopoly under the view that competition affects costs as well as prices. In addition, the rectangle $C_mC_cDB$ is the welfare loss resulting from monopoly and refers to the higher costs used to produce the restricted level of output. This loss has no allocative component since it is not concerned with any change in output. The important implication of this analysis is that the

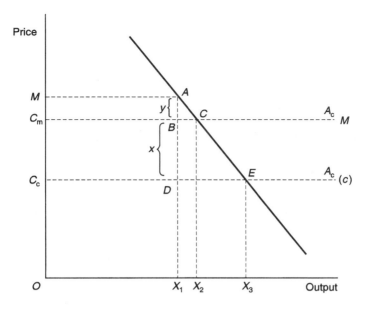

**Figure 8.2**  X-efficiency and monopoly welfare loss

actual degree of allocative inefficiency may be very much larger than the traditional Harberger type measure.

However, Parish and Ng (1972) have argued that even if costs were higher under monopoly than under competition, the resulting technical efficiency loss should not be added to the allocative efficiency loss when calculating total welfare losses. This loss is offset, they argue, by an implicit gain in satisfaction accruing to the managers of the monopoly as a result of the increased leisure time they enjoy, which is the reason for the greater inefficiency in production under monopoly. This gain may be spurious; it is certainly unquantifiable.

Monopoly may also have effects of a much broader kind. A key argument in defence of monopoly is that some degree of monopoly power is conducive to technical innovation and progress. Insofar as this effect operates, dynamic efficiency gains should be considered; Chapter 10 reviews some of the links between structure and technical change.

Market power may also have effects in other areas. For example, it can lead to excessive levels of advertising expenditure in moderate to high concentration industries, as oligopolistic firms engage in mutually offsetting advertising. Furthermore, it may lead to excessive brand proliferation or patenting, or alternatively, to other anti-competitive tactics in a bid to deter entry.

Harberger's study, and a later paper with similar results by Schwartzman (1960) were both limited to the manufacturing sector. This introduces two biases. The average return on capital may be lower in agriculture and most divisions of retailing and services than in manufacturing so that using the average rate of return as a proxy for normal profits leads to an understatement of price distortions in manufacturing. More importantly, both studies cover monopolistic misallocations only in manufacturing, although both relate results to overall national income. Clearly, monopolistic misallocation is not restricted to the manufacturing sector but problems arise in measuring and isolating data from other sectors. The manufacturing sector constituted roughly a quarter of GNP in the period studied by Harberger. If we assume the relative incidence of monopolistic distortions is as great outside manufacturing one must multiply Harberger's estimate by four to achieve an economy-wide measure.

Wahlroos (1984) has argued that Harberger fails to adjust for risk premiums. In competitive equilibrium, rates of return will vary in proportion to the riskiness of each industry. The result of this omission is that Harberger overstates the actual welfare loss by a third, in Wahlroos' view. This theoretical deduction again cries out for exhaustive testing.

### 8.2.5  The role of competition

The notion of perfect competition as a static equilibrium is a relatively new development. For Adam Smith and many classical writers, competition was a process of rivalry occurring over time. This view has been revitalized recently by the Austrian school of theorists and notably Littlechild (1981). According to this school, profits form an integral part of the competitive process rather than monopolistic deviations from a competitive datum. In Littlechild's view, most profits result from windfall gains or losses or because of the creativity and superior fore-sight of entrepreneurs who are 'first in the field'. These profits are a vital feature of a successful, dynamic economy, and not signals for welfare loss. Indeed, any attempt to remove these profits, far from improving welfare, would be likely to be detrimental, since the motive force of entrepreneurship would be capped.

Important reservations exist about the use of partial equilibrium methods when evaluating the aggregate social cost of monopoly. The welfare loss concept is often criticized for failing to consider the effect of the price change on demand and cost conditions in other industries. However, Needham (1978) notes that even though the demand and cost conditions in other sectors may be shifted as a consequence of the price change in the market under consideration, the measure of welfare loss is unaffected provided that price is equated with marginal cost in all other sectors. This is the first best condition of Paretian optimality and would be impossible to judge in practice.

In the real world of monopoly/oligopoly the theory of the second best applies. When price differs from marginal cost in diverse sectors then the measurement of welfare losses is not so straightforward. Conventional measures must be extended to incorporate two extra considerations:

1 Welfare effects occurring in other markets as a result of price changes in the market under consideration.
2 The existence, and nature, of any relevant second best constraint.

Since welfare effects in other sectors depend on cross-elasticities of demand and supply between different products, this greatly increases the amount of information required to produce an estimate.

A further objection to the concept of welfare loss concerns the consumer surplus idea which underlies traditional measures. Consumer surplus, the area to the left of a demand curve between two price vectors, is a monetary evaluation of the change in utility experienced by the individual to which the demand curve applies. The change in satisfaction itself will equal this monetary evaluation multiplied by the individual's marginal utility of income. Only if this is constant at all income levels will the area to the left of an individual's demand curve be proportional to the change in satisfaction experienced. Similarly, areas under the demand curve cannot be summed unless the marginal utility of income is the same for all consumers. Neither of these conditions are ever met in practice. However, this does not invalidate the welfare loss measures based on consumer surplus; it simply means that the monetary valuation of a change utility should be weighted by the individual's utility of income. This, however, may be a testing enterprise to execute.

It is dubious to argue that the average rate of return in 'competitive' manufacturing industry reflects the global competitive rate of return. In fact, Harberger's data indicates that the manufacturing industry was not in long run equilibrium in the period studied, since it was getting a higher rate of return than other sectors. This would cause the price differential due to monopoly, and therefore welfare losses, to be understated.

The main issues in the debate over the magnitude of welfare loss estimates concern the size of price-cost margins and the elasticity of demand. Stigler (1956), among others, has attacked Harberger's assumption that price elasticity is unity. This would imply that marginal revenue was equal to zero. Since marginal costs are unlikely to be zero in any instance, this clearly is inconsistent with profit maximization. Moreover, it is hard to think of realistic conditions under which the deadweight loss would not be small for it involves the square of the relative price distortion $M$, whose average value in the Harberger sample was only 0.036, and which common observation reveals seldom exceeds 0.2 in the long run.

## 8.2.6 Extensions of Harberger's model

Clearly, the majority of welfare loss estimates had uniformly shown very small costs for practices normally deplored. This led Mundell to comment:

Unless there is a thorough re-examination of the validity of the tools upon which these studies are founded ... someone will inevitably draw the conclusion that economics has ceased to be important. (Mundell, 1962)

Harberger and his disciples considered only resource misallocation arising from output restrictions. Thus, in terms of the analysis of welfare loss depicted in Fig. 8.1, they consider only the magnitude of area 3. Several writers, notably Tullock (1967) and Posner (1975), have argued that when monopoly profits exist, they will also attract extra resources competing for those profits, which in turn may lead to an inefficient use of resources. It is to the work of Posner in this field that we now turn.

*Posner's Study (1975)*

The existence of an opportunity to make monopoly profits will attract resources into efforts to obtain monopolies and the opportunity costs of these resources are social costs of monopoly too. (Tullock, 1967)

Posner used theft as a simple example to explain this statement. The transfer of resources from victim to thief involves no artificial restriction of output, but it does not follow that the social costs of theft are nil. The opportunity for such transfers draws resources into robbery and consequently into protection against theft, and the opportunity costs of these resources are the social costs of thieving.

Competition to acquire monopoly profits may take diverse forms. One form might be non-price competition on advertising, product styling, packaging, etc. and bribing or lobbying government officials another form. Given that these expenditures would not arise under competitive conditions, they can be regarded, in the extreme, as socially wasteful. To measure the size of these losses Posner made some heroic assumptions. These were:

1 The costs of obtaining a monopoly equals the expected profits from being a monopolist.
2 The long-run supply of all inputs used in obtaining monopolies is perfectly elastic. Thus the total supply price of these inputs excludes rents.
3 The costs incurred in obtaining a monopoly have no socially valuable spin-offs.

The first two assumptions ensure that all expected monopoly rents are transferred into social costs, and the third ensures that these costs generate zero benefits.

Given the above, the social cost of monopoly in Fig. 8.3 is the total of areas, 1, 2, 3, and 4. Where area 1 represents pre-tax reported profits, area 2 is the traditional welfare loss triangle, and area 3 represents competitive expenditure by the monopolist to maintain entry barriers. Such expenditures include advertising.

Obviously, Posner's methodology provides scope for substantially larger estimates of monopoly welfare losses once competition to obtain or maintain monopoly profit is encompassed. Using Harberger's data, Posner found that total welfare loss is 3.4 per cent of US GNP, clearly much higher than most previous estimates. Posner also argues that even greater social costs are incurred in the regulated sector of the US economy, where typically much higher cost-price mark-ups exist.

The ability of firms to maintain supra-competitive prices must be greater in industries where a regulatory agency limits entry and price competition. Depending on the estimate of demand elasticity, the estimated costs of regulation ranged from 0.05 per cent of sales (for milk) to 0.32 per cent (oil).

These estimates are, of course, very crude but they indicate that the total costs of regulations may be very high. Indeed, the social costs of regulation probably exceed the costs of private monopoly according to Posner.

However, significant reservations exist concerning Posner's use of monopoly profits to estimate wasteful expenditures on competition to obtain monopoly profits. Wasteful expenditures are likely to be less than monopoly profits, both because such expenditures may have socially beneficial effects and since competition for monopoly profits may not be as intense as Posner assumes. Any social costs of competing for excess profits should be considered net of these

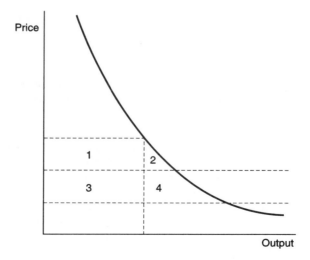

**Figure 8.3**  Posner's model of social welfare loss

effects. Moreover, firms may be able to collude to evade competition for profits. The implications of Posner's work are none the less important and deserve consideration. They are that:

1 Early studies of monopoly welfare losses may have been gross understatements.
2 The social costs of monopoly are potentially greater in a regulated sector of the economy than in the unregulated sector.

### 8.2.7   A firm-level approach to welfare loss

While Cowling and Mueller (1978) adhere to tradition, their work is more robust than Harberger's. Drawing on oligopoly theory they first estimate losses at the firm level before aggregating. Data on the price-cost margin gives estimates of the price elasticity of demand for each firm, and hence the competitive rate of return and level of excess profits. However, this partial equilibrium approach still remains open to the comment that it ignores the interdependencies between industries and firms as did previous studies.

Cowling and Mueller base their approach on four weaknesses of Harberger's methodology. First, they argue that by using separate estimates of the price-cost mark-up and the demand elasticity in the deadweight loss equation (Equation 8.8), Harberger ignored the interdependence between the price distortion and the output restriction due to monopoly. They argue that a firm i will maximize profits according to the Lerner index as follows:

$$\frac{P_i - MC_i}{P_i} = \frac{1}{\mu_i} \tag{8.8}$$

where $\mu$ is the elasticity of demand.

If returns are constant, $AC = MC$, and

$$PCM = \left(\frac{P - AC}{AC}\right) = \frac{1}{\mu_i} \tag{8.9}$$

Given that costs are constant and demand is linear then the deadweight loss is given by:

$$WL = \frac{-1}{2}\Delta P_i \Delta Q_i$$

$$WL = \frac{1}{2}Q_{m_i}\Delta P_i$$

$$WL = \frac{\pi}{2}$$

where $\pi$ is monopoly profit. Thus, the deadweight loss due to monopoly can be viewed as half of the firm's monopoly profits.

Second, Cowling and Mueller attack Harberger for measuring competitive rates of return as mean profit rates in the sample. There are two issues here. Since rents are included in the calculation of the mean profit rate, they will tend to overestimate the competitive rate of return. Also, by measuring deviations from the mean profit rate, Harberger effectively estimated the gains to be made by equalizing rates of return rather than by moving to a competitive rate. Cowling and Mueller avoid these issues by using an independent estimate of the competitive rate of return.

Third, Cowling and Mueller attack most earlier studies, with the exception of Worcester's, for using industry-level data. This will reduce estimates for two reasons. Since industry profits are aggregates of firm's profits they will include below-competitive returns of weaker firms. Further, since price-cost margins are squared to estimate the deadweight loss, the problem is enhanced.

Finally, like Posner, they argue that the deadweight triangle alone does not represent the full reduction in welfare. Expenditure will be incurred in the acquisition of a monopolistic position, for example by advertising. Thus Cowling and Mueller's measure incorporates the indirect effects of advertising ($A$). Compared to perfect competition this will lead to a further fall in output and rise in price and thus reduce welfare. Welfare loss, $WL$, thus becomes:

$$WL = \frac{\pi + A}{2}$$

If advertising itself is also viewed as bad then:

$$WL = A + \frac{(\pi + A)}{2}$$

A fourth measure adds after-tax excess profits $\pi'$ to gauge the resources that are spent in competing for these profits:

$$WL = \pi' + A + \frac{(\pi + A)}{2}$$

Given the arguments above, Cowling and Mueller go on to provide estimates of monopoly welfare loss for both the UK and the USA. Data for the USA relates to the largest 734 firms in 1963–66 whilst for the UK the largest 103 corporations in 1968–69 were used.

Their results put welfare losses as high as 7.2 per cent of corporate output in the UK and 13.1 per cent in the USA. These estimates, however, should be regarded very much as upper limits, given the strong assumptions made. Comparing the UK and the USA one finds almost twice the welfare loss (on measure 4) in the USA. This difference primarily reflects the higher levels of advertising found in the USA. These estimates are far higher than Harberger's.

Cowling and Mueller's results for individual companies in the UK, are interesting since the two major oil companies, BP and Shell, dominate the findings. The social cost associated with BP alone is roughly 0.25 per cent of corporate product in 1968–69, a figure which outstrips Harberger's estimate for the entire US manufacturing sector and serves to underline the vast differences between Cowling and Mueller's results and the early studies.

However, some qualifications are required. While Cowling and Mueller's methodology is more sophisticated than the traditional approach, it still rests on standard analysis, implicit in which is the presumption that monopolies are always bad. Although there is substance in the argument that not all reported costs will be incurred in production and distribution, it does not automatically follow that extra costs are a loss: for example, advertising may provide valuable market data.

Their assumption that firms set profit-maximizing price and output levels may also be attacked. Firms may choose to set a limit-price through fear of new competition or government regulation, or they may pursue non-profit maximizing goals or coordinate their actions with their rivals.

### 8.2.8   The social value of competition

A more recent calculation of welfare loss was offered by Masson and Shaanan in 1984, using limit price theory. This approach is radically different from Harberger's but has similarities with that of Cowling and Mueller. They depart from past studies by taking into account different levels of market power, giving estimates of:

1 Actual social costs arising from actual market structures.
2 Expected social costs that would occur if there were no competition, either actual or potential.

This methodology is based on an empirical model of oligopoly behaviour and limit pricing. Using this model they estimate the mark-up which would occur in the absence of competition. This mark-up is then used to estimate industry demand elasticity at the monopoly price. With these estimates, and the assumptions of linear demand, they are able to exhibit demand, cost and welfare conditions at each equilibrium: monopoly, actual and competitive.

One key difference in the Masson and Shaanan approach involves the way they estimate demand elasticity.

Masson and Shaanan believe an industry-demand approach is more appropriate, despite the costs of losing individual firm differences. Competition policy in the UK and Europe is geared more towards achieving 'workable competition' than towards breaking up individual firms or forcing firms to price at marginal cost. The industry approach is more suitable for dealing with the former, while Cowling and Mueller's methodology is more appropriate for the latter. To avoid the problems that arise in the PCM formula for industry demand elasticity when prices are below the joint profit maximizing level, they first estimate the joint maximizing level of the PCM and proceed from there.

Masson and Shaanan present estimates of welfare loss for a sample of 37 US industries over the period 1950–66. On average they found that actual welfare losses were 2.9 per cent of the value of shipments. The mean potential monopoly welfare loss for their sample was 11.6 per cent of the value of shipments. The social value of competition is thus 8.7 per cent of the value of shipments, of which 4.9 per cent was attributed to potential competition and 3.8 per cent to actual competition. These findings suggest that while significant welfare losses do exist, the existence of competition in actual markets is also a major force in offsetting the potential for full-blown monopoly welfare losses.

## 8.3    Alternative methodologies and the welfare loss problem: the 'Austrian' approach

Empirical studies of market power commonly use a cross-section approach, making the tacit assumption that markets are at, or near to, equilibrium. The view is that any positive relationship between concentration and profits will persist. In other words, when these results are attributed to market power, it is argued that incumbent firms are insulated from potential competition by entry barriers, and so high profits persist. However, at any point, some firms, markets or industries are likely to be in disequilibrium. A positive relation between market concentration and profitability may reflect disequilibrium and so be inadmissible as evidence of market power. Only if the relationship holds through time is the case valid.

Brozen (1970) was the first to test for the persistence of profits over time. He found that even in industries categorized as having 'high entry barriers', above-average rates of return were eroded over a relatively short time. Together with the evidence of Demsetz (1973) and Peltzman (1977), this throws doubts on the view that market power poses a problem. Instead, it tends to suggest that high profits may reflect efficient resource-use.

The conclusions above are no surprise to 'Austrian' economists. Austrians are critical of those who ignore the competitive process and regard competition as a particular sort of market structure. To Austrians, the calculation of welfare loss from monopoly is a misplaced effort resulting in erroneous policy recommendations. Conventional theory pays insufficient attention to the causes of market power and ignores the point that market power is generally ephemeral.

In the static equilibrium models, monopoly is depicted as being durable. There are no forces acting within the model to reduce the loss it causes. In a dynamic process model by contrast, there is both opportunity and incentive to discover new product techniques which might bypass the monopoly, thereby reducing over time the extent of the welfare loss. Secondly, firms may use resources in order to gain or maintain monopoly rents. However, as with entrepreneurial profits, it does not follow that the total value of these spent resources equal monopoly rents, since potential monopolists differ in ability and skill. Similarly, competition to acquire a monopoly may accelerate output of the monopoly product. Monopoly may indeed be socially beneficial. In fact, this is the usual defence for patents and other forms of intellectual property.

Littlechild (1981), arguing from the viewpoint of the 'Austrian' school, offers an alternative interpretation of welfare loss calculations. He views innovating monopoly as one that:

generates a social gain given by his own entrepreneurial profit plus the consumer surplus

Assume that a market corresponds to that shown in Fig. 8.1 (p.98) where a monopolist produces $OQ_m$ and charges a price $OP_m$. Assume that this relates to a pioneering entrepreneur who discovers an unexploited market opportunity for, let us say, mineral water. Austrians argue that the alternative to monopolistic production is no mineral water at all, rather than the orthodox alternative of production by many sellers. Area 3 is no longer regarded as a dead-weight loss to society since without the monopolist there would be no mineral water. Instead society gains area 1 (consumer surplus) and area 2 (abnormal profit) as a result of the innovator's efforts. Society gains still further when other sellers enter the field as monopoly rent is eroded and translated into consumer surplus. As price and output tends towards competitive levels, area 3 is also added to society's welfare gain.

This analysis has radical policy conclusions; radical in the sense that they differ markedly from those of mainstream theory. This (as instanced by Cowling and Mueller) sees excess profit as deriving from market power and hence as indicating inefficiency. Because the object of policy is to promote efficiency in resource-allocation, it follows that steps should be taken to break monopolies down. From a neo-Austrian perspective, such policies would be mistaken. For neo-Austrians, profits are a sign of successful entrepreneurship (unless, of course, they derive from government-imposed barriers to entry). An abundance of firms earning super-normal profits would, in neo-Austrian eyes, be an indication of a innovative economy characterized by firms who were beating their (presumably international) competitors in the race to innovate and be first to market with new ideas. For neo-Austrians, the key role of government is not to strike monopolies down but to make the economy for flexible so that firms can adapt more rapidly to changing circumstances and new opportunities.

Neo-Austrian ideas are arguably sympathetic to the view that monopoly brings dynamic gains to the economy in that the entrepreneurial profits from one innovation can fund the research which creates the next. Thus preventing firms from securing super-normal profits amounts to killing the goose that lays the golden eggs. The argument is often taken a stage further in situations where the costs of innovation become large, as in the cases of aircraft or semiconductors. Many take the view that existing producers should be allowed to form consortia to spread the costs and risks of innovation. This might of course mean the suspension of competition. These matters are reviewed in later chapters on innovation and international trade.

## 8.4   Conclusion

This chapter sets out to present the major developments in the measurement of monopoly welfare loss, stemming from Harberger's pioneering work in 1954, and to examine some of the issues and controversies surrounding this area of economic analysis. Within the orthodox framework, that is implicitly assuming that monopoly power is detrimental to social welfare, the studies of Harberger and others appeared to downgrade the importance of monopoly as a cause of resource misallocation to insignificance. Naturally, these results proved disturbing to economists who had long been condemning monopolistic market structures and advocating policy measures designed to curb market power. However, the work of Posner, Cowling and Mueller and Masson and Shaanan has reinvigorated the controversy. The modern studies include the assumption that not only is monopoly power itself socially undesirable but so too are resources spent on competition to acquire or maintain a dominant monopolistic position. The impact of this assumption on welfare loss measures was huge; for example Cowling and Mueller placed US welfare losses as high as 13.1 per cent of GNP. It would be fair to conclude that the estimates of Harberger and similar studies put welfare losses too small and later developments improved our knowledge of the welfare loss idea and provided a basis for more accurate future research.

A policy of deconcentration is likely to open up the possibility of improved performance. However, the rejection of perfect competition as the ideal benchmark casts doubt on these policy recommendations.

The debate continues in the absence of any cast-iron empirical confirmation for any of the alternative views proposed. If structure is to be the guide for policy it is necessary to obtain some solid empirical backing for the profits-concentration hypothesis. Alternatively, if the evidence for this is ambiguous then more research on the social costs of regulation is needed since the conditions of entry then become the focus of policy.

The broad conclusion is thus that grounds for concern over social costs of monopoly exist in some sectors and that more research, both theoretical and applied is needed in this area.

## Guide to further reading

A useful way to begin might be to look at the controversy between Cowling and Mueller (1978) and Littlechild (1981).

# 9 Mergers

## 9.1 Introduction

Mergers demand the attention of industrial economists for several reasons. First, they are a major feature of the world of business. In the UK between 1981 and 1987, companies spent £50 billion (1986 prices) on 4225 mergers. This compares with some £200 billion spent on new plant and machinery over the same period. In the USA from 1981 to 1986, 17 500 mergers absorbed some $400 billion (1993 dollars). Second, mergers are an important method by which the structure of industry is altered. This may occur in different ways.

## 9.2 Mergers and competition

On the one hand, mergers are vehicles whereby firms may effect entry into a new market, perhaps across national boundaries, so stimulating competition. On the other hand, mergers are a method of suppressing competition: if the producers of the bulk of the output in an industry merge, competition will be replaced by monopoly. Indeed, many of the first mergers of modern times in both the UK and the USA were of exactly this nature. In 1890, for example, 27 companies accounting for 98 per cent of the output of the UK cloth-dyeing industry merged to form one company, while in the USA, Rockefeller's Standard Oil grew by acquisition (and by leasing capacity) until in 1878 it controlled over 90 per cent of US oil refining capacity. These admittedly extreme examples of aggressive restructuring through merger carry important implications for economists of the S–C–P approach, who argue in essence that the structure of an industry forms the framework within which companies formulate their business tactics. If the structure of an industry can be transformed in a short space of time by takeovers, then conduct (that is, merging) can determine the structure of an industry. The implication may be that structure can no longer be taken to be determined exogenously by technological and cost factors acting in concert with consumer demand. Rather, structure may be determined endogenously. Third, mergers often raise many issues for public policy. The mergers of the 1880–1900 period mentioned above fuelled populist demands that governments should take the power to regulate the resultant monopolies; the first US antitrust act was passed in 1890 and the issue of market power has remained a subject of recurrent public debate since then.

This chapter examines the causes and consequences of mergers. Numerous theories of merger have been advanced with one authority noting no fewer than 15 (Ravenscraft, 1987, p.20). Given the variety of mergers and the diversity of participants in the process, the number of theories is perhaps understandable. Indeed, it would be unlikely if one theory were to embrace all instances. The issue is rendered more complex by the fact that many theories of merger are basically theories of diversification in which mergers serve merely as a vehicle. Although means and ends are difficult to disentangle, the focus of this chapter is upon mergers themselves. This permits us to focus upon three broad theories of mergers: those relating to the structure of markets (that is, the pursuit either of economies of scale or of market power), those which centre on management efficiency and finally, theories based on the tax effects of merger. A final section sets out the Austrian perspective on mergers. First, however, it is necessary to introduce some of the basic terminology of the topic.

## 9.3   Some definitions

Mergers may be classified into three categories depending on the industries in which the two companies operate. Horizontal mergers occur between members of the same industry, vertical mergers take place between firms which engage in successive stages of production such as brewing and running public houses, while mergers between firms in unrelated industries are described as 'diversifying' mergers. These last may again be subdivided according to whether there is a link between the two businesses. Where the two share customers, technology or some other asset, the takeover may be described as 'concentric'; where no link is apparent, the merger may be said to be 'conglomerate'. The most numerous category of mergers is horizontal ones, as Table 9.1 shows.

Technically, a merger involves the formation of a new company from the fusion of two (or more) former companies. In an acquisition, by contract, one company retains its identity while absorbing the victim. Mergers are not frequent; the overwhelming bulk of transactions by number (though not by value) are acquisitions of unquoted companies by larger, quoted companies. In the UK in 1988 for instance, 83 per cent of acquisitions fell into this category. (Booz. Allen, 1989, p.15). Since the directors of a non-quoted company could simply refuse an unwelcome offer to sell, it is plain that most acquisitions take place by mutual consent. Only when the company to be acquired (the 'target' or 'victim') is quoted on the stock market is it possible for a would-be acquirer (or 'raider') to attempt to buy the company by appealing to shareholders in the face of opposition from the incumbent management. Such a transaction is a 'takeover' or, in the USA a 'tender offer' (so called because the acquirer tenders to buy all the shares in the victim). Unless the context requires that a distinction be made, the term 'merger' will be used for simplicity to denote any fusion of business units.

Mergers may be financed in a variety of ways. The acquirer can offer cash or shares in his or her own company or a mixture of the two. The cash may come either from reserves, the issue of extra shares or from the issue of bonds. Table 9.2 shows recent trends. A practice which is expanding is that of selling off unwanted businesses. Such divestiture may take the form of a direct sale to another company. In many cases, however, a subsidiary may be sold to its own management team (a management buy-out: MBO). Sale to an outside management team is,

**TABLE 9.1   UK mergers by category** (*Source*: Annual Report, Director General of Fair Trading, 1994, Table G.14)

|  | Horizontal | | Vertical | | Diversifying | |
|---|---|---|---|---|---|---|
|  | Value % | Number % | Value % | Number % | Value % | Number % |
| 1990 | 75 | 89 | 5 | 3 | 20 | 16 |
| 1991 | 88 | 89 | 5 | 5 | 7 | 6 |
| 1992 | 93 | 97 | 1 | 0 | 6 | 3 |
| 1993 | 90 | 81 | 3 | 2 | 7 | 18 |
| 1994 | 88 | 86 | 5 | 11 | 7 | 3 |

**TABLE 9.2   Finance for mergers** (*Source: Financial Statistics*, May 1995, Table 6.1)

|  | Number | Total expenditure £ billion | of which Cash | of which Shares and stock loan |
|---|---|---|---|---|
| 1990 | 770 | 8.3 | 6.4 | 1.9 |
| 1991 | 506 | 10.4 | 7.3 | 3.1 |
| 1992 | 432 | 5.9 | 3.7 | 2.2 |
| 1993 | 526 | 7.1 | 5.7 | 1.4 |
| 1994 | 676 | 8.5 | 5.4 | 3.1 |

conversely, a management buy-in. Where deals are financed largely by the issue of bonds, they are called 'leveraged buy-outs' (LBOs).

Since most larger transactions (and all hostile ones) take place through the medium of the stock market it is clearly important to examine briefly the role of this institution. One of its principal functions is to place the value of the income-stream which the shares will command, that is, the expected dividends and capital growth. To arrive at these valuations, dealers use a variety of information including data on the company's present performance such as the annual report and accounts. They also make use of information about shifts in the demand for the company's products, its reputation as an innovator, the skills of the management team and other factors. Not all of this information consists of hard facts; stockmarket dealers are compelled to exercise a degree of judgement. Nevertheless, many analysts of capital markets adhere to the efficient market hypothesis, which states that share prices reflect all the information known about companies at any point in time. *It is of significance to note that mergers frequently involve the acquirer paying a premium in the region of 30 per cent or so above the market value of the target's share price.* There is thus a paradox: mergers can only take place if there is a discrepancy between the value which the market places upon a victim and its value in the eyes of a raider. Accordingly, all theories of mergers have sought to explain how a victim may be worth more to the raider than it is to its present shareholders.

The procedures used in hostile bids are also of some importance. In such a case the raider generally begins by buying shares in the victim on the stock market. Under US and UK regulations, the raider is obliged (i) to disclose its holding publicly when it reaches 5 per cent of the outstanding shares and (ii) to offer to buy all the shares when its holding reaches 15 per cent (in the USA) or 30 per cent (in the UK). Normally the raider also offers an attractive bid premium. On completion of the transaction, control of the victim passes to the raider. Often this is accompanied by the removal from office of the victim's senior management.

A final feature of mergers is the fact that they are localized in both time and space. First, mergers are far more frequent in the Anglo-Saxon economies than in the European Union (apart from the UK) or Japan. This is partly because it is more usual for companies to seek stockmarket quotations in the UK and the USA and because trade in shares in those stockmarkets is more attractive. To illustrate, in 1988 the total value of all EC stockmarkets stood at 1370 billion Ecu, of which 594 billion (39 per cent) was accounted for by the London Stock Exchange. In that year 191 mergers between quoted companies were launched in the UK against a figure of 104 for the other eleven states (Booz. Allen, 1989, p.15). Even within the US and UK economies, moreover, mergers tend to be grouped into 'waves' such as the years 1898–1901, 1926–30, 1965–72 and 1981–88. Naturally these fluctuations are influenced by environmental factors such as the stance of the government (policy became perceptibly more liberal during the 1980s, for example) and the ability of the financial sector to create new mechanisms such as the 'junk bond' to facilitate mergers. Merger waves have also formed the subject of economic research. This has established a correlation between the incidence of merger and macro economic rates such as movements in interest rates. It is clear that high stock prices encourage mergers in that raiders' shares have greater value and should thus be more acceptable to investors. (At the same time, of course, victims would, *ceteris paribus*, be more expensive when stock prices are high; high prices must operate asymmetrically upon raiders and victims if they are to promote mergers.) As Geroski (1984) points out, the significance of this finding is not clear because high stock prices are associated with general economic expansion. Thus while high stock prices could cause mergers, both phenomena could equally be the effects of an economic boom.

Mergers have traditionally involved the acquisition of small firms by larger ones. Thus the larger the company is, the less likely it is to be a victim. Hughes and Kumar (1985), for example, investigated the rate at which different sizes of firm were taken over in the UK between 1972 and 1982. Ranking firms by turnover in 1972, they found that 12 of the largest 100 firms had been taken over by 1982. Of the firms ranked 801–900, however, 23 had been acquired. This has been encapsulated in the phrase 'the survival of the fattest'.

## 9.4 Economies of scale and market power

Perhaps the most obvious justification for merger is a desire to reap economies of scale. The argument in brief is that a raider (or conceivably, a victim) may have relatively high fixed costs which can be spread over greater output if turnover is expanded. More precisely, the raider may have an asset which is (a) costly and (b) indivisible (or 'lumpy'). Such assets may be available at the level of the establishment in terms of plant or equipment, or at the level of the enterprise, in the form of distribution networks, R&D programmes or brand names. (There are also, of course, assets which are costly, indivisible and 'fungible', that is, capable of being used in several industries. Such assets give rise to 'economies of scope': they make it relatively easier for a company to enter new lines of business. When fungible assets are the motive for merger, the result is likely to be diversification.)

The issue of the importance of economies of scale in mergers was one of many addressed in an extensive research project reported by Professor Dennis Mueller (1980), the results of which will be referred to on more than one occasion in this chapter. The importance of this study arises not least from its scope: it covers merger activity over a ten-year period in each of seven nations (USA, UK, Belgium, France, The Netherlands, West Germany and Sweden). Just over 800 cases were included, with the UK and the USA each contributing about one third of the observations.

Data problems meant that each national study was slightly different. All concentrated on quoted companies and all established a counterfactual by comparing victims and raiders both with control groups and with matched companies which were selected on the basis of size and industry. Thus the studies assumed that targets and raiders would have grown at the same rate as the average for their industries in the absence of merger. To search for evidence of economies of scale as a motive for merger, the studies compared the sizes of merging companies with the sizes of randomly selected non-merging companies matched by industry. The logic was that if mergers were caused by a quest for economies of scale, then merging companies would be smaller than the controls. The study found, however, that the merging companies were as large as or larger than their counterparts. They were, in other words, already large enough to have attained optimum size. Commenting on the seven national sets of results, Mueller concluded, 'The economies of scale motive was consistently rejected' (1980, p.302).

Corroborative evidence was offered in the same year by Cowling *et al.* (1980). Adopting a case study approach, they examined a number of horizontal mergers in British manufacturing during the late 1960s. The industries included motor vehicles, brewing, engineering, cables, paint, confectionery, machine tools, bricks, tiles and computers. In each case the researchers sought for evidence of savings or productivity gains in inputs of real resources. These savings were compared both with an expected rate of productivity growth of 1.5 per cent per annum and with non-merging control companies in the same industries. In the first test, the researchers found evidence of gains in productivity in four of the nine cases. In some companies, however, efficiency actually declined during the seven years following the merger. In none of the cases, however, did gains exceed those of non-merging controls. The researchers went on to argue that such gains that were observed could have been realized without merging: that the pre-merger companies could have reaped the efficiency gains anyway.

The case studies indicated that while economies of scale were sometimes available to merging firms, they could only be unlocked through an active programme of rationalization and investment by which the constituent elements were moulded into a new entity. The merger transaction, in short, could best be seen as the start of a process of joining two companies rather than as its culmination. The results of horizontal mergers is supported by the study by Newbold (1979) which covered the same period, that is, 1967–68. Of the 38 companies surveyed, 17 were unable to report any beneficial effects two years later. In sum, while economies of scale may be a motive for merger, the gains seem to take many years to materialize, if indeed there are any to be found.

### 9.4.1 Mergers and concentration

Besides economies of scale a plausible rationale for merger is a quest for market power. Allusion has already been made to the trusts or combines formed at the end of the nineteenth century. Given the mounting incidence of mergers, it might be hypothesized that a link could be found between merger activity and changes in the structure of industry. Several attempts have been made to identify such links. The most simplistic approach has been to trace the history of a sample of industries, noting concentration levels and the sizes of firms involved in mergers. Thus Hart, Utton and Walshe (1973) examined 30 randomly selected British manufacturing industries during the period 1950–63. Their measure of concentration was the CR5 and the study recorded the mergers which the top five companies undertook. No attempt was made to specify a counterfactual; that is, to assess the growth rates which would be have been observed in the absence of merger for (a) the top five firms, (b) their victims or (c) the industry as a whole. (Growth by a company by means of investment and sales rather than by merger is termed 'internal' growth.) Clearly, differing growth rates for these groups would produce varying counterfactual situations. Implicitly, Hart *et al.* can be taken to have assumed that all three items grew in step; a not implausible assumption, perhaps, given the short time span used. Their findings were that in nine industries, concentration fell, in 10 cases it rose largely because of merger activity while in the remaining 11 industries it rose because the top five firms grew faster (without merging) than the rest of the industry. They concluded first that overall concentration had increased and second that this increase could be attributed to 'internal' growth by large firms and to their merger activity in more or less equal proportions.

A slightly different approach was later used by Hannah and Kay (1977). Again attention was restricted to the manufacturing sector of the British economy and although the period was 1919–69, the analysis was conducted separately for sub-periods such as 1957–69. To measure concentration, the authors devised their own index or, more precisely, their own indices. There were variants of the Hirfindahl index which, as readers will recall, aggregates the squared market shares of all firms:

$$\text{HI} = \sum s^2 \tag{9.1}$$

The Hannah–Kay (HK) indices used the formula:

$$HKI = \left[\sum s^a\right]^{1/1-a} \qquad (9.2)$$

When $a = 2$, this formula gives the square root of the Hirfindahl index. In fact, Hannah and Kay used several values for $a$, including 0.6 and 1.6. In later discussion, Hannah and Kay (1981) used a range of other measures of concentration such as HI and CR5 to show that their findings did not depend upon the index selected. These indices were used to calculate concentration levels for the opening and closing years. To identify the effect of mergers, Hannah and Kay 'demerged' the closing year structure and recalculated the indices. This task, of course, requires assumptions about the rates of growth which those merged assets would have enjoyed in the absence of merger (the counterfactual). These assumptions are not, unfortunately, quantified. Nevertheless, after recalculating their measures of concentration, Hannah and Kay attributed the remaining change in structure to internal growth. Their finding was that during the period 1957–69, mergers accounted for more than the whole of the increase in concentration. In other words, without mergers, concentration would have fallen. This finding is shown in Table 9.3 using CR measures for aggregate concentration (i.e. concentration across the entire manufacturing sector); the findings for individual industries are similar.

These two sets of results are clearly not consistent. The principal problem is the establishment of counterfactual internal growth rates of raiders, victims and non-merging companies in the absence of merger. Rather than the naive assumptions of the studies reported above, it would perhaps be useful to draw more heavily upon developments in understanding of market dominance and in particular of the durability of dominant market positions as discussed in Chapter 3. It is certainly the case that concentration has been falling or remained stable in the UK and the USA in recent years despite large numbers of mergers and there is an obvious need for research into the relationship between these two trends.

## 9.5 Management performance: merger as the 'market for corporate control'

A fundamental insight into the nature of merger behaviour was provided by Professor Henry Manne (1965). He characterized merger transactions as constituting a 'market for corporate control', and it applies principally to hostile takeovers. Participants in this market are the management teams of industrial, commercial and financial companies, together with financiers or investors. Many of the former engage in mutual competition for the control of companies. This competition takes the form of bids: 'raiding' teams bid for the control of other companies ('victims' or 'targets') by offering cash or securities (bonds or shares) to investors. In the case of a contested bid, the incumbent management may well attempt to persuade investors to retain their shares by, for example, promising to pay higher dividends in the future. In other words, the

TABLE 9.3  **Causes of changes in aggregate concentration 1957–69** (*Source*: Hannah and Kay, 1981)

| Measure | 1957 | Merger | Internal growth | 1969 |
|---------|------|--------|-----------------|------|
| CR50 | 48.4 | +14.2 | −2.0 | 60.6 |
| CR100 | 60.1 | +15.2 | −0.4 | 74.9 |

two management teams (the incumbent and the would-be) compete for the backing of the shareholders. If the investors decide to back the raider and accept the offer and, as noted, these offers often contain a premium which shareholders may find irresistible, the takeover goes ahead. Should the incumbents persuade shareholders to let them retain control of the business, the offer will be rejected. Takeover battles are thus the means whereby rival management teams compete for control of industrial and commercial assets.

The implication of Manne's view of merger is that it is a spur to efficiency. If managers fail to maximize profits (or, as it is sometimes phrased, to maximize the wealth of shareholders) they lay themselves open to takeover; that is, to being deprived of control of the business. The novelty of this view derives from the fact that economists have long argued that efficiency is promoted by competition in factor markets (where costs force managers to economize on resource-use) and in product markets (where inefficiency is punished by losses if markets are perfectly competitive). A loophole in this argument is clearly imperfectly competitive markets. Yet the view of merger as a market for corporate control sees the power of competition extending to parts of the economy which other forms of competition cannot reach. (Limitations on the market for corporate control in France and Germany have been noted in Chapter 2.)

The causes of inefficiency are not difficult to list. Attaining least-cost requires attention and vigour and, if the pressures of competition are not too great, it is clear that slackness on the part of management will suffice. Inefficiency may also arise from the incentive structure of the modern business corporation. This has received attention from the two groups of theorists whose ideas are outlined above in Chapter 2: the 'managerial' school and the 'agent–principal' theorists. These relate directly to mergers because managers are the agents of shareholders, that is, managers are employed to further shareholders' interests by maximizing the latters' wealth. Deviations from value-maximizing behaviour should therefore be punished by termination of employment. Moreover, if managers are themselves shareholders, their own interests will be served by value-maximizing policies. As Chapter 2 showed, however, conflicts of interest can occur. Depending on the incentive structure within which they operate, managers may find it more rewarding to expand the operations of the firm, to reduce risk or to lavish funds on executive perquisites than to maximize profits. Furthermore, shareholders may find it difficult to obtain information on business policy, while the work of assembling a bloc of votes to censure management is costly. Such activity could moreover lead to the company's stock being downrated; to the discomfort of shareholders themselves. Shareholders thus have problems enforcing their rights, that is, the heavy agency costs. To compound these problems, the benefits of enforcing shareholders' rights accrue to all shareholders whereas the costs of doing so would fall on the minority with enough interest to tackle the problem. Value-maximization thus has the characteristics of a public good, and is in consequence beset by the familiar problem of the freerider: if all shareholdings are small, no shareholder will find it worth while to enforce his or her own rights. Managers may thus be able to pursue their own interests without hindrance from shareholders.

Inefficiency may naturally take many forms. Some are obvious, such as employing too many workers for a given job, selling old-fashioned designs or owning a little used executive jet. There are, however, more subtle forms of inefficiency. These relate to the correspondence between a company's activities and its environment. Practices which are in themselves efficient in a technical sense may become redundant as circumstances change. Firms must keep abreast of customers' changing preferences as well as with developments in technology and methods of management. Alterations in the prices of inputs (including interest rates) and outputs as well as changes in the regulatory environment also compel management to adjust. Rising interest rates in particular imply that investment programmes should be trimmed. Failure to make such adjustments may mean that a company is earning lower profits than it could; circumstances which present a raider with an opportunity. For example, if a manufacturing firm owns its own premises, rising land values in the locality may mean that the company could make more money by selling the land (and either moving or closing down) than by continuing to operate in its current locality. If these options are not apparent to the incumbent management, a raider could buy the company and make such changes as were profitable.

This line of argument can be illustrated by examples from the USA during the 1980s. Between 1981 and 1984, mergers occurred disproportionately in four industries: oil and gas, banking and finance, insurance and food processing. These industries accounted for 45.6 per cent of total merger activity by value, although they made up only 27.2 per cent of the US stockmarket. The first three were characterized by far-reaching changes in their respective regulatory regimes during these years. The oil and gas industry, furthermore, was subject to abrupt swings in prices and demand. In the early 1980s falling prices and depressed oil sales meant that exploration work brought no advantage: any extra oil discovered could not be sold profitably while the expense of exploration simply squandered the profits made from producing oil already discovered. Takeover riders were thus able to raise profits by merely curtailing exploration programmes (Shleifer and Vishny, 1987). These theories cast important light on several aspects of corporate takeovers. First is the high incidence of horizontal mergers. The fact that a management team is failing to minimize costs would arguably be most apparent to management teams in the same line of business who could make direct comparisons with their own experience and would be most likely to be aware of current best practice. The specific information necessary to identify the inefficiencies of a management team is, in other words, most readily available to other managers in the same industry.

Second is the growth during the 1980s of highly-leveraged management buyouts. In these transactions, the buyers generally issue bonds which are secured on the assets of the subsidiary itself. The attraction of this approach in terms of the discussion above can be seen by comparing their effects upon investors. The securities which investors hold offer a combination of (i) a promised stream of income and (ii) rights to control the assets if the income fails to materialize. In the case of shares, the promises are vague, and pay-outs depend upon profits which are variable and which are moreover at the discretion of management. By contrast, bondholders are offered quite specific rights: the income stream of a fixed-interest bond is guaranteed and, should the company fail and be liquidated, bondholders receive their capital back before shareholders. Indeed, shareholders may not receive anything at all. Shares, in short, are riskier than bonds. To investors these risks have traditionally been acceptable because of the possibility of high returns. When shareholders are unable to exercise control over their agents, however, then the more specific rights and returns which bonds offer may be preferable. Thus management teams which are prepared to offer bonds to investors in highly geared bids may well have their offers accepted. During the 1980s in the USA, such deals (vilified as 'junk bond deals') became increasingly common, being used in some eight per cent of all mergers by 1985.

The theory that the threat of takeover is a spur to efficiency has prompted economists to produce a number of testable hypotheses. One is that raiders should be more efficient, that is, more profitable, than victims, while another is that merging ought to be a profitable activity. Much research, most of which is restricted to mergers involving quoted companies, has been directed to the testing of these and related hypotheses.

## 9.5.1 Distinguishing raiders, targets and non-merging companies

Many studies have tried to test the management inefficiency theory (and perhaps to shed light upon other theories) by identifying characteristics which distinguish raiders from targets, from each other, and from non-merging companies. This work typically involves drawing three-way comparisons between raiders, victims and control groups. Mueller and his collaborators (1980) tried five economic and accounting indicators. Only one (size) was able to distinguish between categories of company: raiders were consistently bigger than both control groups and their victims at the 0.05 confidence level. Victims, however, were indistinguishable from controls in terms of size. The US component of this study, conducted by Mueller himself, covered 287 mergers in US mining and manufacturing industry over the years 1962–72. He found that raiders were over twice as large as the mean for their 2-digit industry, regardless of whether size was measured in assets or sales. Acquired firms, by contrast, were significantly smaller than mean size for their 2-digit industry.

Another indicator, growth, was reasonably successful as a discriminator: raiders were found to be growing faster than victims in five economies, and nowhere did raiders grow more slowly than victims. The profitability of raiders was always at least equal to or greater than that of victims, but raiders were only significantly more profitable than victims in the UK. Finally, Mueller et al. examined the variability of profits and found that raiders' profits were either the same or less variable than those of their victims. In the UK and USA, but nowhere else, raiders were found to be more highly geared than victims.

The importance of size as a discriminator is underlined by a number of British studies using evidence from the same period. Singh (1975) looked at 112 manufacturing mergers between 1963 and 1970, Meeks (1977) examined 233 mergers between 1964 and 1972 and Levine and Aaronovitch (1981) looked at 109 mergers from 1966 to 1971. All restricted their studies to quoted companies and all found victims to be smaller than the median in their industries. Dissent comes only from Kuenhn's (1975) examination of 1554 mergers between 1957 and 1969, which was not able to distinguish victims from non-acquired companies on the basis of size. British researchers have, like Mueller and his collaborators, found characteristics which distinguish raiders and victims to be rather elusive. Levin and Aaronovitch (1981) for example examined 109 mergers between quoted UK companies in the manufacturing, distribution, construction, transport and property industries between 1966 and 1971. Apart from size (noted above) they searched for differences in terms of rates of return on capital, earnings per share as well as growth in these variables. At the five per cent level of significance, they were unable to distinguish between either acquirers or acquired from the population as a whole. Indeed, they failed to detect any differences in terms of these variables between raiders and victims. Singh (1975) in his examination of mergers in four UK manufacturing industries (food, drink, clothing and non-electrical engineering) between 1967 and 1970 searched for differences between acquirers and acquired in terms of profits, growth in profits, growth, liquidity, gearing and retentions. Only one indicator proved significant (at the one per cent level of confidence): victims suffered a significant fall in profits in the two years proceeding the merger. No other indicator proved significant. In sum therefore, the proposition that inefficient firms are taken over by more efficient firms is (if profits are an indication of efficiency) not supported by the evidence from these studies.

Some American studies indicate that European research may have obscured an important distinction between mergers (which are agreed) and takeovers or tenders (which are hostile). Thus Ravenscraft and Scherer (1987) examined over 5000 US acquisitions in manufacturing and extractive industries between 1950 and 1975. As with British studies, they found that victims tended to earn profits which were not below average for the sector as a whole. They also, however, subjected to scrutiny the minority (96) cases of hostile acquisition. For these victims, profits were below average for the (2-digit) industry in which they operated. The difference, 11 per cent as against 12 per cent, was significant at the five per cent confidence level. Overall, however, the same impression is generated that, apart from size, the similarities between acquirers, acquired and non-merging firms are greater than their differences.

Studies which are based (such as those described above) on accounting data are dogged by serious problems. Meeks and Meeks (1981) note three. One is that measures of growth and of profit frequently use data on sales. Mergers, however, often affect sales: vertical mergers in particular can turn transactions from sales between independent companies into cashless transfers between different branches of the enlarged company. Second, the act of merging can permit a company to alter its capital structure by raising the number of bonds it has outstanding. This can in turn affect its tax liability and thus its profits. The third problem is, however, the most serious. It is that profit and asset figures depend upon accounting conventions. In entering the victim's assets in the annual report and accounts, the raider has two broad options. One is to value these assets at their pre-merger 'book value'. This is the value stated in the companies' annual report and accounts and is normally determined by their purchase price minus depreciation to date. Both figures are usually thus based upon historic (as opposed to replacement) cost and the latter is determined by the firm's depreciation conventions: rapid depreciation will give assets a lower value while slower depreciation will show them at a higher value. (Entering the assets of victims at their book value is sometimes termed 'pooling'.) The alternative is to value the assets at the price which the raider actually paid, a price which normally includes a premium. In other words, the second method can give a value which is 30 per cent higher than the first. To illustrate, a raider with assets of £100 million pays £40 million to acquire a target with assets which have a book value of £30 million. Post-merger, the raider could declare assets of £130 million (pooling method) or £140 million (purchase price method). The choice between the pooling and purchase price method, each of which is legitimate, can make a significant difference to the reported assets and thus to the reported rate of return of the post-merger company, particularly when the victim is large in relation to the raider. Reported profits can change, therefore, for reasons which are only obliquely related to the act of the merger.

Partly in response to problems of this nature, researchers have turned increasingly to data on share and bond prices. The rationale, as discussed above, is the hypothesis that capital markets are efficient at placing a value upon the expected stream of future earnings of a company. This implies that raiders and victims should be distinguishable in terms of their share values, inefficient victims having relatively low share values and more efficient raiders having relatively higher values. Morck, Shleifer and Vishny (1988) tested this hypothesis by looking at 371 companies, all from the top 500 US quoted corporations, which were involved in acquisitions, both hostile and friendly, between 1981 and 1985. The indicator used was Tobin's $q$: the ratio of the market value of the company's shares and bonds to the replacement value of its physical capital. A low $q$ suggests that the company's assets are not being used as well as they might. The new share price-based approach, however, was no more able than the accounting-based studies reported above at distinguishing between acquired and non-acquired companies on the basis of their $q$s. On the other hand, Morck *et al.* found that victims of the 40 hostile takeovers in their sample had a substantially lower $q$ than the average for the entire sample: 0.524 against a figure of 0.848.

Some British studies have taken a similar line by examining the 'valuation ratio' (VR), that is, the ratio of market value to the book of assets. Given the arbitrary nature of book values, these studies cannot provide as consistent a measure of the value of assets as the replacement-cost approach. Thus Levine and Aaronovitch (1981), looking at 109 mergers in manufacturing and services between 1966 and 1971, reported that while acquiring firms tended to have higher valuation rations than acquired firms, the overlap between the two groups was substantial. For example, although 30 per cent of acquired firms had a VR of less than 1 (and could *a priori* be deemed vulnerable to takeover), 14 per cent of acquirers were in the same position. Thus attempts to use share values to distinguish victims from raiders have, like the accounting studies, demonstrated the overlap between them.

### 9.5.2   The results of mergers

Another major research effort has been devoted to assessing the results of mergers. As with the attempts to distinguish raiders from victims, many researchers have used accounting data on sales, profits and assets to measure company performance. The basic hypothesis is, of course, that if mergers are indeed a market for corporate control, then a merger should be followed by an enhanced performance in terms of higher sales and/or an increase in profits. In the USA, Mueller (1985) examined data on the 1000 largest manufacturing and mining firms over the period 1950 to 1972. The data related not to companies' entire operations but were broken down into 'lines of business' (LBs) which related to 5-digit product classes. Mueller identified a group of 209 companies which had been acquired by another group of 123 firms which were present both in 1950 and 1972. These acquisitions were divided into horizontal, vertical and conglomerate mergers. As a control, Mueller selected a group of firms which had not been involved in acquisitions. He proceeded to compare the market shares of acquired units with those of non-acquired units. Results were obscured by the fact that definitions of product groups had changed over the period; hence the importance of the control group which was subject to similar influences. The findings are nevertheless of interest. The non-acquirers had, over the 22 years, retained 50 per cent of their 1950 market shares. For the LBs which had been acquired horizontally, the equivalent figure was a startling 4 per cent. (For comparison, the victims of conglomerate acquisitions retained 12 per cent of their initial market shares.) Although there is no means of seeing whether these losses had occurred before or after acquisition, the findings do not offer support for the proposition that mergers raise efficiency. Ravenscraft and Scherer (1989) also used data on LBs during the years 1975–77 to assess the performance of merged units. The data were linked to acquisitions made by LB respondents between 1950 and 1974. This procedure provided Ravenscraft and Scherer with a database of 6000 acquisitions, making this the most comprehensive study to date. Many of the acquisitions were of non-quoted companies, information on which was obtained through the statements which the raiders filed with the New York Stock Exchange. Most studies, by contrast, are restricted to quoted companies. The study is also notable for attempting to control for the accounting problem of the value given to the assets of the victims. This is done by dividing raiders into two groups: those following the pooling convention and those using the purchase-price rule: and then analysing the groups separately. One finding was that, at the time of acquisition, the victims were on average more profitable than industry averages. The 1975–77 LB data was then used to examine the outcome of those mergers, which were then on average eight years old. The data showed that profits, even after the accounting bias had been taken out, fell back sharply. Control groups of small firms which stayed independent also experienced a reduction in profit, but the rate of fall for them was much slower than for acquired firms.

The 1980 study by Mueller et al., which, as noted, used accounting data, found mixed results for the decade up to the mid 1970s. In the UK, the USA, Belgium and West Germany, after-tax profits of merging firms, were found to be higher than those of control groups of similar cases. There were, however, qualifications to be entered. First, the Belgian and American merging firms failed to outperform their industry peers. Second, the superiority of merging firms in the USA appeared only after tax; pre-tax profits were no higher than those of control groups. Thus the evidence of superior performance was not clear-cut. In three other countries (Sweden, France and The Netherlands), there was evidence of a deterioration in the performance of merging companies. Certainly, evidence of a definite increase in profitability was not found. Nor was any evidence found of declining prices (as rising efficiency might suggest) or of an acceleration in growth on the part of merging companies.

One of the earliest British studies was undertaken by Meeks (1977) whose work merits attention because, unlike many of his successors, he made adjustments for accounting bias. He restricted attention to firms making only one acquisition in the period 1964–71. As a counterfactual, Meeks assumed that a company would, in the absence of merger, have retained its rate of profit relative to this counterfactual by 6 per cent while five years after merger the fall was 11 per cent. Both results were significant at the 1 per cent level and Meeks pithily entitled his published results, *Disappointing Marriage*. It should, however, be observed that there was some variation around these averages so that a substantial minority of raiders recorded rises in profits: 47 per cent in year 3 and 36 per cent in year 5. Similar findings of falling post-merger profits relative to controls coupled with a degree of variation around the mean were also noted by Utton (1974a), Singh (1971), Kumar (1985) and Cosh, Hughes, Kumar and Singh (1985). After discussing these and other studies, Hughes comments that 'there is not much evidence here for the view that merger raises relative profitability' (p.79). In view of the work of Newbold and of Cowling *et al.* which were discussed previously, the results of these larger scale enquiries come as little surprise.

As with the surveys of pre-merger characteristics, research on post-merger performance began, during the 1980s, to exploit data on share prices. In essence, the approach was to track movements in the share prices of victims and raiders for varying periods prior to and after the act of merger. To establish a counterfactual, several techniques are possible. Comparison can be made with the mean past price level of the company's shares, or with the average for the stockmarket as a whole (a 'simple market index model'). A more sophisticated approach is to attempt to make some explicit allowance for the degree of risk to which the company is exposed. The logic behind this 'capital asset pricing model' is that companies which are involved in risky industries would, even without the merger transaction, plausibly be expected to experience rather different price movements from those of the market at large. Other methods of specifying a control group are also available; Mueller *et al.* were also able to use the share prices of the control groups which they have utilized in other comparisons in their study. Differences in methodology have, in the event, had little effect on the results, which display a pleasing degree of unanimity. These are (i) that shareholders of target companies earn a substantial return while (ii) returns to raiders' shareholders are highly variable with a tendency to·be, on average, rather low. A widely-cited (though unpublished) study is that by Franks and Harris (1986). They noted that during a six-month period commencing four months prior to the bid announcement, the victim's shareholders gained a weighted average of 26 per cent (the bid premium). They also looked at raiders' share values and found, over the same period, a weighted average gain of 2.5 per cent. They also examined the share prices of raiders two years after the merger by using a market model to specify the counterfactual position. Franks and Harris found that the raiders' share values had fallen, relatively, by 13 per cent. The international study by Mueller and his collaborators similarly found that share prices of acquiring firms rose relative to those of control groups in four countries: France, the UK, the USA and The Netherlands. Three years after the event, however, this premium had disappeared and, in the UK, it had gone into reverse: raiders' shares were lower than those of non-acquiring controls. Other studies by, for example, Firth (1980) and Magenheim and Mueller (1988) confirm these results, allowing Caves (1989) to describe the finding of large gains for victims' shareholders as the 'conventional wisdom'.

## 9.6  Short termism

The argument that mergers are a spur to management to run companies efficiently has its converse side. It is that mergers (or even simply the threat of merger) force managers to maintain profits and dividends in the short run for the sake of bolstering share values. This could, it is argued, lead to a tendency to reduce capital spending or investment in R&D. Evidence on the issue is provided in work by McConnell and Muscarella (1985), again from the USA. Their study examined the reaction of share prices to announcements of capital spending or, more precisely, to changes in capital spending. The data covered 658 announcements, made by 375 quoted companies from the New York Stock Exchange or American Exchange between 1975 and 1981. Financial companies were excluded. Public utilities, whose profits are subject to regulation in the USA, were then treated separately, reducing the sample to 547 announcements by 285 firms. A problem facing the researchers was the fact that announcements of changes in capital spending are sometimes combined with the release of other information which could affect a firm's share price. Such 'polluted' announcements were also treated as a separate group leaving 349 unpolluted announcements. The method used was to establish a counterfactual rate of return for the securities of each firm by averaging their prices movements over a period beginning 60 days before the announcement and ending 60 days after but excluding a central 20 days on either side of the announcement.

The next stage was to record price movements for the securities over the 'announcement period' defined as the day of the announcement and the next day. The final step was to compare the two. Three tests were used: first, a straightforward comparison of the mean rates of return and second, a t-test to see if the difference between the two sets of returns was statistically significant. Third, the number of positive changes was subjected to a binomial test to see whether the number of positive returns was significantly different from that which would have been expected.

The results were consistent with expectations. McConnell and Muscarella found that share prices reacted positively to announced changes in investment intentions for industrial corporations: prices rose when investment was increased and fell when investment was cut. The changes in share prices were small (between 1 per cent and 2 per cent) but they were nevertheless statistically significant at the 0.01 level. (Although share prices of public utilities moved in the same direction, the changes were not found to be statistically significant.) The implication appears to be that investment (provided, of course, that it is based upon a realistic assessment of business opportunities) does not serve to depress share values but rather enhances them. The thesis that R&D is deterred by the threat of takeover was also investigated in the same study. The problem, however, was numbers: of McConnell and Muscarella's original 658 announcements, only eight related to changes in R&D spending by industrial corporations and two of those were 'polluted' with other information. The remaining six were all related to rises in R&D. On average, these announcements produced excess returns of 1.4 per cent, in line with the effects of other announcements. Nevertheless, three of the announcements produced negative returns and because of the small sample the results were not statistically significant.

Another researcher, Bronwyn Hall (1987) attempted to examine directly the relationship between takeovers and R&D. Taking manufacturing firms in the USA between 1977 and 1986 as her sample, she found first that takeovers tended to be directed towards industries and firms which are less R&D intensive than average. Second, she found that following a takeover, victims showed little change in their R&D levels compared with their performance before the merger. Taken together, these findings give little direct support to the 'short-termism' thesis. They are, however, confined to the US economy and much work remains to be done in examining the mechanisms which support the ability of other manufacturing concerns in other economies (notably Japan and western Germany) to devote more resources to investment and innovation.

## 9.7  Taxation

A final hypothesized cause of mergers is taxation: merging may have the effect of reducing the aggregate tax liability of the companies concerned. It will be recalled that Ravenscraft and Scherer (1989), for example, observed that while their sample firms earned low returns in gross terms, their after-tax returns were positive. The possibility that mergers may be advantageous for tax reasons arises from the treatment of different transactions by the tax authorities. First, interest payments on companies' borrowed funds are tax-deductible so that there is an incentive to issue bonds against shares. Rebalancing a company's capital structure so that there are fewer shares and relatively more bonds is not easy to negotiate, but mergers can provide an opportunity. Second, while company profits are taxed, losses entitle a company to a refund or a reduction in future tax. These losses may be 'carried forward' from the year in which they are sustained and used in a year in which profits are made, a process of smoothing or averaging. Such credits can also be transferred to an acquiring company. This feature of the tax system in both the UK and the USA means that a profitable raider which acquires a victim with tax losses can use those losses to reduce its own tax liabilities. In the USA, both of these effects were investigated by Auerbach and Reishus (1988). Their sample was composed of 318 mergers occurring between 1968 and 1981 between quoted companies from the manufacturing sector of the US economy. These were examined to see how many mergers offered tax advantages, with data being sought from annual accounts and stock exchange returns. A tax advantage was identified as a situation in which one or both firms had 'tax losses', that is, losses which could be carried forward and used to reduce the other firm's tax liability. It was found that such tax advantages were obtained in only 20 per cent of the cases. Even then, the gains were small: gains amounting to over 10 per cent of the value of the victim were seen in only 6.5 per cent of the cases. The researchers were, however, unable to assess other possible gains arising from the tax treatment of depreciation, so that their initial findings might, they concluded, have been understated. Auerbach and Reishus were also able to look for changes in the debt-equity ratio of merging companies. While such changes were found, they were no larger than normal year-to-year swings in the ratio, leading the researchers to conclude that capital restructuring was not an important factor in mergers.

## 9.8  Austrian perspective on merger activity

'Austrian' economists take the general view that, since the fundamental data of economic life are not objective conditions such as market structure but subjective assessments of the possibilities for entrepreneurial action, much mainstream research is misplaced. For example, Austrians would look askance at the effort to identify factors distinguishing raiders, victims and others. Since merger is (presumably) an entrepreneurial decision, it would be argued that the idea would be as likely to present itself to the boss of one company, whether it be large, small, dynamic, highly-geared or whatever, as another. Moreover, from an Austrian perspective there is little surprise in finding that mergers are not always profitable for the raider.

Austrians would emphasize that business is driven by the expectation of profit; the fact that previous attempts have brought little net gain would not indicate that the next merger was bound to fail. Further, Austrian economists would draw attention to the variation in returns experienced by raiders; although average returns are not great, the possibility of large returns is demonstrated by the high returns which are sometimes earned. Second, Austrians and mainstream economists tend to part company markedly over the significance of mergers for industrial structure.

From an S–C–P perspective, mergers can be a problem because they are a means whereby firms can raise concentration levels, creating either an outright monopoly or a concentrated industrial structure which is conducive of collusion. In other words the S–C–P model suggests that mergers affect structure which in turn affects the degree of competition in the industry and thus its performance. Austrians, however, do not consider conduct to be limited by environmental factors such as industrial structure but rather to be controlled by creative entrepreneurship. From this perspective, mergers are to be viewed not so much in terms of their effect upon structure but rather as conduct, that is, as one of a range of tactics open to entrepreneurs as part of the process of completion. If an entrepreneur can make better use of a collection of assets than their current owners by incorporating them into his or her own business, Austrians can see no grounds for objection. While Austrians would acknowledge that firms can create market power through mergers, they tend to deny its importance. For Austrians, monopolies and cartels (other than those created by governments) are essentially temporary; competition from other entrepreneurs is bound to overturn any monopoly sooner or later as long as access to the market is free. Thus for Austrians, structure is not the fixed bedrock of an industry but rather a temporary phenomenon which is constantly formed and changed by the process of competition between entrepreneurs.

The final point of importance from an Austrian perspective relates to property rights; in this context, the rights which are conferred by the ownership of bonds and shares. Bondholders have narrow but specific rights: they have a legal claim to a known payment each year plus a claim on the company in event of it being liquidated. Shareholders, by contrast, have wide but unspecific rights, such as the rights to appoint and dismiss management, to determine the level of dividends and to wind up the company and sell assets. Many have argued that in practice these rights are difficult to enforce because of the power of management; particularly their power over information. Neo-Austrian economists argue that an effective antidote to this development is competition between management teams in the market for corporate control, that is, the merger market. Viewed in this light, the creation of 'junk bonds' and leveraged buy-outs are to be applauded since they facilitate more active competition in this market.

## 9.9   Conclusion

On the one hand it is clear that mergers are an inescapable part of the free-market economy. They serve as a useful means of entry into new industries and, by the same token, as a means of exit whereby investors can recover funds expended on ventures which are not as successful as hoped. Industrial economists point to the dangers of mergers, namely, the possibility that competition may be suppressed; concerns like these have given rise to the regulation of mergers in most industrial economies. Industrial and financial economists have also established that the rewards that mergers bring are often elusive; while many acquire other firms in anticipation of higher profits, the record shows that often these profits are not always realized. The persistence of the practice of merging in the face of this evidence is perhaps a puzzle, although two factors must be borne in mind: first, the averages conceal a wide spread of results, so that while most mergers may not bring discernible benefits, a large fraction do in fact succeed; second, merging serves a variety of company strategies, not all of which could be expected to generate profit in the immediate period.

The possibility that mergers can distort industrial structure and suppress competition clearly exists. It is one that politicians have been aware of (in the USA if not in the UK) for over a century. The consequence has been a policy, followed across the industrial world at national and, in the EU at international level, of monitoring mergers for their effects on competition. We discuss this topic in Chapter 12 which deals with competition policy.

## Guide to further reading

Fairburn and Kay (1989) contains a wealth of useful material. Franks and Mayer (1989) gives an invaluable insight into the contrasts between Anglo-Saxon, German and French capital markets.

# 10  Innovation

## 10.1  Introduction

Innovation is the creation and use of new products and processes. It encompasses the use of new materials, sources of supply, services, organizational forms and the sale of existing products in new markets. Its importance in industrial economics is self-evident: the outstanding characteristic of the capitalist system is its ability to generate a constant stream of innovations whose cumulative effect is a rising level of industrial output and its corollary, a higher standard of living. Innovation is, of course, not free: like any economic activity, it absorbs resources, with most industrial economies devoting between 1.5 and 3 per cent of GDP to R&D. A common error, of course, is to identify innovation with R&D work. Firms constantly modify their products in the light of experience in manufacture, feedback from customers, changing external conditions and the creativity of their workers; recall Aoki's J-form firm. In fashion industries, innovation never ends, but it has little connection with scientific R&D. The benefits of innovation, however, are estimated to outweigh the costs by a substantial margin. Moreover, the benefits to the economy at large are estimated to exceed the returns to the firm which bears the cost of the innovation. These spillovers come in the form of lower product prices (after allowing for changes in quality), while the direct benefits to the innovator come in the form of higher profits deriving from reduced costs or increased sales revenues. Mansfield (in Landau and Rosenberg, 1986) estimated that in the USA private returns to R&D expenditures ran at 25 per cent but that spillovers or social returns raised that figure to over 50 per cent.

Economists have concerned themselves with several aspects of innovation; this chapter will focus on three. The first two are both potential determinants of innovativeness, namely industrial structure and so-called 'intellectual property rights' such as patents, while the third is the process of the diffusion of innovations across the economy. A preliminary step, however, is an introduction to the basic vocabulary of the topic.

## 10.2  Innovation: the basics

A first distinction is that between product innovations and process innovations. The former denotes the creation of an entirely new product while the latter the development of a new technique for making an existing product. In reality, this distinction is easier to state than to recognize. Product innovations are in practice not easy to define because while some companies develop their own production technologies, most buy in productive resources from suppliers. For the supplier, a new piece of equipment may thus appear as a product innovation but for the downstream industry it is a process innovation.

A second distinction, due to Schumpeter (1954) divides the innovation process into three stages: invention, innovation and diffusion. The first relates to the creation of a new idea; an event which could occur outside a business context in a university or elsewhere. Innovation denotes the first commercial application of the idea. Diffusion refers to the spread of the invention through the relevant industry. In practice, the three stages are not easy to isolate. In particular, inventions are normally improved drastically as they are put into wider use. Ray (1984), analysing the diffusion of process innovations, reported that all were subject to substantial modification. Thus invention and innovation continue even when a new piece of equipment is in the process of diffusing.

Resources devoted to R&D in industry are not spread evenly but tend to concentrate in certain industries and in larger firms. Tables 10.1, 10.2 and 10.3 give details. Clearly such patterns cry out for explanation. This chapter will attempt to show how successful economists have been in finding them.

Other important concepts are development costs, learning curves, research-to-sales ratios and 'advance pricing'. Development costs pertain to the innovation stage. Their existence underlines the proposition that technological change, although it improves welfare, is not free but demands resources. In high-tech industries these are far from trivial. The creation of the Boeing 747 jet aircraft, for example, is estimated to have cost $1.2 billion (Tyson, 1992, p.167). The implication of high development costs is that new products typically face negative cash flow before they begin to earn a return. To fund such investment, firms generally allocate a certain percentage of turnover to R&D by following a research-to-sales ratio (sometimes also called the 'research intensity ratio').

Learning curves relate to the way production costs fall with cumulative production. In other words, later batches of a new product can be substantially cheaper than the early ones. In the manufacture of jet aircraft, for example, when cumulative production doubles, average costs of

TABLE 10.1    **Expenditure on intramural R&D by industry**[1] (*Source*: *Business Monitor*, MO 14, Table 15, 1989)

| Industry | £ billion |
|---|---|
| Chemicals | 1.6 |
| Mechanical engineering | 0.2 |
| Electronics | 2.1 |
| Other electrical engineering | 0.1 |
| Motor vehicles | 0.5 |
| Aerospace | 1.1 |
| Other industries | 1.6 |
| Total | 7.2 |

[1]Intramural denotes R&D work undertaken on firms' establishments. This is largely 80 per cent funded by business.

TABLE 10.2    **Expenditure on intramural R&D by size band of enterprise** (*Source*: *Business Monitor*, MO 14, Table 15, 1989)

| Size band in number of employees | % of total expenditure |
|---|---|
| 200–499 | 3.7 |
| 500–999 | 3.8 |
| 1000–4999 | 11.9 |
| 5000–9999 | 7.0 |
| 10 000–19 999 | 22.7 |
| 20 000 + | 51.3 |

**TABLE 10.3** **Enterprises with the largest expenditure on R&D** (*Source: Business Monitor*, MO 14, Table 9, 1989)

| Enterprises | Cumulative | | Cumulative | |
| --- | --- | --- | --- | --- |
| | £ billion | % | 000s | % |
| First 5 | 2.45 | 32 | 58 | 33 |
| First 10 | 3.52 | 46 | 81 | 46 |
| First 15 | 4.25 | 56 | 94 | 53 |
| First 20 | 4.68 | 62 | 105 | 60 |
| First 50 | 5.82 | 77 | 129 | 73 |
| First 100 | 6.51 | 86 | 145 | 82 |
| Total | 7.60 | 100 | 177 | 100 |

production fall by 20 per cent (Tyson, 1992). One implication of learning curves is the practice of 'advance pricing' whereby firms set prices on the basis not of present costs but of costs that they will obtain when they have moved down the learning curve. In other words, they set prices below present costs. Such prices can, of course, look suspiciously like predatory prices or dumping. These ideas, though not incorporated into many formal models, are of some importance in relation to trade and thus to trade policy in high-tech products, a topic which we shall develop in the following chapter. For the present, this chapter (to repeat) deals with three major aspects of innovation. First we shall look at the economics of research and development: the industries and firms that undertake R&D and the conditions that stimulate it. We shall then turn to intellectual property rights, which provide the legal framework for inventive work. The third topic is diffusion.

## 10.3 Market structure and the incentive to innovate

### 10.3.1 Monopoly vs. competition

For economists who, like those of the S–C–P tradition, accept the structure of industry as data, the obvious starting-point is: 'which market structure provides the greatest incentive to innovate: monopoly or competition?'. To answer this question, Arrow (1962) devised an elegant model which indicated that the advantage lay with competition. Figure 10.1 shows how. The innovation in question is a process innovation, since this can be treated as reducing the costs of a given product (a product innovation would mean the creation of new cost and demand curves).

Figure 10.1 shows a market demand curve AB with an associated MR curve, AC. Costs are assumed to be constant so that the line DE shows both average and marginal costs. If the industry is competitive, price will equal marginal cost at OD. If, however, it is a monopoly, the firm will maximize profits in the normal way by selecting the level of output at which margin cost equals marginal revenue ($OQ_1$), so that price will be OH and supernormal profits of DIGH will be earned. Now consider the impact of a process invention which reduces costs substantially (KL). The invention, we assume, is made by an outside inventor in the case of the competitive industry and by the monopolist itself in the case of the monopoly. In the competitive case, the inventor is assumed to have patent rights over the invention which the inventor can make available to the industry by (let us assume again) licensing the ideas in return for royalties. To make the maximum profit, the inventor sets a per unit royalty of KM earning an income of

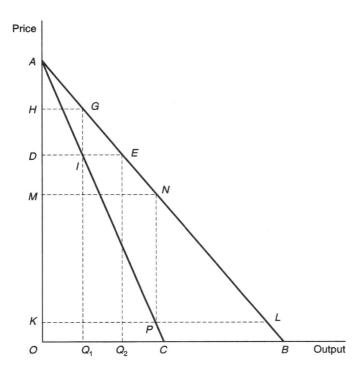

**Figure 10.1**    Incentives to innovate: competition versus monopoly

KMNP. This is, in effect, the inventor's incentive to invent: it is worth spending a capital sum equal to the present value of the stream of KMNPs to develop the invention. What of the monopolist? The monopolist could make the same revenue, KMNP, by inventing the idea. Bringing it into practice, however, would mean foregoing the old profits, DIGH. Thus the incentive of the monopolist is lower.

Two points merit attention. One is that even the incentive of the leasing inventor does not capture all the benefits which the invention produces. These benefits are, of course, measured by the area DELK. Of this, KMNP accrues to the inventor while the area MDEN goes to the consumers and cannot be captured by inventors. Thus consumers cannot communicate the full strength of their wish for lower-priced products, incentives will be too small and insufficient resources will be committed to invention. A related point is that if the invention were to be given away freely to competing users, the rise in consumer surplus would be rather greater at KDEL. Certainly, such a method would earn nothing for inventors, a point to which we shall return later in the chapter.

This analysis has naturally been subject to criticism. Demsetz (1969) argued, for example, that monopolies' smaller use of resources was simply a reflection of the commonplace finding that, when facing similar cost and demand conditions, monopolies produce less and thus use fewer resources in general. In Fig. 10.1, for example, the competitive industry produces at $OQ_2$ while the monopolist is at $OQ_1$. If one were to compare two industries of equal output (say by assuming that MR were the demand curve for the competitive industry so that both produced $OQ_2$) then with some small changes in assumptions the monopolist could offer the greater incentive.

### 10.3.2 Innovation, game theory and asymmetry

In Arrow's analysis (1962), the basis for the superior performance of the competitive industry is the fact that the monopolist has to subtract the lost profit arising from doing nothing from the gains of innovation. This assumes some inviolable barrier protects the monopolist's existing business: that is, no one else could find and exploit the innovation under analysis. Does the conclusion hold when this assumption is relaxed? To investigate this question, Martin (1989) uses game theory. Consider an incumbent monopolist who could earn a profit of £10 million per year if that monopolist were to innovate. If an entrant were to undertake the innovation, the entrant could enter the industry and the two firms could operate as an oligopoly. Joint profits are typically less than monopoly profits so these could amount to £8 million. Suppose these to be divided £5 million to the entrant, £3 million to the incumbent. The entrant thus has an incentive equal to the present value of £5 million, while the incumbent has an incentive of £10 million – £3 million = £7 million. The incumbent thus has the greater incentive. Algebraically, if a = the monopolists' post-innovation profit, b = the entrants' post-innovation profit and c = the monopolists' shared post-innovation profit, then

$$a > b + c \text{ (monopoly profits exceed shared oligopoly profits) so that}$$
$$a - c > b \text{ (monopolist's incentive must exceed the entrant's)}$$

Martin's model is open to the objection that, like Arrow's, it treats the two firms asymmetrically: if the incumbent innovates, then the incumbent retains a monopoly but if the entrant innovates then the incumbent shares the market. In other words, the incumbent is assumed to be able to copy the innovation (a 'fast second strategy') while the entrant cannot. This asymmetry protects the fruits of the incumbent's innovative efforts from retaliation, hence the greater incentive. Clearly in reality incumbents may have some special expertise or legal protection which produces such an asymmetry. If so, then arguably these factors should be placed in the foreground by the analysis.

### 10.3.3 Intellectual property rights (IPRs)

One factor which allows an inventor to maintain a monopoly over a new idea is a patent or, more generally, intellectual property rights. Baldwin and Scott (1987) compare a situation in which the first firm to innovate can establish a watertight monopoly round its market (e.g. by taking out a patent) with one in which no such property are available. This they term 'perfect appropriability' because the fruits of innovation can be appropriated by the successful firm. To highlight the consequences of this situation, they also consider a situation in which there are no property rights over innovations. Let us take these in turn. First, with perfect appropriability, we assume that there is competition in the pre-innovation market, that is, firms can engage in an R&D race to be first to find the innovation. Once the first firm registers the idea with the patent authority, however, competition ceases and the winner proceeds to enjoy its monopoly. Will innovation be under- or over-resourced under these circumstances? Assume the monopoly profits of the winner to be Z, the (known) number of potential entrants to be r and the (known) costs of innovating to p. These last are assumed to be the same for all entrants.

For each entrant, there is therefore a $1/r$ chance of making profits of Z, so that each one has an expected gain of $Z/r$. If Z is greater than the cost, p, then more entrants will arrive, driving down the value of $Z/r$ until it is equal to p. At this point, the cost to the economy of creating the innovation will be $r \times p$, which is equal to the benefits which it brings, Z. With perfect appropriability and perfect foresight, therefore, innovation will be neither under- nor over-resourced but resourced to an optimum degree. It is, however, possible to argue that this conclusion depends upon some unrealistic assumptions which could be modified, for example, by allowing for the possibilities that firms will under-estimate the number of competitors, over-estimate their own likeliehood of coming first or over-estimate the profits to be made. Baldwin and Scott note that under these (quite plausible) conditions innovation will be over-resourced, that is, there will in effect be 'over-bidding' for the profit stream which the innovaton will create.

In the second case, there are no property rights over the post-innovation market. The consequence is that innovations will simply be copied and profits will be driven down to zero. Baldwin and Scott term this the 'appropriability problem'; the problem is that innovation will be under-resourced, that is, few innovations will be worth considering since no innovator will recoup expenses.

A related approach to the issue of market structure, technological opprtunity and innovation was formulated by Nelson and Winter (1982). Like Baldwin and Scott (1987), they took the view that market structure, R&D spending and innovativeness could be seen as being determined by underlying factors such as property rights over innovations and technological opportunity. The implication of this approach, of course, is that empirical work like that of Acs and Audretsch (1988) fails to examine the real relationships but remains at a surface level: it traces symptoms rather than causes. To examine these more fundamental relationships, Nelson and Winter set up a computer-based model in which firms of equal initial size compete for market share by producing homogeneous products. Firms compete by engaging in process innovation which has the effect of reducing costs and thus boosting profits for reinvestment, either in plant or in R&D. R&D can be spent in two ways: innovating, that is, developing new processes or an imitation, that is, copying others' innovations. All firms in the simulation spend the same on imitative R&D, while half the firms spend the same again on innovation.

To widen the scope of their model, Nelson and Winter introduced a number of novel relationships. One was that R&D efforts meet with mixed success. Rather than results being proportional to expenditure, R&D only yields results probabilistically. In effect, firms face a lottery in which they have a chance (but not a guarantee) of reducing costs; large cost reductions having lower probabilities than small ones. Larger R&D expenditure still confers an advantage in that it buys more 'lottery tickets', while a large scale of output means that cost reductions apply to more production and thus have more effect. Lower costs in turn mean higher profits, more investment, more sales and thus more R&D. Innovative R&D spending permits a firm to reduce costs in line with a set of technological opporunites which advances at a given rate (presumably, in line with research in universities or elsewhere). This technological frontier can advance rapidly or slowly.

In a modification termed 'cumulative technology', Nelson and Winter made the cost-saving potential of innovative R&D relate not to a technological frontier but to an improvement on the firm's current practice. Thus the progress which a firm has made to date through its history of R&D related cost reductions sets the platform for any further improvements. In the science-based case, by contrast, a firm can leap to the front of the industry even when it has done no previous R&D simply by virtue of luck with its innovative R&D. Imitative R&D by contrast allows a firm to reduce its costs in line with current best practice in the industry, that is, to catch up with the industry's lowest-cost producer. The various R&D lotteries thus have different prizes. In fact, innovators are at a competitive disadvantage because they have fewer funds for investment while their R&D expenditure brings only an uncertain pay-off. Indeed, one prime purpose of the model was to investigate the relative performances of innovators as compared with imitators.

To compensate innovators for the disadvantages of devoting resources to innovation, Nelson and Winter allowed other features of the model to vary. One allowed firms to invest not all their profits, that is, to moderate the competitive pressure which they placed upon their rivals. In another, the speed of technological advance could be varied from slow (2 per cent p.a.) to rapid (6 per cent). Yet another feature describes the ease or difficulty of imitation of an innovation, proxied by the time taken to imitate an innovation. Innovators could thus be sheltered by restrained competition, difficulty of imitation or a rapidly-developing science base.

On running the simulation, it emerged that when imitation was easy, the science base moved slowly, competition was ruthless and innovators lost ground to imitators. The effect of such an outcome, of course, is that the pace of advance of the industry as a whole tends to slow as the volume of resources devoted to pure innovation across the industry as a whole diminishes. Conversely, when innovators were defended by a difficulty of imitation, a fast-growing science base and restrained competition, innovators maintained their share of the market. The simulation thus points to the importance of these factors as determinants of technical progress; it also suggests (like the work of Baldwin and Scott) that industrial structure is the reflection of the processes of innovation and imitation rather than their determinant.

### Forms of intellectual property rights

The previous discussions have rather taken patents and other forms of intellectual property for granted. Before going further, we examine these. IPRs come in many forms, perhaps the best-known being patents. Although their origins lie in concepts of natural justice, for economists they serve two conflicting objectives. One is to encourage people to innovate. The paradox of innovating, of course, is that by setting an innovation to work, the innovator demonstrates the new idea to the world at large. The innovator thus paves the way for the imitator who can, of course, reap the benefits of the innovation, leaving the innovator with nothing. To encourage innovation, therefore, IPRs give the inventor the right to control the use of an invention. The other economic objective, however, is to encourage the widespread use of innovations, that is, their diffusion. Such an objective is best served by permitting uncontrolled use.

Patents serve these objectives in turn. An inventor can, for a fee, register an invention with the Patent Office, where the plans can be seen by anyone. The patent-holder can then license others to use the invention, usually for a fee known as the royalty. He can also sue anyone using the invention without permission. These rights expire after 17 years. If the holder fails to exploit the invention (directly or via a licence), the patent lapses. A patent thus confers a temporary monopoly upon an inventor; the duration, as we shall see, is typically far shorter than 17 years. The monopoly profits encourage innovation while the eventual extinction of the rights permits diffusion.

Related IPRs are trademarks, by which a producer can identify its products; servicemarks which perform the same role for services, and copyrights which prevent the duplication of creative works like images. Like patents, trade- and servicemarks have to be registered but, unlike patents, then they exist in perpetuity. Copyright need not be registered but comes into existence automatically for a span of 50 years.

The principal alternative to patents and other legal forms is secrecy. Naturally this strategy gives a firm no redress against imitators. Its advantage is that there is no obligation to file the plans or designs with the Patent Office and thus would-be imitators have no clues to help them. (It also avoids paying the registration fee.) To exploit innovations by this means, firms usually rely upon sheer speed. That is, they calculate that although imitators will eventually destroy their monopoly, it will last long enough to allow them to recoup their costs and make a return. They thus rely upon the difficulty of imitation. If an innovation is difficult to replicate because it requires special knowledge or materials, the innovator will enjoy a monopoly while the imitators work upon the task. Another mechanism which allows the innovator to reap a profit is the 'learning curve'. This refers to the average costs of production. As a firm gains experience in making a product, these costs tend to fall. Thus the innovator will tend, at any point in time, to have lower average costs than an imitator and profits will accordingly be higher. In time, the innovator ceases to reduce costs and the imitators catch up, prices fall and profits are reduced to normal level. Viewed from this perspective, patents can be seen not as a unique mechanism for exploiting an innovation but rather as one means among many of delaying would-be imitators.

*Effectiveness of IPRs: some empirical results*

Light was shed on the working of the patent system in the USA as a delaying tactic by two pieces of research: one by Mansfield, Schwartz and Wagner (1981) and the other by Richard Levin (1986). Mansfield *et al.* sought data from firms in the drugs, chemicals, electronics and machinery industries in the north-eastern USA about the time and costs of imitating an innovation. They obtained information on 34 imitations and received estimates on imitations from 14 innovators. Seventy per cent of the innovations were patented, with only one being licensed. It might thus appear that the innovations were safe from imitation for 17 years. This, however, was far from being the case. Imitations were still created for an average cost of 65 per cent of the innovator's cost and in 70 per cent of the time. There was, however, considerable variation around both these figures. In half the cases, the time taken for imitation ranged from 40 per cent to 90 per cent of the innovator's time. Only in 14 per cent of cases did imitation costs exceed innovation costs. Patenting was estimated to raise imitation costs by 11 per cent. (In drugs, patents were thought to add 30 per cent to imitators' costs.) Moreover, 60 per cent of patented innovations were imitated within four years. Imitators can evidently circumvent patents; the effect of patents is to delay or hinder imitation, not to prevent it. (Mansfield *et al.* also found, consistently with Nelson and Winter's simulation, that easier imitation is associated with lower levels of concentration.)

Levin's (1986) survey of 630 R&D executives in 130 industries in the USA cast even more doubt on the power of patents. He asked his respondents to rate, on a 7-point scale, the efficacy of six methods of protecting both product and process innovations. The six were patents taken out to prevent duplication, patents taken out with the intention of licensing the innovation, secrecy, lead time, learning curve and sales-and-service efforts. Eighteen industries were denoted as research intensive by virtue of having 10 or more replies. In none of these was patenting the most efficacious method of protecting an innovation for most respondents for either processes or products, with the exception of pharmaceutical products.

## 10.3.4   Firms and innovation

Besides the neo-classical Arrow–Demsetz and the property rights approaches there is a third strand associated with the names of Joseph Schumpeter and John Kenneth Galbraith. Schumpeter (1953) argued that economists' traditional definitions of industries were too narrow and tended to overlook the fact that often the fiercest competition took place not between firms in the same trade but rather between industries. The classic example is the railway industry, where companies face intense competition not from other rail companies but from another industry, namely, car producers as people decide between different modes of transport. For Schumpeter, the structure of the first industry is irrelevant since that is not the locus of the competitive struggle. Indeed, if it were a monopoly, its high prices and super-normal profits would simply raise the incentives for the outside entrepreneurs to create new industry.

In later writings, Schumpeter took a slightly different line, arguing that monopolies (or rather oligopolies) provided the most conducive environment for innovation. This arose, he argued, by virtue of the funds which their super-normal profits provided and from the fact that a high market share provides a relatively secure base from which to withstand the risk of launching a new product. A variant of this argument was offered by J. K. Galbraith (1968). He suggested that innovative activities are characterized by risk and economies of scale or synergy. The uncertain nature of R&D projects means that a larger portfolio of projects has a safer return than a smaller one. Synergy between projects arises from the possibility that a research establishment may need to reach a particular size in order to attract talented workers or simply from the ability of a large programme to use discoveries from one field in other areas. Galbraith thus concluded that large size (which may or may not accompany large market share) was the organizational form most likely to foster innovation. These theoretical approaches have supplied empirical researchers with a fund of hypotheses to test. The following sections report some findings.

### 10.3.5   Industrial structure and innovativeness: some findings

One hypothesis which has been be tested is the Arrow–Schumpeter hypothesis that competitive industries offer superior incentives to monopoly (or, by extension, oligopoly). Researchers had, however, first to address a series of measurement problems, relating principally to innovation. (The problems of assessing concentration are discussed in Chapter 3.) Quite simply, there are no simple, objective indicators to use and researchers have been forced to use a variety of proxies. One approach has been to compile a database of innovations by surveying industrialists or by inspecting trade magazines. The former method was used by the UK Science Policy Research Unit (SPRU), which gathered data on over 4300 innovations in British manufacturing since 1945. The second was used by, among others, Acs and Audretsch (1988). Although this method has much to commend it, it rests upon the interpretation which the people providing information place upon the ideas of 'innovation' and 'significant'; one person's breakthrough could be another's minor improvement. Another line has been to examine data on patents, on the supposition that significant innovations will be protected by this means. One problem here is that registration costs money, so that firms may use cheaper alternatives such as simply keeping the invention a secret if possible. Another is that many (in the UK, up to 40 per cent) are not exploited, that is, many inventions never turn into innovations. An easier route (particularly in the USA, where data is published) is to look not at innovative outputs as do the previous methods but rather at inputs. Researchers can thus focus upon the employment of qualified engineers and scientists or of research personnel or again at expenditure on research and development (R&D). These are, of course, inferior proxies in that inputs are not guaranteed (particularly in the risky area of R&D) to produce results. Another problem is that in fashion- or style-dependent industries such as clothing or furniture, innovation can occur with little or no formal R&D.

Problems of measurement not withstanding, researchers have come to a broad consensus that the highest level of innovation is associated with oligopoly (four-firm CRs of about 50 per cent). Lower or higher CRs are associated with lower levels of innovation, producing a relationship which can be plotted as an inverted U-shape. For example, Levin et al. (1985) examined some 130 3- or 4-digit US manufacturing industries during the 1970s. For their indicator of concentration they took CR4. They used two indicators of innovativeness. The first was taken from a questionnaire sent to companies' R&D managers who were asked to rate, on a scale from 1 to 7, their industry's innovativeness in terms of products and processes. (Clearly, such an approach involves a degree of personal judgement.) The mean of the two scores was then used as one indicator. The other was the ratio of R&D expenditure to sales or research intensity.

The first stage in the process was to regress both indicators against concentration. The results for research intensity using 2SLS were:

$$RD/S = 1.810 + 0.166C - 0.159(C4^2 \times 100)$$
$$(1.402) \quad (0.067) \qquad (0.068)$$

where $RD/S$ is research intensity and C4 is concentration. Both independent variables were significant at the 99 per cent confidence level. The CR4 which produced the highest level of research intensity was 52 per cent: research intensity seems to follow an inverted U-shape, the highest level being found with a moderate degree of oligopoly while competition and monopoly are associated with lower levels. These findings are in line with previous findings, as reported in a survey by Kamien and Schwartz (1982).

The main problem with this regression is that industries face different opportunities to engage in technical innovation. There are also different conditions governing the appropriability of innovations in different industries. Scherer (1967), after finding a significant role for concentration, attempted to correct for these factors by dividing industries into groups such as chemical, electrical, mechanical and traditional. The effect was that concentration ceased to make any significant contribution. Levin and collaborators (1985) took a more complex approach, using their questionnaire to examine three aspects of the situation. The first was the industry's closeness to science on the grounds that science-based industries have greater opportunities. The second was the usefulness of outside sources of innovations: suppliers of plant or materials, customers or government agencies. The logic here was that such sources could act as substitutes for the industry's own R&D. The third was the industry's maturity (i.e. the age of its plant) on the grounds that technological opportunity is higher in new or expanding industries. The managers were also asked about the conditions of appropriability in their industry; whether secrets could be kept easily and how long it would take to imitate a major innovation.

The replies from these questions were then used in a second set of regressions using again both research intensity and innovativeness as the dependent variables. In both cases, the importance of concentration fell away dramatically, with the t-statisitics falling by an order of magnitude. The variables which were found to be significant were the maturity of the industry (or rather its newness), its proximity to science and the role of users and government agencies in providing innovations. The preliminary finding of support for the Schumpeterian hypothesis (and against Arrow's) appears, on deeper probing, to have been mere coincidence, with innovativeness being driven by certain aspects of an industry's technological opportunity.

## 10.3.6 Firm size and innovation

Table 10.2 noted the concentration of R&D among larger firms. The issue, also raised by Schumpeter and Galbraith, of which category of firms produce innovations, was addressed by Acs and Audretsch (1988). As previously noted, their source of information was a databank compiled by the US Small Business Administration, of innovations reported in the press in 1982. Of the 8800 identified, 4938 were found to be in the manufacturing sector. These were allocated to size categories of firms, with small firms being defined as those with fewer than 500 employees. (This is a rather generous definition of 'small'; Johnson *et al.* observe that in 1986 over 40 different definitions of this terms were in use among researchers and policy-makers.) The innovations were likewise allocated to four categories depending upon their significance. There were no category 1 innovations (the most important) and 80, 576 and 4282 of categories 2, 3 and 4 respectively. Small firms were found to account for 37.5 per cent of innovations in categories 2 and 3 and 43.3 per cent in category 4. A chi-squared test indicated that these proportions were not significantly different, that is, small firms' contribution to category 2 innovations was as large as their contribution to category 4. When compared with their resources, however, small firms appeared to be more innovative, having on average 43 per cent more innovations per employee than large firms (although variations about this average were wide). In the more innovative sectors of industry, small firms recorded six times as many innovations per worker as large firms. At first pass, these findings run contrary to the Schumpeter–Galbraith thesis that the large firm is the natural breeding ground for innovation.

To tease out more detail, Acs and Audretsch (1988) undertook a series of multiple regressions relating the shares of innovations attributable to small and large firms in each of 247 4-digit industries, considering R&D spending, capital intensity, the level of concentration (CR4), the share of output taken by large firms, the use of skilled labour and the level of advertising. The last factor was used as an indicator of the importance of fashion or style. No atttempt was made to take account of technological opportunity, a factor which had effectively undermined previous attempts to explain innovativeness at industry level. It could, of course, be argued that the share of skilled workers in the labour force was a plausible proxy for technological opportunity. In this context the most significant findings related to the conditions under which small firms made a relatively large contribution to innovation. These were found to be industries with the following characteristics: a high level of R&D in the industry, a high share of output for large firms, high levels of capital intensity and a greater reliance on skilled labour. It therefore seems that under these circumstances, the best way for small firms to survive is to compete through innovation rather than by other means.

Evidence from the UK on the size of innovative firms is provided by Pavitt et al. (1987). This study used a methodology similar to that of Acs and Audretsch (1988) in that it began with the SPRU database already mentioned of over 4000 innovations in British manufacturing. Unlike the American study which classified firms simply into large and small, the British research divided firms into 10 classes according to the number of employees in the UK. At this level of detail, the study found evidence for a U-shaped relationship, with both very small and very large firms contributing more innovations than their employment shares. Table 10.4, on the periods 1976–80 and 1981–83, shows ratios of shares of innovation to employment share for each size band, so that values greater than unity indicate greater fecundity.

The results appear to be consistent both with the Schumpeterian perspective that larger firms are the best producers of innovations and with the converse idea that small is beautiful. These simple conclusions, however, need to be set in the context of two considerations. One is that the study did not systematically allow for technological opportunity, the bane of previous work in the field. The second relates to the sample of firms under analysis. To merit inclusion, firms have

**TABLE 10.4   Ratio of shares of innovation to shares of employment** (*Source*: Pavitt et al., 1987)

| Size band | 1976–80 | 1981–83 |
|---|---|---|
| 1–99 | 0.59 | 0.63 |
| 100–199 | 1.19 | 2.07 |
| 200–499 | 1.49 | 1.58 |
| 500–999 | 1.00 | 0.92 |
| 1000–1999 | 0.82 | 0.34 |
| 2000–4999 | 0.65 | 0.91 |
| 5000–9999 | 0.45 | 0.37 |
| 10 000–19 000 | 1.22 | 1.07 |
| 20 000–49 000 | 1.00 | 1.09 |
| > 50 000 | 1.90 | 1.90 |

to innovate. The data set does not relate to all manufacturing firms. The research simply tells us, therefore, that of those manufacturing firms which do innovate, very large and very small enterprises make disproportionately large contributions. Since all size bands contain non-innovators to an unknown degree, the question of whether large or small firms *as groups* contribute disproportionately to innovation remains an open one.

## 10.4   Diffusion

The final aspect of innovation to be examined is the diffusion of innovations. From the standpoint of economic growth and the prosperity of national economies, this is arguably the most important. As Freeman (1989, p.215) notes, 'ultimately, it is only the successful *diffusion* of innovations which leads to perceptible and widespread effects on the growth of productivity or trade competitiveness and on agregate economic performance'. This perspective is reinforced, of course, by the strong implication from Nelson and Winter's simulation to the effect that, in the absence of strong defence mechanisms, imitators tend to prosper at the expense of innovators.

### 10.4.1   Modelling diffusion: the Sigmoid curve

Much attention has been given to modelling the processes of diffusion (Davies, 1979; Metcalfe, 1988 and Dasgupta and Stoneman, 1987). Models have frequently started from assumptions about the decision to invest in innovations. They have thus attempted to take account of the availability of information about innovations and the degree of perceived risk. When an innovation appears, adoption is slow because few potential users know of it and because its capabilities are relatively uncertain, its purchase represents a risk. As time passes, more potential users come to hear of the process and the experience of the initial users becomes known through the industry, so reducing the risk to buyers. In these conditions, diffusion proceeds more rapidly. As sales approach saturation, the number of non-users falls with the effect that pace of diffusion slows once more. A typical model thus concludes that, when the share of output attributable to a new process is plotted against time on a graph, the diffusion path will not follow a simple straight line but rather an s-shaped (or sigmoid or logistic) curve as shown in Fig. 10.2 (Davies, 1979).

### 10.4.2   Diffusion paths: empirical results

Alongside the theoretical work has been a strong effort to collect relevant data on the diffusion paths of various innovations. Important work in this area was undertaken by Nabseth and Ray (1974) and Ray (1984). Ray's studies covered an array of process innovations in (initially) six countries. The innovations studied were numerically-controlled machine tools, paper-making presses, tunnel kilns, the basic oxygen process in steel-making, float glass production, the use of giberellic acid in brewing, continuous steel casting and shuttleless looms. The economies involved were those of the UK, France, Italy, Sweden, West Germany and Austria. Japan and the USA were added later. The study sought to identify the date at which an innovation was first introduced into the country and the share of the output of the relevant industry for which it accounted at later dates. Obtaining the latter information was far from easy since firms typically use an array of old and new equipment at the same time. Ray and colleagues nevertheless were able to arrive at some significant conclusions. First, diffusion is typically a slow process. Table 10.5 shows the number of years which selected processes took before they accounted for high levels of output for the various countries taken in aggregate. Tunnel

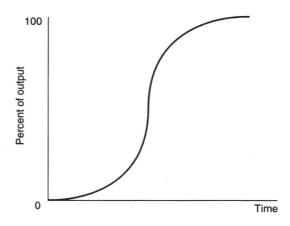

**Figure 10.2**   Sigmoid diffusion curve

kilns, for instance needed 30 years to account for 90 per cent of brick output. Of equal importance are the differences between countries; Table 10.6 shows the levels of diffusion reached in different economies in 1981.

Second, it was found that innovations improved as they diffused. Whereas the researchers had anticipated that certain innovations such as, for example, float glass would only be applicable to the manufacture of certain types of glass, they found that as time passed the process was developed so that it could produce other kinds of glass as well. Its 'saturation level' thus retreated before it. Third, the data were not precise enough to differentiate between sigmoid diffusion paths as indicated by theory and simple straight lines. Fourth, countries differed substantially in their diffusion paths, with Germany and Japan performing notably well. This is a topic to which we shall return later in the chapter. Finally, Nabseth and Ray also found that the size of companies had no effect on diffusion: large companies were as likely to adopt a new process as were smaller ones.

The last point has been unambiguously contradicted by a large volume of subsequent work and must now be regarded as erroneous (Gibbs and Edwards, 1985; Northcott and Walling, 1988; Rees *et al.*, 1984; Stead, 1994; Thwaites, 1982). The study by Rees *et al.* in the USA is a useful example. During 1982 the research team surveyed plants (not firms) in 4-digit industries

**TABLE 10.5   Time lags in innovation and diffusion** (*Source*: Ray, 1984, p.84)

| % diffusion | *BOP* | *CC* | *TK* | *SL* |
|---|---|---|---|---|
| 1 | – | 7 | – | – |
| 2 | – | – | – | 6 |
| 10 | – | 13 | 7 | 19 |
| 20 | 7 | 17 | – | 23 |
| 50 | 13 | 20 | 22 | – |
| 90 | 18 | – | 30 | – |

*Time in years to reach degree (%) of diffusion Process:*[1]

[1]BOP Basic Oxygen Process   CC Continuous Casting
TK Tunnel Kilns   SL Shuttleless Looms

**TABLE 10.6   Diffusion indicators by country, 1981** (*Source*: Ray, 1984, p.81)

| | | | | % diffusion | | | |
|---|---|---|---|---|---|---|---|
| | *Germany* | *UK* | *France* | *Italy* | *Sweden* | *USA* | *Japan* |
| BOP | 80 | 68 | 82 | 49 | 45 | 61 | 75 |
| CC | 54 | 32 | 51 | 51 | 65 | 21 | 71 |
| SL | 9 | 22 | 16 | 12 | 35 | 16 | 4 |
| TK | 90 | 72 | 90 | 90 | 95 | – | – |
| FG | 100 | 100 | 100 | 89 | 100 | – | – |
| NCMT | 2.2 | 2.6 | 1.9 | 2.2 | 3.0 | – | – |

BOP Basic Oxygen Process            CC Continuous Casting
SL Shuttleless Looms                 TK Tunnel Kilns
FG Float Glass production            NCMT Numerical-controlled machine tools

making electrical and mechanical machinery including electrical apparatus, aircraft and metal-working machinery. All were asked about their use of seven process innovations including numerically-controlled machine tools, computers and robots and one product innovation: the incorporation of microprocessors in the final product. Respondents were analysed by a range of factors such as their size, regional location, their urban location (i.e. the size of the city they were in), the size of the owning company and, naturally, by industrial sector. Size of plant and ownership status were found to be decisive for all eight technologies: plants which were members of multiplant groups were roughly twice as likely to adopt new technology than were single-plant enterprises; plants with over 1000 workers were between one and a half and ten times more likely to have new processes than plants with under 100 employees. Regional location was not found to be important for six of the eight technologies: plants in the South were as likely to use the innovations as those in the industrial heartlands of the North-East. A strong regional pattern did, however, emerge in the restricted case of single-plant firms in respect of two technologies: microprocessors in products and numerically-controlled machine tools. It emerged that small single-plant firms in the areas where these technologies had been invented and developed (the North-East (New England) and the Mid-West respectively) were more ready to use them than their counterparts in other regions. Since this was not a longitudinal study, the data cannot directly support or refute the idea that diffusion paths follow an s-shape.

An explanation for the superior performance of larger plants and multiplant enterprises is not difficult to propose. Larger firms (multiplant firms are almost invariably larger than single-plant firms) have more sophisticated procedures for gathering and evaluating data, while for them investing in a piece of new equipment represents less of a risk, given their larger stocks of capital, their use of specialized staff and easier access to finance.

## 10.4.3   National systems of innovation and diffusion

An outstanding feature of the research undertaken by Nabseth and Ray was the variation in diffusion rates between countries. This line of analysis was developed by Henry Ergas (1986) of the Centre for European Policy Studies. Ergas argued that the performance of various economies in terms of the diffusion of innovations coud be attributed to a range of institutional factors. In the USA, diffusion is facilitated by the mobility of factors of production: new firms are easy to create, venture capital is readily available and people change jobs frequently, naturally, carrying new ideas with them. In Germany, diffusion is prompted first and foremost by high levels of education and training which ensure that firms are easily able to assimilate new techniques. Besides this there is a system of certifying new products to ensure that they meet national standards. This work is undertaken not by government agencies but rather by trade associations, with the result that information about new products spreads across the relevant industry relatively quickly. Third, much industrial research is undertaken not in firms' own laboratories but in research facilities which are run by trade associations. The result again is that news of innovations tends to spread rapidly. At the time the research was undertaken, the UK lacked equivalent institutions.

Since rapid diffusion is strongly associated with high productivity and strong economic growth, the policy implications of this analysis are of some interest: if diffusion (that is, imitation) is more important than innovation, then it is the former and not the latter which should occupy the thoughts of policy-makers.

## Guide to further reading

Much of the theoretical literature starts from the assumption that intellectual property rights are watertight. Since they are not, it is useful to start perhaps with Mansfield *et al.*'s (1981) study of the limitations of patenting. Ergas (1986) on the approaches to technological development found in different countries is of substantial importance. Christopher Freeman, Margaret Sharp, Pavitt and Pavel and Kirsty Hughes have all written extensively on innovation and technology policies; see, e.g., Freeman, Sharp and Walker (1991). Stoneman (1995) is also useful.

## Appendix: optimal timing in a patents race

Game theory can be used to analyse the class of problems dealing with timing decisions in a competitive environment. In such cases the actions which players may use are given in advance, but the timing of the actions utilized by players is determined by the strategic decisions of the players (Dasgupta, 1988). Games of this type are common in oligopoly and feature the following conflict of interests: each oligopolist wishes to postpone its decision as long as possible, but it may be punished for waiting. The speed of innovation as characterized by Dasgupta and Stiglitz (1980(a) and (b)); the innovation scenarios sketched by Kamien and Schwartz (1982) and Fudenberg *et al.* (1983) capture the essence of patents races as games involving optimal timing decisions. This paper follows this tradition insofar as it delivers a 'winner-takes-all' result but differs from other approaches insofar as it embraces uncertainty both at the start and the end of the 'patent race'.

Uncertainty is the core issue facing a potential innovator. The uncertainty stems from several areas: namely uncertainty as to whether R&D will successfully generate a new technology, uncertainty as to the market reaction once the innovation hits the market. Coupled with these sources of uncertainty, oligopoly creates additional uncertainty as to rival reactions. Rivalry in oligopoly may take the form of beating others in the patents race or imitating the patented good. Despite these complexities, analysis focuses sequently on timing issues.

Clearly in oligopoly, timing of a win in a 'patents race' may be as significant as the prize itself. As Dasgupta (1988) makes clear weighed against the market advantage of being first in the race is the uncertain costs of developing the project. Moveover, in some patent races it may pay to come second especially if the initial innovator has suffered adverse market reactions. Crucially therefore innovation involving patents of products (or processes) is a phenomenon stretching through time.

## A patents game: two players and a race against time

In this game two identical firms (hereafter, firms I and II) are engaged in a patents race against a rigid time constraint. These two players may be conceived as natural duopolies, potential entrants, or perhaps bidders for a franchise which requires a successful prototype before a bid could be considered. In all cases there is a fixed time allocation, $T$, which cannot be exceeded.

A rational strategy for firm I instructs it to patent if the rival has not done so, but if the rival had already done this and failed to capture (enter) the market then firm I knows that it will succeed with a probability of 1. Hence a rational invention strategy for player I is to patent its invention when $x$ units of time are left, where $0 \leq x \leq T$. Similarly a rational strategy for player II is to patent its invention when $y$ units of time remain where $0 \leq y \leq T$. Let the probabilities of a successful patent be $P_1(x)$ and $P_2(y)$ respectively. So $P_1(x)$ is the probability of firm I cornering the market when $x$ units of time are left to complete the race. Assume that the probabilites of success for both players increase as the time available to complete the game decreases.

Let the payoffs be $+1$ to the player who captures the new market and 0 to each firm if both fail. Moreover, once engaged in the race neither player opts out prematurely before the game ends. So this game delivers a 'winner takes all' result.

The payoff $E\pi(x, y)$ to player I is that player's expectation of success for three possible 'patent' dates; there are: patenting before player II, simultaneous patenting by both players, and patenting after player II has patented. So the payoff is given by

$$E\pi(x,y) = \begin{cases} P_1(x)(1) + [1 - P_1(x)](-1) = 2P_1(x) - 1 & \text{if } x > y \quad (10.1) \\ P_1(x)[1 - P_2(x)] + P_2(x)[1 - P_1(x)] - 1 = P_1(x) - P_2(x) & \text{if } x = y \quad (10.2) \\ P_2(y)(-1) + [1 - P_2(y)](1) = 1 - 2P_2(y) & \text{if } y > x \quad (10.3) \end{cases}$$

Since $P_1(x)$ and $P_2(y)$ increase with falling values of $x$ and $y$ respectively it follows that:

$$\max_x \min_y E\pi(x, y) = \max_x \min[2P_1(x) - 1, \ P_1(x) - P_2(x), 1 - 2P_2(x)] \qquad (10.4)$$

The time span available for the patents race $[0, T]$ can be split into three arbitrary phases as follows:

| Time phases | Consists of x for which | |
|---|---|---|
| $Q$ | $P_1(x) + P_2(x) \geq 1$ | (10.5) |
| $W$ | $P_1(x) + P_2(x) = 1$ | (10.6) |
| $Z$ | $P_1(x) + P_2(x) \leq 1$ | (10.7) |

Such a time scheme is useful because:
Let

$$q(x) = \min[2P_1(x) - 1, P_1(x) - P_2(x), 1 - 2P_2(x)] \qquad (10.8)$$

Then

$$\max_x \min_y E\pi(x,y) = \max_x q(x) = \max[\max_{x\in Q} q(x), \max_{x\in W} q(x), \max_{x\in Z} q(x)] \tag{10.9}$$

For all $x$ in $Q$ there is:

$$P_1(x) + P_2(x) \geq 1 \tag{10.10}$$

which yields:

$$1 - 2P_2(x) \leq P_1(x) - P_2(x) \leq 2P_1(x) - 1 \tag{10.11}$$

so if:

$$x \in Q, \text{then } q(x) = 1 - 2P_2(x) \tag{10.12}$$

In phase $W$ which is a point the following exists:

$$P_1(x) + P_2(x) = 1 \tag{10.13}$$

Hence:

$$1 - 2P_2(x) = P_1(x) - P_2(x) = 2P_1(x) - 1 \tag{10.14}$$

So, if $x \in W$, then:

$$q(x) = P_1(x) - P_2(x) \tag{10.15}$$

Phase $Z$ is defined by those $x$ for which:

$$P_1(x) - P_2(x) \leq 1 \tag{10.16}$$

Obviously therefore

$$2P_1(x) - 1 \leq P_1(x) - P_2(x) \leq 1 - 2P_2(x) \tag{10.17}$$

So for all $x$ in $Z$:

$$q(x) = 2p_1(x) - 1 \tag{10.18}$$

If $x^*$ is defined as:

$$q(x^*) + P_2(x^*) = 1 \tag{10.19}$$

Then:

$$\max_{x\in Q} q(x) = 1 - 2P_2(x^*) \tag{10.20}$$

$$\max_{x\in W} q(x) = P_1(x^*) - P_2(x^*) \tag{10.21}$$

$$\max_{x\in Z} q(x) = 2P_1(x^*) - 1 \tag{10.22}$$

Therefore:

$$\max_x \min_y E\pi(x,y) = P_1(x^*) - P_2(x^*) \tag{10.23}$$

where $x^*$ satisfies the equation:

$$P_1(x^*) + P_2(x^*) = 1 \tag{10.24}$$

Similarly it is straightforward to show that:

$$\min_y \max_x E\pi(x,y) = P_1(y^*) + P_2(y^*) = 1 \tag{10.25}$$

where

$$y^* \text{ satisfies equation } P_1(y^*) + P_2(y^*) = 1 \qquad (10.26)$$

So it has been shown that $E\pi(x, y)$ has a saddle-point at $x^*$, $y^*$. The optimal strategy for each player is to patent the invention when it has $t$ units of time left in the patents race. The optimal strategy is given by:

$$P_1(t) + P_2(t) = 1 \qquad (10.27)$$

The value of the game is $P_1(t) - P_2(t)$.

The best strategy for each player is to patent their inventions simultaneously with $(t_0)$ unit of time left, which satisfies the following equation:

$$P_1(x_0) + P_2(x_0) = 1 \qquad (10.28)$$

If player I uses this strategy it is sure of getting at least $P_1(x_0) - P_2(x_0)$. If player II uses this strategy too, it will lose a maximum of $P_1(x_0) - P_2(x_0)$. If player I's success probability is given by $P_1(x) = 1 - x$ and player II's is given by $P_2(y) = 1 - y^2$, then each should patent their inventions when time left in the race $x$ is determined by:

$$x + x^2 = 1 \qquad (10.29)$$

or $x \approx 0.62$. The value of the game is $x^2 - x = -0.24$ to player I and $+0.24$ to player II. If both players have equal chances of success in the race they should patent their inventions when their success probabilities are both 0.5. The value of this patents game is therefore zero.

## Implications of the patents race game

The results given for this game illustrate some of the paradoxical issues often featured in oligopoly/innovation studies. When there are two (or more) identical firms involved in a race against time, each firm in the game might be willing to commit marginally more money to R&D to be first with a patent. But, if all the identical oligopolists behave like this expected profits are zero. So, for an oligopoly group, patenting is unappealing given zero or negative profits, despite the fact that from the viewpoint of a single oligoplist patenting looks profitable. However, these paradoxes wane somewhat when the players are permitted to compete for multi-patent prizes.

## A multi-patents game: two players and race against time

The symmetrical nature of the previous game with identical firms is rather unrealistic. Intuitively it is reasonable to assume that in oligopoly patents races some basic asymmetries in R&D between players is allowed. These asymmetries can be ascribed to the fact that one or more players are existing patent holders, or established in the market whereas others might be trying to innovate to gain the next patent or enter the industry.

The fact that oligopolistic firms are not identical means that different players possess different incentives to win the patents race.

Let us consider a patent race against time when both players can patent more than one invention and where the two players are asymmetrically placed. If we assume as previously, that payoffs in this race are $+1$ to the winner and zero otherwise then the optical timing strategy for patenting for both players is relatively straightforward to compute. Imagine that at time $t$, players I and II possess $g(t)$ and $r(t)$ inventions to patent respectively. Imagine also that both have equal chances of market success per patent, $p(t)$. Now one optimal strategy for either player is to patent one invention whenever:

$$P(t) = \frac{1}{g(t) + r(t)} \tag{10.30}$$

However, given the asymmetrical nature of this game, the player with fewer inventions to patent at any such time, should not patent until:

$$P(t) > \frac{1}{g(t) + r(t)} \tag{10.31}$$

Hence this 'weaker' player should delay its patent temporarily and then patent only if its rival has not already done so. The value of this multi-patent game is then:

$$k = \frac{g(0) - r(0)}{g(0) + r(0)} \tag{10.32}$$

where $k$ is the value of the game.

Given these asymmetries, if player I has two patents and player II has three and both use optimal strategies, then player II patents when its probability of success is $p(t) = 0.2$, both patent at $p(t) = 0.25$, again both should patent at $p(t) = 0.5$, and $k = -0.2$ to player I. In particular, if $p(t) = t$, then player II patents at $t = 0.2$, both patent at $t = 0.25$ and again both should patent at $t = 0.5$.

## Implications of the patents game model(s)

The models outlined above imply that the players compete vigorously until the end of the game. The multi-patent race game illustrates the differential incentives for different phases of the game, issues which are not always evident in some analyses of patents races. Moreover, the models discussed here highlight the innate uncertainty embraced by a patents race and indicate precisely when a waiting game is the best strategic response.

The arguments outlined above are predicated on the assumption that the players possess the same risk preference functions and expectations. Moreover, the results delivered here are consistent with several others in the area, namely Gilbert and Newbery (1982) and Harris and Vickers (1985a and 1985b) insofar as 'winners take all' and monopoly ensues. However, in the models discussed here the route to the monopoly conclusion results from a two-player game where neither player drops out until it is beaten. This is because the focus here is entirely on optimal timing of the patents. This is true in both the symmetrical (identical players) and the asymmetrical cases.

Finally, in the models discussed here two key sources of uncertainty in a patents race, namely the value of the payoffs and completion time for the race are central to the discussion. In the models utilized here the player with the largest expected payoff does not necessarily win because it cannot set a research budget so as to pre-empt the rival by ensuring the rival's expected payoffs net of costs are negative. Once again it is because the stress is on optimal timing, given the rival's best response, rather than differential innovation rates or speeds.

The models developed in this section seek to formulate optimal timing scenarios for single- and multi-patent game races. Hence the objective is to analyse the issue of optimal timing given that both players compete strongly to the end without retiring. This is an important class of game in oligopoly and is likely to be a key industry feature either when a race involves several phases of R&D, or where R&D expenditure cannot be monitored accurately by the players so that imperfect information colours the play of the game. Fudenberg and Tirole (1983a and 1983b) have discussed rich scenarios of industrial competition as have others (Grossman and Shapiro, 1987). The significant strength of these approaches is that the competing firms make insightful attempts to understand each other's behaviour. This paper focuses almost entirely on patent competition as a game of timing rather like a duel between two equally gifted (or otherwise) marksmen albeit in the multi-patents race, the 'duel' between the players involves one duelist with extra bullets as a market leader might have.

# Questions on Part II

1 Review your understanding of the following concepts:

Intellectual property rights          Product life cycle
Fast second strategy                  Diffusion-oriented systems
Market for corporate control          Vorstrand and Betreibsrat
Tobin's $q$                           Disappointing marriage
Raiders                               Victims
Tender offer

2 Name as many definitions of profits used in company annual reports as you can.

3 Using data from 'Oversease Trade' (for the UK) and/or from the OECD, examine trends in imports and exports of electrical and electronic equipment for the UK, France, Germany, Japan and the USA over the last 10 years. What does this tell us about European technology policy? What are the limitations of such data for evaluating these policies?

4 'Efficiency is sustained by competition in three markets: product markets, factor markets and the market form corporate control.' Explain and comment on this statement.

5 Chief executives of privatized utilities have been criticized for overpaying themselves. Overpayment is, of course, an indication of weak competition. In which of the three markets above is competition weak in these cases?

6 Describe the ways in which economists have tried to understand or integrate advertising into economic theory.

7 Many advertisements on television and film have voice-over but no dialogue. Why do you think this is the case?

# PART III  POLICY

# 11 International trade, technology and the multinational enterprise

## 11.1 Introduction

What is the connection between international trade and industrial economics? Traditionally, trade was considered by economists as an inter-industry matter: in David Ricardo's famous exposition, English cloth trades for Portuguese wine; England produces no wine, and Portugal, no cloth. Ricardo's model and all that have followed leave two salient matters unanalysed. First, it is clear that much international trade consists not of countries swapping different products (so-called inter-industry trade) but of countries swapping similar products: cars built in the UK against cars built in Germany for example (intra-trade). Second, even when countries engage in Ricardian inter-trade, how does it come about that some countries have an advantage in certain types of goods? What, in other words, are the bases of comparative advantage? In Ricardo's example, although Portugal has a climate that favours grape production, there is no climatic reason for England to specialize in cloth. Nor are natural forces responsible for Japan's present prowess in electronic housewares. To find explanations for these puzzles, and to discover guidelines for policy, economists have been turning to industrial economics. This chapter looks at explanations of intra-trade via reaction-curve models and then at work on trade and technology, ending with some case studies in policy.

## 11.2 Intra-trade and oligopoly theory

How can international trade be integrated into oligopoly theory? In principle, the analyses of earlier chapters can easily be extended to accommodate the peculiarities of cross-border traffic such as commercial factors (for example, transport costs) and political factors arising from the presence of more than one government. Let us begin with reaction-curve oligopoly models of the Cournot variety. We recall that, with homogeneous goods and the Cournot conjectural variation, each producer takes rivals' output as given, the market is divided equally between the participants. If there are two countries with identical levels of demand but with unequal numbers of identical producers, that is, producers with identical costs (and zero transport costs), trade will occur (though only in one direction). The absence of transport costs means that there is in effect only one market and one industry, and the country with the more numerous producers (that is, with the larger industry) will export to the other. Transport costs or tariffs (the two are here conceptually the same) will be the same as any other cost differentials: the reaction curve of the firm(s) suffering the cost is shifted towards the origin of the graph. This is because, at any level of production by its rival, a firm with higher costs would maximize profits by supplying less output. Thus overseas producers, suffering relative cost penalties, find themselves with a smaller market share and correspondingly smaller profits than would otherwise be the case. This logic is, however, not satisfactory, since it predicts that trade will only go in one direction, from low-cost or large to high-cost or small. Modern intra-trade, however, goes in both directions.

The introduction of differentiated products alters the conclusions slightly. As Chapter 3 argued, a Cournot oligopoly with differentiated products can be analysed with reaction curves which are rather less responsive to the decisions of others than is the case with a homogeneous product. Higher costs for overseas producers would not under such circumstances be quite so damaging for them; given the right kind of differentiating characteristics, market shares (and profits) of overseas producers would tend to hold up in the face of cost penalties. In this situation, two-way trade could easily occur as firms in each country served their local and overseas consumers.

In pure Bertrand situations with a homogeneous product, price competition as described in Chapter 3 eliminates super-normal profits. It would not, however, eliminate trade, which would again depend on the relative sizes of demand and production in the two countries. The absence of transport costs, tariffs or other cost differences has, however, a huge impact: higher-cost producers are simply eliminated from the industry. If transport costs are high, the market becomes two separated national markets (no trade), while if one country's production costs are relatively high, its industry is eliminated and it imports the total consumption of the product. If products are differentiated, then, as with Cournot, interaction between competitors is restrained so that firms can survive competition and trade can take place.

## 11.3    The EU and intra-industry trade

The traditional Heckscher–Ohlin factor proportions model of trade patterns focuses on inter-industry trade (IIT) between nations. To use the classical Heckscher–Ohlin approach to explain IIT is both convoluted and tentative. Indeed, neo-Heckscher–Ohlin explanations of IIT rely almost exclusively on horizontal product differentiation models to explain trade patterns between countries with similar industrial structures. For example, some neo-Heckscher–Ohlin explanations of IIT extend the standard Heckscher–Ohlin configuration to include human capital embodied in skilled labour. So if higher quality versions of a standard good embody a large quantity of skilled labour (and hence human capital) then the basic Heckscher–Ohlin prediction applies: countries rich with human capital will export capital intensive goods.

Neo-Chamberlain models of IIT accept an industry structure of many competing firms which produce a rich variety of horizontally differentiated goods, where the varieties differ in proportion to the 'characteristics' (real or imagined) developed. In these cases where the industrial structure exhibits 'perfect monopolistic competition', only normal profits are earned and freedom of entry and exit colour the analysis.

Still more explanations of IIT have been offered by Krugman (1987) and Brander (1981) where models of homogeneous oligopoly explain the existence of the phenomenon, but where strict assumptions of Cournot closed entry models give a basis of homogeneous IIT between two home market monopolists who then compete for a larger market once trade is opened up.

However, a more satisfying model of IIT would include vertical product differentiation, national oligopolies and non-price competition to explain the dominant IIT flows of trade between the UK, Germany and France. The largest volumes of trade recorded in the EU since the implementation of the Single European Market (SEM) have been seen in three broad industry groups: namely motor vehicles, chemicals and machinery. Neven (1990), and Smith and Venables (1988) have sought to show that greater economic integration will lead to increased gains for consumers due the removal of tariff barriers and non-tariff barriers. These 'gains' result from specialization and exchange gains, or, 'gains' because consumers have wider choice. The study by Neven sought to identify gains and comparative advantage resulting from removal of non-tariff barriers in 1993. Economies of scale factors, greater contestability and convergence of labour costs were cited by Neven and others to measure the potential gains. Neven and other studies (for example, Jacquemin *et al.* (1980)) suffer from the weaknesses that:

- their explanations of IIT differ
- their conclusions as to future trade patterns are inconsistent.

There are not serious weaknesses because the actual causes of IIT have not been fully understood or modelled. The plethora of econometric studies reported in Greenaway (1985) also produce conflicting and different explanations of IIT. If reliance on some variant of neo-Chamberlain oligopoly models of IIT is made, efforts must be made to consider in more detail elasticity of demand for traded goods, levels of concentration, market structure and the models of oligopolistic competion.

It seems to us that the class of models developed by Shaked and Sutton (1984) on vertical product differentiation and natural oligopoly are the most robust explanations of IIT in the EU between the UK, Germany and France, especially in motor vehicles, chemicals and machinery.

The generic Shaked–Sutton type models of trade assume:

1 All consumers possess similar tastes and rank goods on an accepted scale in terms of perceived quality.
2 The distribution of income is unequal so different consumers buy goods in relation to their incomes. Thus, higher income consumers buy higher 'quality' goods.
3 Firms are profit maximizers operating in natural oligopolies in home markets with high market shares.
4 R&D is required to enter new markets for quality. R&D is therefore a fixed long-run investment in the home and overseas markets.
5 Scale economies are evident in home markets, so European-wide costs of production are constant.

Most of these assumptions accord with evidence produced in the last few years. In particular, the evidence from Venables (1985) and Jacquemin (1989) underscore the realism of these assumptions in developing EU IIT for the UK, Germany and France.

Duopoly equilibrium with vertical product differentiation is shown in Fig. 11.1. with no trade the home market duopoly competes internally but with no threat of foreign competition. In Fig. 11.1, the home market duopoly attains a Nash equilibrium when variable costs are constant and do not alter when quality changes.

In Fig. 11.1, $T(V)$ is the cost of R&D needed to develop a variety of quality and $SR_1$ and $SR_2$ are sales revenues for home firms 1 and 2 respectively. Imagine firm 1 is the home market incumbent and firm 2 enters with higher quality good $V_2$. The incumbent gets no total revenue if it attempts to produce $V_2$, but gets positive revenue if it makes a lower quality variant, however, it cannot continually reduce quality or consumers will 'trade up' to the higher quality good. The incumbent is in equilibrium at $V_1$ and the entrant is at equilibrium at $V_2$.

A move to free trade between two identical countries, each of which features an industrial structure dominated by duopoly with differentiated goods. If trade occurs between a bilateral pair of traders such as these two countries, the firm making high-quality goods in one country will find itself in direct competition with the firm making higher quality goods in the other country. One pair of producers might exit from the market since neither can make profits with

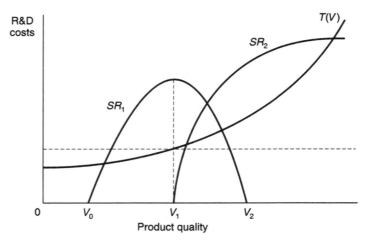

**Figure 11.1**   Oligopoly equilibrium with quality competition

competition from the other being present. Free trade can easily result in there being a single monopoly producer of each of the two qualities, with each monopolist supplying both markets, home and foreign. It cannot be predicted from *a priori* reasoning which producer will flourish and prosper. Consumers may gain from price reductions which will flow from market growth. However, in this model, if one firm leaves from each country we will see ITT occur, with one country specializing in higher or lower quality goods. If, however, both firms in one country exit one should observe inter-industry trade patterns.

## 11.4   Technology and trade in industrial economics

### 11.4.1   Evidence for the shifting advantage

The models above show merely that intra-trade might, under some circumstances, take place. Casual observation, however, suggests that there is one vital factor driving international trade: technology. In general it is clear that there is a broad correlation between inventiveness and trade performance. In the eighteenth century, the British were the world's foremost innovators, and its foremost exporters. In the nineteenth century, the USA and Germany successfully challenged the UK in both these roles. The late twentieth century belongs to Japan, again in terms of both innovativeness and export performance.

The performance of the British economy has been subjected to rather more detailed scrutiny by Patel and Pavitt (1987) of the National Institute for Economic and Social Research. US patent data is used to generate an indicator of 'revealed technological advantage' (RTA), defined as the ratio between Britain's share of patents in a particular industrial sector and its share overall. Thus if Britain's overall share is 7 per cent, a sector in which the UK registered 14 per cent of the patents would have an RTA of 2. Any figure above 1 indicates strength while any figure below 1 shows a relative lack of competitiveness. Tracing data over several years also allowed Patel and Pavitt to identify sectors in which Britain's strength was growing, shrinking or remaining stable. A similar set of calculations was then performed upon exports. The two researchers generated an indicator of 'revealed comparative advantage' (RCA) by relating

**TABLE 11.1   UK revealed comparative advantage** (*Source*: adapted from Patel and Pavitt, 1987)

| Sector | RCA | |
|---|---|---|
| | *1977–81* | *1981–84* |
| Aircraft | 2.15 | 2.04 |
| Drugs, medicines | 1.39 | 1.54 |
| Instruments | 1.06 | 1.32 |
| Office equipment | 1.29 | 1.27 |
| Other chemicals | 1.11 | 1.21 |
| Non-electrical machinery | 1.09 | 1.11 |
| Electrical machinery | 0.94 | 1.02 |
| Food, drink, tobacco | 0.81 | 0.84 |
| Fertilizers, pesticides | 0.72 | 0.86 |
| Textiles, cloth | 0.92 | 0.85 |
| Radio, TV, telecommunications equipment | 0.74 | 0.72 |
| Vehicles | 0.87 | 0.72 |

Britain's export share in particular industries to its share of all manufactured export. The results are reproduced in Table 11.1.

The research sought links between the two indicators; high-RTA sectors should also be high-RCA sectors, and so on. In the event, consistency between the two sets of data is high but not perfect. Aircraft, drugs and non-electrical machinery conform to expectations in being areas of high RTA and RCA while textiles (with a weak but stable RTA) and vehicles (with a medium but declining RTA) conform in a negative way by showing low RCAs. The improved showing of fertilizers and pesticides in exports is also consistent with their medium but growing RTA. On the other hand, office equipment (including computers) confounds the pattern by showing a low RTA and a high RCA, while food, drink and tobacco conversely shows a high RTA yet a low RCA. The picture is thus less clear than expected, suggesting perhaps that competitive strength in exports rest on factors other than US patents (such as price) or that US patents fail to capture important aspects of the innovation process. The evidence of a relationship, however, remains strong.

## 11.4.2   Game theory

The implications of a relationship between innovativeness and trade are far-reaching. For governments, they provide temptations to intervene in markets. Since export success is connected with economic growth and employment, it is possible that policies to aid innovativeness could, through the latter's effect on exports, be the foundation of macro-economic success. At a micro-level, the models analysed above suggest that in imperfect markets, that is, oligopolistic markets in which competition is restrained by Cournot behaviour or by differentiation, producers earn excess returns. Such returns, of course, vary with the number of actual and potential entrants; they are highest when the industry in question is a natural monopoly. (These returns, of course, need not be restricted to profit but could be shared by labour.) If production can be shifted from one country to another by government intervention, then so too can the excess returns. Moreover, if technological advantages derive from learning by doing then they may be expected to persist: this period's producers have a head start in the next period, when they may earn excess returns once again. Thus government assistance now may yield benefits which last into the future. Given the possibility of such gains, governments have frequently tried to promote innovativeness and exports, often thereby inhibiting free trade. They may, for example,

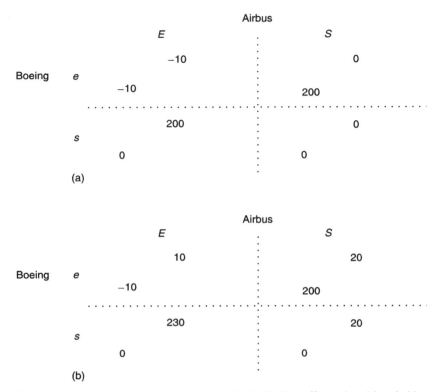

**Figure 11.2** (a) Payoff matrix without subsidy (b) Payoff matrix with subsidy

subsidize domestic producers of advanced equipment or, as major customers, refuse to buy weapons or industrial equipment from other nations. Such practices violate the precepts of traditional theories of international trade, which argue strongly for *laissez-faire*. Naturally this raises the questions of whether these interventions can succeed and of their effect on welfare in the two countries. These issues have been modelled by economists, one of the foremost in this regard being MIT's Paul Krugman. It is to his work that we now turn.

Krugman (1987) uses a simple pay-off matrix to develop his argument (see Fig. 11.2). In the model, two producers, Boeing and Airbus, prepare to enter a market for a new product, a 150-seater aircraft. The producers are located in different countries and are assumed to produce only for export. If there are domestic consumers then the producer's excess returns come in part at their expense; assuming that there are no such consumers allows us to identify the income of the producer with the national interest. In the pay-off matrix, each firm has to choose between entering the market or staying out. Airbus' choices are shown in upper-case letters (E, S) while Boeing's are in lower case (e, s). The matrix shows Airbus' returns in the lower left-hand corner of each cell and Boeing's in the upper right-hand corner. It is clear that if both enter the market (top left cell), both make losses. If both stay out (bottom right), no returns are made; but if one firm alone enters (top right and bottom left), then that firm makes an excess profit of 200. Once one firm has entered, there is no incentive for the other to enter since it would make a loss by doing so. With these numbers, there is no indication who would in fact enter first, but in the real world one potential entrant would have some advantage in terms of preparedness and would be able to set up first. In this context, the advantage would probably lie with Boeing.

This model of producer choices can easily be extended to accommodate action by government. The natural choice here is the European Commission, because the US government would presumably be satisfied with the outcome of an unregulated market. The European Commission could offer a subsidy to Airbus so that its returns were boosted by 20 in all circumstances. This would remove the possibility of loss for Airbus, who would thus face no risk in its enter/stay out decision. Knowing this, Airbus would enter. If the European Commission's promise were made early enough (before Boeing had committed itself to production) and publicly enough (so that Boeing knew of Airbus' changed circumstances) then Boeing would simply not enter the market; if Boeing knew that Airbus would enter regardless, then Boeing's only choice would be between a loss (arising from entry) and breaking even. Why does the presence of government make a difference? The answer lies in the concept of commitment. We have seen in Chapter 4 that oligopolists can engage in strategic behaviour by committing themselves to action (normally, high levels of production) which would damage potential entrants. A public subsidy can thus be seen as a form of commitment. By declaring its willingness to subsidize, the government commits 'its' producer to a certain level of production, thus deterring rivals. From the viewpoint of the EC, the exercise is a success: a subsidy of just 20 raises European GNP by 200 as economic activity is transferred from the US to Europe.

The logic of this argument is one that appeals to a wide audience. In summary, it is that a little protection can raise national income while the only losers live overseas. As we have emphasized, this runs counter to the *laissez-faire* teaching of Ricardian trade theory. The conclusions, however, depend upon certain conditions which repay examination. First, the case above was a duopoly; when one company decided to stay out of the market, its rival had a monopoly so that excess returns were maximum. With larger numbers of producers, present and potential, in the system, competition would be more intense, reducing producers' excess returns. In fact, the argument for rent-shifting is strongest when the industry is a natural monopoly, that is, when all demand is most economically supplied from only one producer. The example above is consistent with such a situation in that returns are highest when there is only one producer in the market, whether it be Airbus or Boeing.

Second, the model above assumes that the US government does not retaliate. If it were to offer Boeing a subsidy of 20 to match the EC's, then the industry would in effect return to the first payoff matrix and Boeing would capture the market. Now, however, both firms would be receiving subsidies from their governments, distorting both economies without altering the outcome in the aircraft market. Both governments could proceed to raise subsidies again. It is, of course, to prevent such mutually-damaging escalations that countries have joined GATT. A third objection is of neo-Austrian derivation. It is that the model assumes that all actors have perfect information. In reality, the returns from the sale of a new aircraft, both with and without competition, are only conjectures; there is no certainty that excess returns would be earned.

## 11.5   Trade and protection: case study in aircraft production

Krugman's example is not plucked from the air: Boeing and Airbus are in fact duopolists in the market for wide-bodied commercial jets. Boeing is the largest producer with some 55 per cent of the market. Airbus (a consortium of British, French, Spanish and German producers) was formed in the late 1960s. All the participants were (and many remain) in state ownership. Since then it has captured some 40 per cent of the market, with allegedly appreciable help from European governments in terms of preferential purchasing by state-owned airlines, low-interest loans and loan guarantees. At the same time, the Japanese and Taiwanese governments have shown interest in helping local producers to enter the industry, while US producers such as McDonnell Douglas and Lockheed have lost market share or quit the market altogether. Krugman's model has, arguably, some semblance of reality.

The basic economic feature of the industry is its economies of scale. These derive in large measure from the design costs of creating a new airframe, estimated at $4 billion upwards. These costs have risen as technology has progressed. Production also provides economies of scale, notably from learning curves. Producers thus tend to offer families of plane, that is, designs which are essentially variations on one basic concept, so that components can be shared. Given the costs of a new design, producers have some incentive to innovate by adding to a family rather than designing a new aircraft. Producers recoup their development costs over the entire life-cycle of the model. Prices are set on the assumption that over 400 planes will sell and the first 70 planes or so do not cover even their direct costs; producers rely on learning to bring costs down later in the cycle so as to generate profits. (This practice, of course, raises barriers against entry; indeed, it bears a resemblance to predatory pricing.) New entrants to the industry would clearly have to bear both up-front design costs and the early losses associated with learning curves before going into profit. The industry thus tends towards a natural monopoly or duopoly. Secondly, there are economies of scale for users; pilots, for example, have to be trained for each type of aircraft and it is thus cheaper for an airline to have only one type. Maintenance is likewise cheaper when an airline has only one type of plane. This has the effect of an entry barrier; customers switching suppliers have to bear adjustment costs. Thus to break into the US market in 1979, Airbus felt compelled to offer their first customer, Eastern Airlines, an attractive deal including free use of the aircraft for six months in order to demonstrate their value. Finally, the industry has economies of scope in that commercial manufacturers frequently make military aircraft as well. Governments, seeking local sources of military hardware, often have an interest in the continued existence of commercial-come-military plane-makers. This leads to preferential purchasing of locally-made warplanes and thus, if the terms of sale are advantageous, to the effective subsidy of plane-makers. Governments also promote exports of civilian and military aircraft by granting or guaranteeing credit to overseas buyers. When this credit is offered at low rates of interest, the effect is to reduce the price of the planes, that is, to subsidize the domestic producer.

Before the growth of Airbus, the industry was dominated by American producers. Several factors went to create this situation. Apart from the enterprise of US companies and the abundance of technical skills in the US economy, the home market for aircraft was shaped by the regulation of its customer, the air transport industry. From 1938 to 1978, Federal authorities regulated fares and schedules so that airlines could only compete by offering their passengers better flights on better aircraft. This put pressure on manufacturers to upgrade their aircraft. Thus when Boeing led the field in the early 1950s with a commercial jet, Douglas was compelled by its customers to follow suit. Another favourable factor was state support for R&D. In part this came in the form of tax deductions. More important was the help of the American armed forces, who regularly purchased advanced designs. Notable among these was the C–5A, a large transport plane which went out to tender in the mid-1960s. The ideas developed in this process were used by McDonnell Douglas and Boeing to create jumbos: the DC-10 and the hugely successful 747.

Rising development costs meant that by the 1960s European producers (mainly with only national airlines as captive customers) were in difficulties. The Plowden Report on the British airframe industry of 1965 concluded that the future lay with cooperation; essentially, the British market was too small to support even one domestic producer of commercial aircraft; Europe as a whole would provide sufficient demand but this would require Europe's producers to consolidate. As we have seen, this eventually came about in the form of Airbus.

While part of the success of Airbus is attributable to public support (estimated by some to be as high as $25 billion), the company also brought in new designs. In the early 1980s, while Boeing pursued the conservative strategy of modifying existing designs, Airbus developed the A320 which used many new technologies including the 'fly-by-wire' system of control which economizes on fuel and personnel.

Using the auspices of GATT, the US negotiated an agreement with the Airbus countries in 1979. This liberalized trade in aircraft components (hitherto subject to tariffs) so that it grew rapidly as manufacturers diverted orders from expensive domestic sources to other, cheaper or better producers. The American side had hoped for an agreement to end subsidies such as cheap loans to cover development costs which Airbus had been granted, but no firm declaration was forthcoming. During the 1980s, Airbus continued to make headway against US competition. In 1992, the US was driven to bring a case against Airbus before GATT, on the grounds that exchange-rate guarantees given by the German government violated the GATT. A GATT committee ruled in favour of the US, forcing the Airbus partners to negotiate a second bilateral agreement with the US. This second agreement limited any future subsidies and interest rate concessions. From an economic perspective, the agreement appears beneficial: subsidies to innovation are retained but controlled, in recognition both of their usefulness and of the dangers of escalating, mutually-damaging subsidies. It can also be seen that Airbus, having secured a significant market share and moved down the learning curve, was quite prepared to see further entry (for example, by Japan or Taiwan) barred by GATT rules.

Studies of the effects on economic welfare of Airbus' subsidized entry have tried to quantify several elements. First are the lower prices of planes caused by competition among manufacturers: an increase in consumer surplus for passengers in Europe, America and, of course, in economies which purchase but which do not produce aircraft. These gains would, of course, continue for as long as competition is enhanced; they are not restricted to any single generation of aircraft. Second are the changes in producer surplus: lower profits for shareholders and lower pay for workers in Boeing and McDonnell Douglas plus profits, if any, and wages for Airbus owners and employees. Clearly 'consumer' nations would be expected to gain, while for the US and Europe producer losses and consumer gains work in opposite directions. The magnitude of changes also depends upon what is taken to be the situation without entry by Airbus. The alternatives here include a simple monopoly by Boeing or a Boeing-McDonnell Douglas duopoly. Reviewing studies by Baldwin and Krugman (1989) and others, Tyson (1992) finds that most ignore wage payments in the calculation of producer surpluses. With this item included, Katz and Summers come to the conclusion that European and consumer-nation welfare rose while American welfare fell (because producer losses outweighed consumer gains in the USA). From a European perspective, the Airbus operation appears to have been a successful exercise in rent-shifting. Besides static effects, Tyson notes that Airbus' entry has raised the rate of innovation in the industry, complicating any computation of welfare.

## 11.6   Trade and technology: case study in semiconductors

At the forefront of technology in the second half of the twentieth century has been the semiconductor industry, which began with the production of transistors and then moved into electronic chips. (A distinction which later becomes important is that between more complex microprocessors and the simpler memory chips.) Although highly innovative and entrepreneurial, the industry bears the clear imprint of a supportive environment including positive contributions from public policy. The industry began in the research labs of Bell Telephones in America in the late 1940s. Although the creative genius of the early inventors was clearly vital, so too was the commitment of US industry to basic research as well as the relative abundance of skilled engineers. For the development of the industry from invention to innovation, it was also important to have a flexible labour market and a venture capital industry ready to lend on the basis of new products and their potential. During the 1950s and 1960s, the industry expanded with the growth of sales of a major user, computers. Here again, public policy played a vital role in that the US Department of Defense readily bought advanced products for military purposes, effectively funding their research costs.

The industry shows many of the more familiar patterns but in a highly exaggerated form. Foremost is the rate of innovation. New powerful chips (the 286, 386 and so on) appear every four to five years, each being superseded in its turn by one even more powerful. Innovation affects costs. As chips become more complex, both design costs and the costs of an MES plant rise: the latter climbed from $3 million in 1970 to $75 million in 1980, $150 million in 1985 and $500 million in 1990. Learning curves in production moreover are steep, so that costs per chip fall as cumulative production increases.

These cost features have brought economic consequences. First, in the 1970s certain manufacturing operations were moved from the US to 'export platforms' in Southeast Asia. Second, prices are volatile or rather cyclical. Each new product sells at high prices at the start of its period of dominance by virtue of its new capabilities, but prices fall relentlessly as more producers offer the design. Companies thus race to be first to market with new designs so as to make good prices and profits to recoup their outlays and to finance the next generation. A practice also developed of 'advance pricing', that is, of setting low prices during the early stages of a product's cycle, on the basis not of current cost but of anticipated costs (as did aircraft manufacturers). While damaging to the company adopting the practice, the damage to rivals could be more severe. Indeed, the difference between advance and predatory pricing is not easy to perceive. (In an international context, predatory pricing is called 'dumping'.) Technically defined as selling at a price below the marginal cost of production, it is illegal under international treaty.)

Under the impact of innovation and policy, the structure of the industry has changed. When the costs of an MES plant were low, new US producers came into the industry: between 1966 and 1972, 30 new firms opened for business in the USA. Because of innovation, however, even incumbents have to invest anew in each round simply to stay in the game. As the costs of so doing rose, entry ceased in the USA and was replaced by exit as firms left the industry. On an international scale, however, entry increased as Japanese producers of electrical and electronic goods established their own in-house production units. Latterly Korean firms have also entered the industry.

The impact of policy is evident in both Europe and Japan. In Europe, governments attempted to protect their computer industries (the chip-users) by a variety of means including preferential purchasing. The British government, for example, bought only ICL machines for the public sector up to 1980. They also imposed tariffs on imported chips. This, of course, penalized the European computer-makers who were already relatively uncompetitive.

European governments were, however, willing to exempt from tariffs semiconductors made in European plants, encouraging US firms to manufacture in Europe and compete with locally-owned producers. European chip manufacturers found difficulty in withstanding such competition and their share of world production remained below 15 per cent. In Japan, policy was more effective (if expensive). The Japanese initially imported chips from US 'merchant' producers (companies which make chips for sale rather than for internal consumption as does for example IBM's 'captive' chip-maker). Up to 1978, foreign investment in Japan was restricted and US semiconductor firms were therefore unable to consolidate their position in the Japanese market by establishing local subsidiaries. At the same time, the Japanese Ministry of International Trade and Industry sponsored industrial research into semiconductor manufacturing so that by 1978 Japanese companies had taken a significant share of the home market from their American rivals. Despite the superiority and cheapness of US chips, Japanese users, it is argued (Tyson, 1992), discriminated in favour of domestic producers, who were normally their own in-house subsidiaries. This vertical integration naturally gave Japanese chip-makers access to funds to help them to survive their early period. One estimate is that Japanese electronics companies sustained losses of some $4 billion while building their chip-making subsidiaries (*The Economist*, 22 January, 1994, p.61). Secure in this home market, the Japanese semiconductor industry proceeded to capture 17 per cent of the US market by 1985 while US exports to the booming Japanese market stagnated. These developments were particularly pronounced in the market for memory chips.

Concerned about the loss of market share both at home and worldwide, the US industry lobbied for action on the grounds that Japanese firms were dumping in the US and blocking imports at home. In 1986 the two governments negotiated the SCTA (Semiconductor Trade Agreement) which forced Japanese firms to raise prices in all markets and promised US chip-makers help from the Japanese government in doubling their market share to 20 per cent. The result of the agreement proved to be mixed. The price of memory chips duly rose in Europe and America as Japan curtailed production. This, of course, acted to the detriment of chip-users in those places, who found themselves at a disadvantage in relation to chip-users based in Japan, where chips continued to be 'dumped'. It also benefited chip-makers, who in effect had a cartel organized for them by the US and Japanese governments. With US firms leaving the industry, the chief beneficiaries were the Japanese who were thus able to fund more R&D and investment for the next round of innovations. These profits must, however, be set in the context of their earlier losses. Attempts to open the Japanese market to US chips did not succeed: although many relationships between US firms and Japanese electronics companies were formed, possibly building the foundations for later growth, the Americans' share of the Japanese market rose only to 13 per cent by 1991. The most arresting fact is, however, the sharp decline in Japan's share of the world market that began in 1988. Although partly caused by the SCTA, other forces were at work. One was the continuing encroachment of the Koreans into the memory chip segment. The other was the success of US merchant producers in creating yet another generation of sophisticated microprocessors, a segment which the Japanese had not entered. This development reversed the decline in the US share of the market. The Americans' fear that Japan's expertise in making memory chips would prove transferable to microprocessors proved groundless in a way that no one foresaw, underlining the objection to protectionist policies that they require accurate foresight.

## 11.7 Foreign direct investment

Although foreign trade has grown rapidly in the second half of the twentieth century, it has been outdistanced by the expansion of foreign direct investment (FDI), that is, the creation of subsidiaries on greenfield sites in overseas locations. A substantial proportion of international trade is now conducted between subsidiaries, that is, while it is trade between countries, it is internal to firms. How can this 'globalization' be explained?

First, Bertrand and Cournot models suggest that FDI is a profitable strategy when it reduces marginal costs in the foreign market. This would depend on the relative sizes of the costs of exporting from the home base (marginal production costs plus transport costs) and the costs of creating an overseas subsidiary. These would comprise the fixed costs of establishing the plant together with its lifetime operating costs. Export costs should, however, also take account of any tariffs which would have the effect of boosting overseas costs and thus reducing market share and profits. Similarly, game theory models can be used in that an FDI decision involves sunk costs and is thus a clear commitment to remain in a market and thus to retaliate against entry by others.

Such models, however, omit the salient fact that not all firms in an industry engage in FDI. The same could be said of most models: they treat firms as being identical. This suggests that FDI is driven as much by firm-specific factors as by industry-level forces. Thus Buckley and Casson (1976) argue that FDI should be considered as merely one option among a range which includes, as well as exporting from a home base, licensing or franchising the firm's technology or brand to local producers. Selecting FDI would indicate that its costs and risk were lower than these alternatives. While the costs of FDI can be imagined, those of licensing are perhaps a little less obvious. The difficulties relate to the problems of selling information: the potential buyer has no easy way of appreciating the value of that information without actually being given access to it. Once access has been given, however, the buyer has reason to pay. A firm with specific advantages in terms of its technological or other prowess may find, therefore, that it can only use those advantages by organizing distant production through its own subsidiary. (There is, of course, another consideration: local producers with some understanding of the advantages of a firm's technological or other informational assets are most likely to be potential or actual competitors. Franchising to such firms would be disadvantageous.) The argument is surely a variant on the logic of Coase (1937) and Williamson (1981), set out in Chapter 2, where it was argued that the costs of using the market may lead firms to internalize transactions by integrating operations.

There is evidence to support this line of argument. Martin (1991) surveyed 40 US industries in 1977 for characteristics which were associated with foreign direct investment in the US. He found that FDI was higher in industries which were more concentrated in the US and which had higher than average advertising-to-sales ratios. Since advertising is plausibly associated with firm-specific characteristics which need to be communicated to consumers, this evidence is supportive of the thesis that firm-specific advantages lead companies to adopt FDI as the most efficient means of serving foreign markets.

John Dunning (1988) has taken these ideas further, arguing that 'international production', as he terms it, can only be explained by reference to an 'eclectic paradigm' or theory, which he avers has three elements. That is, firms will turn into multinationals if three conditions are met. First, the firm must have some unique advantage in terms of skill, efficiency or reputation. These Dunning terms 'ownership' advantages, but in reality they are inherent not to ownership but to the work team. Second, there have to be location-specific advantages; that is, the firm must need for some reason to use the resources of some remote (overseas) location. Third, there must be advantages in 'internalization' à la Coase, that is, it must make sense to integrate certain operations rather than contracting across markets for them. Thus contracting should not be a viable method of exploiting the overseas location. One case study Dunning uses is the hotel industry, where US firms, by virtue of their experience with the American consumer, have developed a certain level of expertise. Clearly the hotel industry needs location-specific features: the hotels have to be where the guests wish to stay, in holiday resorts or business centres. Integration is required (although this can take many forms such as ownership, management contracts or leasing) in order to guarantee standards of service and to exploit fixed-cost items such as computerized reservation services.

The growth of FDI is not without consequences for industrial economics. Indeed, it serves to undermine some basic concepts. Whereas Ricardo was able to identify countries with industries (Portugal with wine) and Krugman identifies countries with companies and their products (the USA with Boeing), large-scale FDI means that these devices may no longer be legitimate. Complex products require components from diverse souces which are increasingly located in several different countries; the original design work may have been undertaken in another country, and shares in the parent company may be distributed among investors around the world. While ownership of the brand may reside with the parent firm, whose headquarters still take key decisions, it is with diminshing conviction that one can identify products with a country of origin. These trends, of course, point to a need for an even closer union between industrial economics and trade theory.

## Guide to further reading

Krugman (1987) is useful. Tyson (1992) is a lively discussion of modern issues in high-tech trade policy.

# 12  Competition policy

## 12.1  Introduction

In the course of this chapter we will be surveying a range of policies which are known generically as competition policy or, less commonly, as antitrust. Underpinning these policies are matters of principle which have been addressed in Chapters 3 to 8; this chapter concentrates upon issues of policy implementation.

The primary emphasis in what follows is upon mergers. This arises for a variety of reasons, not least because of the effects upon UK industrial structure of a series of merger waves this century, and the recent European Union (EU) legislation in this area. The sections on mergers are accordingly kept separate for the most part from those on monopolies and restrictive practices. These sections are also of relevance to the discussion of industrial policy in Chapter 14.

## 12.2  Terminology

Before going any further, two matters require explanation: namely 'markets' and 'restrictive practices'. For the purposes of administering policy against alleged monopoly abuse, it is necessary to define a market. We touched on this matter in Chapter 3, and readers will recall that the ideal way to define a market is to identify a group of products that are close substitutes; that is, which have high mutual cross-elasticities of demand but which collectively have low cross-elasticities against (are poor substitutes for) other groups of products.

This information is, unfortunately not usually available, and policy-makers have to be more pragmatic. In the USA, policy guidelines (US Attorney General, 1988) state that the market is to be defined as sales of the product in question together with those products which 75 per cent of the first product's buyers would consider to be acceptable substitutes. To this is added new production which would enter the market from whatever source within one year's time if prices were to be raised by 5 per cent. This gives the basis for calculating how large the market share is of the first supplier. The figures 75 per cent, 5 per cent and 1 year are plainly pragmatic; yet British and EU policies are even more pragmatic in that clear guidelines are not made available and markets are defined case-by-case (Frazer, 1992).

Restrictive practices are many and varied. The clearest examples are agreements to set common prices, to reserve market segments for each member of a cartel, to compare tender prices or to coordinate the compilation of inflated tenders for contracts. Where companies are already well-rehearsed in the art of avoiding price competition, information agreements can suffice. These are horizontal arrangements which restrain competition between members of the same industry. To these must be added vertical restrictions which restrain competition between firms in 'downstream' industries, usually distributors. Such restrictions mean that new manufacturers face greater obstacles in finding outlets for their products. One example is exclusive dealership or the tying of outlets whereby a distributor is obliged, if it is to continue receiving the manufacturer's products, to stop selling the products of rival manufacturers. 'Full-line forcing', by contrast, obliges a distributor to stock everything made by a manufacturer, whereas resale price maintenance refers to the practice whereby manufacturers dictate the price at which distributors should sell to their customers. In addition, franchising agreements often in effect divide markets territorially, with the difference being that these have not been deemed to be anti-competitive.

## 12.3  Monopolies and Restrictive Practices Policy

No formal anti-monopoly legislation existed in the UK prior to 1948. During the late nineteenth and early twentieth centuries monopolies were regarded as special cases within an economy characterized by a high degree of competition, and insofar as it did prove necessary to restrain the abuse of a monopoly position, this could be done using the common law. However, the common law tended to be narrowly interpreted such that only the parties specifically concerned in a case, rather than the public at large, were given proper consideration.

As a result, there existed no general restraint upon the acquisition of monopoly power, and the depressed economic conditions of the 1920s and the 1930s proved to be decades during which opinion swung around positively to favour cartelization in order to protect industry from the ravages of excessive price competition. The authorities continued to support cartelization during the Second World War because of the overriding need to control the allocation of scarce resources, but at the end of the war it began to be felt that a more competitive environment would be needed, in order to ensure that the post-war UK economy would be able to survive and prosper in the vastly different circumstances of the time.

### 12.3.1  Monopolies and Restrictive Practices Act 1948

In 1948, the Monopolies and Restrictive Practices Act appeared, somewhat to the surprise of industrialists who had become used to government support for the trend towards a more concentrated industrial structure. The Act did not define a monopoly as such but applied to markets where:

1  At least one-third of all the goods supplied or processed in the United Kingdom were supplied by a firm and its subsidiaries (scale monopoly);
2  Two or more firms, which together supplied at least one-third of the market, were parties to a restrictive agreement, whether oral or written, tacit or overt, or so conducted their affairs as in any way to prevent or restrict competition (complex monopoly).

The existence of monopoly power was not condemned out of hand; instead the Board of Trade (currently the Department of Trade and Industry) was empowered to refer to the Monopolies Commission any firm or firms falling within the above two categories. The Board of Trade could request the Commission either to report back without judging the issues involved, or to attach a judgement as to whether or not the public interest was being contravened, together with possible remedies as appropriate. It was then up to the Board of Trade to take action upon a report as it saw fit. The Monopolies Commission was thus an *independent administrative tribunal with no powers either to select cases for examination or to execute judgements.* The real power lay with the Board of Trade, which could resolve cases without recourse to law where the firms under investigation were willing to cooperate voluntarily. Alternatively, it could draw up a Statutory

Order, subject to Parliamentary approval, requiring the parties concerned to desist from certain specified practices.

It can reasonably be argued that the 1948 Act was set up to test the feasibility of monopoly legislation. The emphasis was upon enquiry, and investigations proceeded very slowly. The procedures were intended to be flexible, with each case being judged upon its own merits, and no fixed penalties were laid down. Although a structural rule was employed to select out suitable cases for investigation, the cost-benefit approach was to be used in the actual investigation which would concentrate upon conduct and performance matters. The Commission was empowered to conduct follow-up enquiries to determine whether or not any condemned practices had in fact been terminated.

The real stumbling block of the 1948 Act proved to be the lack of a workable definition of the *public interest*, and the clause in the Act giving guidance to the Commission in this area proved to be far too general to have any practical value. In effect, the Commission was left to its own devices in determining what was or was not economically and socially desirable. The Commission conducted 20 investigations between 1948 and 1956. Their investigations were slow, only taking place one at a time, and many of the references were either to small industries or to small parts of larger industries. No investigations of service industries or nationalized industries were permitted, and it is difficult in retrospect to see any rhyme or reason about the choice of references.

Of the 20 industries investigated, 3 were not condemned in any major way, whereas in 16 cases the majority of the Commission members found evidence of serious malpractices. Exclusive dealing and tying arrangements were condemned in almost every case, as were other measures to exclude competitors such as brand proliferation and measures to control supply or productive capacity. Unfortunately, whereas public opinion was influenced by these discoveries, the Board of Trade remained largely unmoved. Only one Order was submitted to Parliament, and that proved unacceptable because it was incorrectly drawn up. In all other cases rather weak voluntary agreements were reached with the industries concerned, and no proper follow-up procedures were set in motion to ensure that these agreements were honoured to the letter.

### 12.3.2 Restrictive Trade Practices Act 1956

This Act came into being largely as a result of the discovery of widespread restrictive practices prevalent in the industries investigated under the terms of the 1948 Act (HMSO, 1955). The Monopolies Commission was left to deal only with specific monopoly situations, while provision was made for the compulsory registration of trade-association agreements with the Registrar of a Restrictive Practices Court.

Such agreements included those between two or more parties concerned with the production or supply of goods who agree upon prices to be charged, the terms and conditions of sale, quantities and types to be produced, the process of manufacture, the persons to whom they sell or the persons from whom they buy. Such agreements did not have to be explicitly laid down in writing but could be of a more informal nature.

Unlike the Act of 1948, the investigatory process was to be set in motion by the Registrar rather than the Board of Trade; it was judicial rather than administrative; and treated the firms in question as *guilty unless proven to be innocent rather than innocent unless proven to be guilty*. This latter change stemmed from the fact that scale economies are not normally of relevance in cases of restrictive practices given that the parties to the practices are not joined together into enlarged operating units. Hence, there is little obvious benefit to the public from restrictive practices.

However, the Act still embodied elements of the cost-benefit approach in that parties to an agreement were permitted to justify the agreement by pleading one or more of the so-called 'gateways'. These gateways, seven in number, were the way in which the concept of the public interest was embodied in the Act, and they were as follows:

(1) that the restriction is reasonably necessary to protect the public against injury in connection with the consumption, installation, or use of goods;
(2) that the removal of the restriction would deny to the public as purchasers, consumers or users of goods, specific and substantial benefits;
(3) that the restriction is reasonably necessary to counteract measures taken by someone not party to the agreement with a view to preventing or restricting competition in the relevant trade;
(4) that the restriction is reasonably necessary to enable parties to the agreement to negotiate fair terms with major suppliers or customers;
(5) that the removal of the restriction would be likely to have a serious and persistent adverse effect upon unemployment in the locality of the firms concerned;
(6) that the removal of the restriction would be bad for exports;
(7) that the restriction is reasonably required for the purposes of supporting other restrictions deemed to be in the public interest.

In cases where one or more of the gateways was successfully pleaded, the Court nevertheless had to satisfy itself that no further disadvantages arising out of the restrictive agreement outweighed the benefits claimed for it. This was known as the 'balancing item' or 'tailpiece'.

Unfortunately, that nature and extent of the gateways, and in particular the vagueness of gateway (2) above, left the Court with no option but to make up its own mind, on a case-by-case basis, how to measure in a meaningful way the costs and benefits associated with a particular agreement. This proved to be an arduous requirement, and it is hardly surprising that the decisions conveyed an element of the unpredictable. In effect, the Court was obliged not only to make economic predictions and forecasts, but also to evaluate the economic effects of agreements in the light of the interests of different groups and of competing policy objectives.

At first the Court was unwilling to let any agreements at all through the gateways, with the result that many firms preferred to claim that agreements had been allowed to lapse rather than bother to present a seemingly hopeless case before the Court. Subsequently the Court's piecemeal approach allowed several agreements through the gateways, and in particular some rather dubious decisions came to be associated with gateway (2). By the end of 1959, 2240 agreements were entered into the register, the great bulk of those then in existence. By the end of 1975 this number had grown to 3100. Of the original registrations some 2000 were either abandoned voluntarily or altered to the Court's satisfaction, rising to some 10 000 by 1991. Altogether, fewer than 100 agreements had been approved by 1980, and rather fewer had been contested before the Court because key decisions by the Court tended to indicate to firms indulging in broadly similar practices that little benefit could be expected from repeating the contest.

Voluntary terminations, therefore, were the order of the day. This appeared on the face of it to be a highly beneficial outcome, but it did not necessarily imply that practices would be altered in such a way as to ensure a more competitive atmosphere in the trades concerned. The fact that most agreements were no longer officially in existence did not necessarily imply that the parties to them had ceased to behave in accordance with their provisions. Because of this factor one cannot state unequivocally that the Act was a success, although most commentators would appear to take the view that the impact of the Act was impressive, and that the performance of the economy was thereby improved.

### 12.3.3 Resale Prices Act 1964

The 1956 Act contained clauses to the effect that whereas collective action to prevent price cutting was prohibited, an individual firm could enforce resale price maintenance (RPM) on its products. RPM obviously has the effect of restricting competition among retailers. At that time RPM covered some 35 per cent of consumer expenditure on goods and services, but the practice came under increasing pressure as self-service outlets selling consumer goods sought to undercut maintained prices. Initially, many suppliers neglected to take out injunctions enforcing RPM, but in 1962 the Net Book Agreement was accepted by the Restrictive Practices Court whereby publishers as a group were permitted to enforce RPM on books, and individual suppliers subsequently enforced RPM with more vigour.

Nevertheless, the spread of supermarkets and the like forced the breakdown of RPM in the grocery trade, and threatened the same result for electrical goods. Once the benefits to the consumer of these developments became widely appreciated, the authorities reacted by passing the 1964 Resale Prices Act. This Act extended the powers of the Restrictive Practices Court to include cases involving RPM where suppliers either try to impose RPM contractually, refuse to supply outlets which undercut maintained prices, or refuse to supply such outlets except on unfavourable terms. The general presumption of the Act was that RPM was contrary to the public interest and that firms imposing RPM were to be considered guilty unless proven innocent. As in the Act of 1956, gateways were introduced whereby firms could plead that the abolition of RPM would prove detrimental to consumers. There were five gateways concerned with:

1 the effects on the quality and variety of goods for sale;
2 the possible reduction in the number of retail outlets;
3 long-run increases in retail prices;
4 danger to health inherent in the nature of differing retail outlets;
5 the effects on the provision of pre- and post-sales services.

Once again, a tailpiece ruled that any benefits to the consumer arising from any of the above should not be outweighed by other detriments. It was also stipulated that no supplier could withhold supplies from a trader who either had sold, or was about to sell, specified goods at below the maintained price, unless the trader was using those goods as an obvious 'loss-leader'.

The Act set down that the Registrar should compile a register of suppliers who wished to claim an exemption within three months from mid-August 1964, and arrange those suppliers into appropriate classes. A representative case from each class would then go before the Restrictive Practices Court. Until the Court had judged each case, all the suppliers within the relevant class could continue to enforce RPM. Once, however, a decision had been reached in a particular case, this decision would be binding upon all suppliers in that class.

The Registrar collected applications for exemption pertaining to over 500 classes of goods, which were grouped into 157 notices of reference. Some notable failures to apply at all related to grocery products and motor cars. However, only three cases eventually went to court. The case of the chocolate and sugar confectionery manufacturers was rejected in 1967, and that of footwear manufactureres in 1968. The ethical and proprietary drug manufacturers obtained an exemption in 1970, and the court reaffirmed the continuance of RPM on net books. The paucity of cases largely reflected the high costs of fighting a case, and a reaction to the adverse judgements in 1967 and 1968.

Although in most cases price competition has resulted from the abolition of RPM, the structure of some markets and/or an adverse price-elasticity of demand has prevented this result from proving universal. Overall, however, what evidence there is supports the view that the abolition of RPM did lead to a general reduction in prices (Pickering, 1974).

### 12.3.4 Restrictive Trade Practices Act 1968

With the effective prohibition of formal market-sharing and price fixing agreements, many industries had moved to a more subtle strategy of 'information agreements' by which they informed their competitors of their prices and, in some instances, their costs. If companies were Cournot oligopolists with no intention of competing on price, then such information was sufficient to allow a tacit cartel to operate. Naturally, in retail markets, prices are in the public domain, but in intra-business markets list prices are often subject to negotiation and discounting such as to render them unhelpful; hence the usefulness of information agreements. Moreover, they fell outside the scope of the 1956 definition of restrictive practices.

In order to deal with this problem, the 1956 Act was amended by the Restrictive Trade Practices Act of 1968, which empowered the Board of Trade to require registration of exchange of information agreements by which firms inform one another of their prices, and occasionally of their costs. On the other hand, the 1956 Act was simultaneously weakened by the addition of an eighth gateway to the effect that an agreement is exempted where it 'does not directly restrict or discourage competition to any material degree in any relevant trade or industry, and is not likely to do so'. More severe penalties were introduced for failure to register.

Subsequently, a series of related Acts were passed as follows: The Restrictive Trade Practices Act 1976; the Restrictive Trade Practices Court Act 1976; the Resale Prices Act 1976; and the Resale Trade Practices Act 1977. The first three Acts simply served to pull together the various threads of previous legislation into a more coherent pattern. The fourth Act basically exempted from investigation agreements concerned with lending between financial institutions.

### 12.3.5 Competition Act 1980

Three distinct processes were in operation before 1980, namely:

1 monopoly and merger cases dealt with under the 1973 Fair Trading Act (discussed below) with limited resources and a requirement to investigate the market as a whole, including all those supplying the reference products, rather than an individual firm;
2 restrictive practice cases dealt with under the Acts of 1976;
3 any cases being dealt with under EC legislation (see below).

The innovation of the 1980 Competition Act was to concentrate upon the areas which complemented the existing legislation, namely practices which did not fall within the scope of any of the above Acts. Thus agreements subject to the provisions of the 1976 Acts were excluded from the scope of the Competition Act, and the now renamed Monopolies and Mergers Commission (MMC) was authorized to investigate *anti-competitive practices of individual firms* and to concentrate upon their effects.

Section 2 of the Act defines an anti-competitive practice as one which:

has or is intended to have or is likely to have the effect of restricting, distorting or preventing competition in connection with the production, supply or acquisition of goods in the United Kingdom or any part of it.

The same principle applies to services. The practice must normally be pursued in the course of production or trade, and must either be, or be expected to be, part of a course of conduct rather than a single instance.

The procedure is as follows:

1 The Director-General of Fair Trading (see Section 12.4.2), quite possibly on the basis of a plausible postal complaint, conducts a preliminary investigation, on his own initiative, of an alleged anti-competitive practice.
2 The Director-General of Fair Trading is obliged to publish a report stating, with reasons, whether there is *prima facie* evidence of such a practice. No direct reference to the concept of the public interest can be made at this stage. If there is sufficient evidence, then
3 The Director-General of Fair Trading approaches the firm informally. If the Director-General of Fair Trading is satisfied within two months either that the practice is trivial in effect, or that the firm is prepared to renounce or modify the practice, the Director-General of Fair Trading may decide to proceed no further. Where, however, a voluntary undertaking is abrogated, or where no such undertaking is forthcoming, then
4 A 'competition reference' is made to the MMC between 4 and 8 weeks (exceptionally 12) after the publication of the preliminary report.
5 The MMC then has six months (plus a possible three-month extension) to report whether the practice is taking place;
   whether it is anti-competitive in effect; and
   whether it is against the public interest.
   At this stage the 1973 Act procedures, including the public interest definition, are brought to bear upon the case. If all three conditions above are answered affirmatively, then
6 The Secretary of State may ask the Director-General of Fair Trading to seek voluntary undertakings. If these are not forthcoming a ministerial order, enforceable through a subsequent court order if necessary, may be made prohibiting the practice. Two further powers are made available. Firstly, the Secretary of State may ask the Director-General of Fair Trading to investigate prices of 'major public concern'. Secondly, under Section 11 the Secretary of State may refer nationalized industries and certain other bodies (water authorities, bus companies and agricultural marketing boards) to the MMC for an audit of their efficiency, costs and service to consumers, or possible abuse of monopoly power.

The emphasis of the Act is, therefore, very much upon conduct in the form of, for example, price discrimination, predatory pricing, full-line forcing, rental-only contracts, exclusive supply and selective distribution. Of particular interest are practices which frustrate 'the legitimate efforts of competitors to expand their own business'. Yet the approach is very different from that embodied in the Acts of 1976, which are also concerned with restrictive practices, and this had led one commentator to conclude that 'a silent revolution in the operation of competition policy in Britain has occurred' (O'Brien, 1982, p.218).

### 12.3.6 The 'Bicester Agreement'

In July 1991 a Court of Appeal judgement in the case of *Director General of Fair Trading v. Smiths Concrete Ltd* had damaging implications for the Office of Fair Trading's (OFT) ability to investigate secret cartels, refer them to the Restrictive Practices Court and seek fines for contempt where an injunction had been granted against an earlier unlawful agreement. The key point was that the company had taken all reasonable steps to prevent its employees from making unlawful agreements, and that the local manager had acted outside the scope of his authority. In future, therefore, the OFT will be obliged to prove not merely that an unlawful agreement is in force but that employees party to it are acting with the company's authorization.

## CASE STUDY: WHITE SALT

An example of UK competition policy is the report on the supply of white salt, which came under scrutiny in 1986. In 1983, the situation was noted by the Director-General of Fair Trading who referred it to the MMC. A panel of the MMC was duly set up and, after hearing evidence from suppliers, buyers and others, it reported in 1985. In 1983, the industry was a duopoly, the market being shared between Staveley Industries' subsidiary, British Salt, with some 50 per cent of sales, and ICI's then Mond Division, which dealt with general chemicals, with some 45 per cent. Salt is mainly produced in Cheshire by pumping natural brine (salt dissolved in water) or by dissolving solid salt in water pumped to deep levels underground. The brine is then purified and evaporated to make salt. Salt is a relatively heavy product in relation to its value, making transport difficult and so keeping imports and exports to marginal levels. Salt is refined into various grades: the least refined is used for de-icing roads, with other grades going as an input for the production of chemicals such as chlorine and caustic soda, for dye manufacture and as an ingredient in food-processing. Other uses include water-softening and tanning.

Demand for salt had been in slow decline for some time, falling from 1.3 million tons in 1978 to 1.06 million in 1984. Customers tended to be local and loyal to one of the two large producers. In the 1930s, the industry had been characterized by price warfare, but this was ended by the 1937 British Salt Federation's price agreement. During the 1970s, salt prices rose faster than the general level of inflation; it was also notable that the prices of the two companies moved in step. In fact, the two producers notified each other and their customers of price increases some weeks in advance, so that the increases were only implemented when each producer had informed its competitior (and usually learned that the increases were to be matched). Both companies were more profitable than the average for the chemical sector, with British Salt showing better returns than ICI. This was partly explained by better efficiency, although both companies had invested in important process innovations.

The production of salt is hedged with entry barriers because of the environmental consequences inherent in the nature of the process. Salt is found in only a few locations, of which Cheshire is the richest. New producers would naturally prefer this location. One problem, however, is that salt extraction brings subsidence, and areas have accordingly to be set aside for brine production. All areas so designated are owned by the present producers and new entrants would be unlikely to receive permission from the local authorities to work other deposits. Another barrier to entry operates in conjunction with the first; namely that demand is falling, making the industry unattractive to new firms and strengthening the argument that new areas do not need to be designated. Finally, there are economies of scale in brine extraction and in evaporation, which mean that any entry would have to be on a large scale. The incumbents, of course, have large sunk costs and thus incentives to fight.

*Prima facie*, the industry appeared to be a cartel in which prices were effectively coordinated by the two firms. Indeed, it seemed that the less efficient operator, ICI, was raising prices and that British Salt, faced with the choice between charging the same price or undercutting it, opted for the former in order to avoid a bruising, and possibly fatal, price war. Faced with the accusation of collusion, the companies argued to the MMC that a common price was natural for a 'commodity' (a product which is relatively unprocessed) like salt. They argued that there was competition between the two firms in the form of discounts offered to loyal customers, although it was conceded that the two sets of discounts were similar. The companies also argued that the barriers to entry were not high.

The MMC found that a monopoly did indeed exist, and that it was reinforced by barriers to entry. Within this market, British Salt had declined to exert competitive pressure on ICI's less efficient operation, in effect colluding. The MMC felt this to be unsatisfactory, and recommended more active price competition by limiting the prices of the lower-cost producer, British Salt. The recommendation was not acted upon by the Secretary of State, and it is not difficult to see why. A period of aggresive price-cutting by British Salt would, if sustained, have led to one company leaving the market. This could have been British Salt, given ICI's larger possibilities for cross-subsidization, but this was not certain. The industry would then have been a monopoly; out of the frying-pan and into the fire! Given the downward trend in sales, such an outcome was likely over the medium term in any event.

## 12.4  Mergers policy

Mergers are an inherent part of the capitalist system. As we saw in Chapter 6, they permit management teams to compete in capital markets as well as in product and factor markets. Mergers make an important contribution to flexibility in that without them entry costs would be much higher. That is, firms entering a new market can, if their plans do not succeed, sell the business to another firm by arranging for it to be taken over. Without this option, exit costs would be substantial and competition would accordingly be muted. Mergers also allow for economies of scale in production or R&D to be realized. Mergers do, however, carry the danger that incumbents could, through mergers, forge rival organizations into a monopoly. Moreover, action against mergers could, as it were, prevent rather than cure a monopoly given that the time that an intention to merge is declared is an opportune moment to prevent the emergence of a monopoly even before it takes concrete form.

It is evident that whereas a firm which has grown through internal expansion must have done so despite some degree of competition, and must therefore be reasonably efficient. Growth by merger has no such efficiency connotations and its sole purpose might be the acquisition of monopoly power. However, during the postwar period the authorities accepted that economies of scale might be forthcoming, as well as improvements in respect of R&D expenditure, invention and innovation, and hence preferred not to outlaw mergers *per se* but rather *to deal with each case on its merits*.

### 12.4.1  The Monopolies and Mergers Act 1965

The 1965 Act accordingly mirrored the approach first established in the Act of 1948. The then Monopolies Commission was once again to be the body to which cases would be passed by the then Board of Trade, advised by a Mergers Panel. At the same time, the Commission was empowered to investigate monopolies and restrictive practices in the service sector, and the powers of the Board of Trade to act upon the Commission's Reports were extended to enable it to require the publication of price lists, to regulate prices and to prohibit or impose conditions on acquisitions. Specifically, the Board of Trade could either dissolve a business, sell a part of its assets or forbid a perspective merger to take place. In principle, therefore, the powers of the authorities under the Act were far-reaching although, in practice, merger activity continued unabated.

A proposed merger *qualified for investigation* either where it produced a firm having a share of more than one-third of the available market for a given commodity or where the *value of the assets taken over* exceeded 5 million pounds. The market-share criterion was designed to catch out horizontal mergers. Conglomerate mergers involve companies in non-related sectors, so their introduction into the legislation clearly reflected a belief that company size could of itself be a source of market power.

Certainly, conglomerate mergers were beginning to take over from horizontal mergers by the mid-1960s as the availability of potentially attractive horizontal mergers dried up, although the latter have remained much the more numerous in absolute terms. Unfortunately, the definition of the public interest contained in the 1965 Act was less than clear-cut, and the resources of the Commission were modest. As a result only a handful of qualifying mergers were referred in most years, of which roughly one-third dropped out, one-third were allowed to proceed and one-third were disallowed (see Table 12.1)

## 12.4.2  The Fair Trading Act 1973

The response of the authorities was to introduce the Fair Trading Act in 1973 which is still in force. This Act repealed the Acts of 1948 and 1965 and set up a new body called the Office of Fair Trading, with a Director-General, known respectively as the OFT and DGFT. The OFT first took over the functions of the Registrar of Restrictive Trading Agreements in registering restrictive practices and referring them to the Restrictive Practices Court. It also took over from the Secretary of State of the Department of Trade and Industry certain responsibilities in respect of the renamed Monopolies and Mergers Commission (MMC) in that the DGFT would henceforth normally initiate monopoly enquiries and would provide the necessary background information for the Secretary of State in respect of merger enquiries, although the latter retained the specific power of refrence to MMC and the sole right to act upon its findings. However, the DGFT was given the right to overrule a MMC decision against a merger, the DGFT could not overrule a favourable decision.

The Secretary of State was given new powers to initiate enquiries into the activities both of nationalized industries and of other publicly sponsored bodies such as Marketing Boards. The Secretary of State was also empowered to look into restrictive labour practices, via the MMC, although no legally-enforceable remedies were made available for where such practices were found to exist. See Fig. 12.1.

A monopoly situation was re-defined as existing where a firm controlled one-quarter rather than one-third of the market, and a proposed merger qualified for investigation either where the value of assets taken over exceeded £5 million or where the new company would control one-quarter of the relevant market. In the course of a merger two or more enterprises had to *cease to be distinct*, which occurred when they came under *common ownership* or *control*. By this was meant either that more than 50 per cent of the equity was acquired; less than 50 per cent of the equity was acquired but *de facto* control could still be imposed by, say, the largest shareholder, or one company had the ability materially to influence the policy of another.

**TABLE 12.1  Numbers of mergers examined and references to the Commission: 1981–94** (*Source:* Office of Fair Trading)

| Year | Total numbers of cases examined | Found not to qualify and proposal abandoned | Qualifying cases Nos | Qualifying cases % change | Confidential guidance cases | Pre-notified cases[1] | References to the Commission Recommended by Director-General | References to the Commission Recommended but not made | References to the Commission Made but not recommended | References to the Commission Total references | References as % qualifying cases |
|---|---|---|---|---|---|---|---|---|---|---|---|
| 1981 | n/a | n/a | 164 | − 9.9 | 15 | — | 8 | — | — | 8 | 4.9 |
| 1982 | n/a | n/a | 190 | +15.9 | 32 | — | 9 | — | 1 | 10 | 5.3 |
| 1983 | n/a | n/a | 192 | + 1.1 | 37 | — | 10 | 2 | 1 | 9 | 4.7 |
| 1984 | n/a | n/a | 259 | +34.9 | 43 | — | 5 | 1 | — | 4 | 1.5 |
| 1985 | n/a | n/a | 192 | −25.9 | 34 | — | 6 | — | — | 6 | 1.9 |
| 1986 | 524 | 211 | 313 | +63.0 | 55 | — | 15 | 2 | — | 13 | 4.2 |
| 1987 | 478 | 157 | 321 | + 2.5 | 40 | — | 6 | — | — | 6 | 3.1 |
| 1988 | 456 | 150 | 306 | − 4.7 | 45 | — | 11 | — | — | 11 | 3.6 |
| 1989 | 427 | 146 | 281 | − 8.2 | 32 | — | 14 | — | — | 14 | 5.0 |
| 1990 | 369 | 108 | 261 | − 7.1 | 22 | 51 | 21 | — | 4 | 25[2] | 11.3 |
| 1991 | 285 | 102 | 183 | −29.9 | 15 | 38 | 8 | 1 | — | 7[3] | 4.2 |
| 1992 | 200 | 75 | 125 | −31.7 | 21 | 9[4] | 10 | — | — | 10[5] | 9.6 |
| 1993 | 309 | 112 | 197 | +57.6 | 46 | 13 | 5 | 2 | — | 3 | 2.0 |
| 1994 | 381 | 150 | 231 | +17.3 | 76 | 7 | 8 | — | — | 8 | 5.2 |

*Notes*
1 The prenotification procedure was introduced under provisions of the Companies Act 1989.
2 This figure counts the four acquisitions by South Yorkshire Transport Ltd as one reference, and excludes divestments in lieu of reference: 1, Rank/Mecca; and 2, Hillsdown Holdings/Strong and Fisher.
3 This figure excludes divestments in lieu of reference: 1, International Marine Holdings Inc/Benjamin Priest Group plc; 2, Trafalgar House plc/The Davy Corporation; and 3, Williams Holdings plc/Racal Electronics plc.
4 One other merger notice was withdrawn.
5 This figure excludes three divestments in lieu of reference: Redland plc/Steetley plc; Bowater plc/Assets of Pembridge Investments plc (DRG Packaging); Schlumberger Ltd/Assets of the Raytheon Company (Seismographic Service Group). It includes The Gillette Company/Parker Pen Holdings Ltd reference.

DIRECTOR-GENERAL
OF FAIR TRADING

MONOPOLIES
AND MERGERS
COMMISSION

SECRETARY
OF STATE

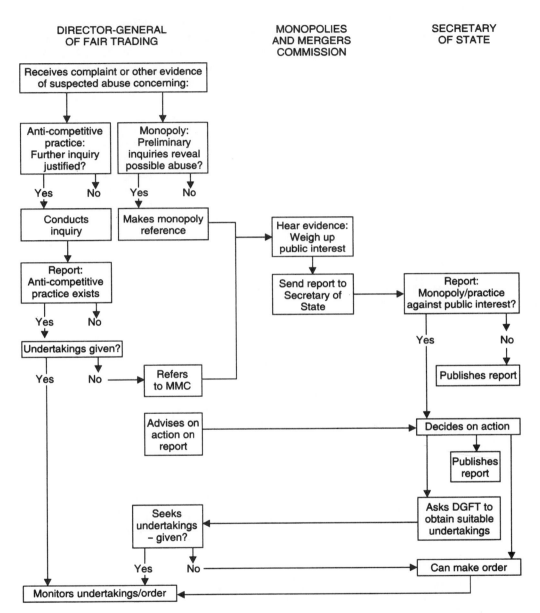

**Figure 12.1** Procedures under the Fair Trading Act and Competition Act (*Source*: House of Commons. Fifth Report Session 1994–95, *UK Policy on Monopolies*, HC249.1, p.x)

Enquiries had to be completed, as before, within six months, although the Secretary of State was also empowered to impose time limits on monopoly enquiries. Once a merger had been completed it could only be referred up to six months after it had taken place, except that where material facts about the transaction had not been disclosed to the authorities or made public, the six-month period would run from the date the authorities became aware, or could have become aware of those facts. A summary of the procedures is set out in Fig. 12.2. There was also a (non-statutory) confidential guidance system whereby a party could request advice whether or not a reference was likely on a proposal it wanted to keep confidential. A new procedure for voluntary pre-notification was introduced in the Companies Act 1989. The Act also introduced new provisions (new sections 75G–75K of the Fair Trading Act) which allow the Secretary of

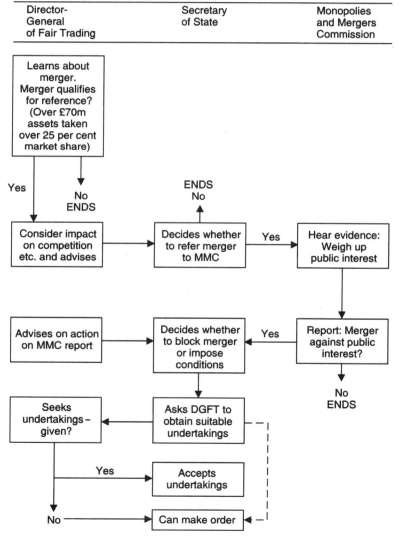

**Figure 12.2** Mergers: who does what (*Source*: DTI, *Competition policy: how it works*)

State to accept binding undertakings for the divestment of part of the merged companies' business, as an alternative to a reference.

A key factor was the redefinition of the public interest as set out in section 84 (2). Enquiries could be narrowed down to a consideration of whether or not specific aspects of a monopoly or a proposed merger were against the public interest, and a new emphasis was placed upon *maintaining and promoting effective competition*. In looking at the relevant market, this could be deemed to be regional rather than national (as in the case of brewing), and competitiveness could also be viewed as international where appropriate.

Specifically, section 83 (2) enjoined the MMC to

take into account all matters which appear to them in particular circumstances to be relevant and, among other things, shall have regard to desirability:

(a) of maintaining and promoting effective competition between persons supplying goods and services in the United Kingdom;

(b) of promoting the interests of consumers, purchasers and other users of goods and services in the United Kingdom in respect of the prices charged for them and in respect of their quality and the variety of goods and services supplied;

(c) of promoting, through competition, the reduction of costs and the development and use of new techniques and new products, and of facilitating the entry of new competitions into existing markets;

(d) of maintaining and promoting the balanced distribution of industry and employment in the United Kingdom;

(e) of maintaining and promoting competitive activity in markets outside the United Kindom on the part of producers of goods, and of suppliers of goods and services, in the United Kingdom.

During the 1980s, the authorities remained largely inactive in relation to mergers. Partly this reflected a reduction in the number of qualifying cases as a result of raising the assets criterion to £15 million in 1980, to £30 million in 1984 and to £70 million in February 1994. It also reflected the so-called Tebbit doctrine as enunciated by the then Secretary of State for Trade and Industry, Norman Tebbit, in 1984. In essence, in the face of (often justified) complaints about inconsistency in relation to referrals, competition considerations were to be given a position of primacy. To some extent this has necessarily diverted attention away from conglomerate mergers where there are no common products and hence no issues of competition.

Conglomerate mergers constituted more than half of the total by value in 1985, 1988 and 1989, although the recent recession temporarily much reduced conglomerate activity. A further significant factor has been the importance of foreign companies both as targets and, more crucially, as bidders. The threat of foreign predators became so great that, in 1990, the Secretary of State, Peter Lilley, announced that he would particularly take into account whether the predator was a foreign nationalized concern. However, attempts to discourage these through references to the MMC resulted in a rebuke from the European Commission on the grounds that he was not operating with a level playing field.

The outcomes of MMC investigations are unlikely to discourage either foreign or domestic predators. As noted, there have been remarkably few references and only a trivial number have been found to be against the public interest. To some extent this reflects the increasingly important role played by the European Commission, as discussed below. It is also the case that individual references have become very sizeable, involving bids for companies worth in excess of £1 billion. Conglomerate bids may necessitate prior divestments (so as to avoid creating high levels of concentration in particular markets) and if successful may lead to the dismemberment and sale of various parts of the target, both of which are factors which have led to increased merger activity. Nevertheless, the inescapable conclusion is that the odds in favour of a merger avoiding a reference, let alone an adverse judgement, are excellent.

*How substantial is 'a substantial part of the UK'?*

In August 1990, the MMC published a report on *South Yorkshire Transport (SYT) Ltd Acquisitions* (Cm 1166). Its recommendations that SYT should sell the four rivals it had acquired in 1989 was accepted by the then Secretary of State. This decision was subsequently challenged by SYT which claimed that the MMC had no jurisdiction since the acquisitions did not affect a 'substantial part of the UK' within the context of the 1973 Fair Trading Act.

In March 1991, the High Court overturned the MMC recommendation, and this decision was upheld by the Appeal Court in November 1991. This appeared to place a severe limitation on the powers of the competition authorities to vet mergers leading to concentration in local markets. However, in December, the House of Lords held that it was up to the MMC to satisfy itself that the affected part of the market was 'of such size, character and importance as to make it worth consideration for the purposes of the Act'. In this case the MMC had applied the market share test fairly, and the Court accordingly ruled unanimously that the MMC had been entitled to investigate. In principle, therefore, the MMC now has *carte blanche* to investigate large numbers of small local mergers.

### 12.4.3  Administrative or judicial?

It is worth reminding ourselves at this stage that the legislation concerned with monopolies and mergers is essentially concerned with *administrative* procedures, operating through the MMC, with a legalistic fall-back only where firms refuse to cooperate in implementing recommended changes in working procedures. Restrictive trade practices, on the other hand, are dealt with by the Restrictive Trade Practices Court in a primarily *judicial* manner. Prior to 1980 there seemed to be little debate about the validity of this dichotomy of approach, although legislation in other countries proceeded somewhat differently. It may be, therefore, that there was a widespread failure to observe that the emphasis upon administrative discretion embodied in the Competition Act applied in an area of antitrust where it had previously been largely disavowed.

Furthermore, although the procedures are similar to those applicable in monopoly and merger cases, there is even more discretion in the Competition Act because voluntary undertakings are sought both prior to, and at the conclusion of, an MMC reference. One interesting consequence of this is that, whereas it is the duty of the MMC to examine the question of the public interest, the DGFT is expected to negotiate undertakings without explicit reference to this concept. As a consequence, voluntary undertakings are often forthcoming at the initial stage, since this will forestall the time and expense of an MMC investigation, after which similar undertakings are likely to be demanded anyway. The ultimate sanction of a court order, on the other hand, does not much frighten firms, since the same facility has been available since 1948 without noticeable effect. This being the case, the discretionary emphasis of the 1980 Act creates the need for a degree of supervision of undertakings well in excess of that applicable under past legislation.

O'Brien argued strongly (O'Brien, 1982, pp.223–30) that the discretionary element in policy had increased steadily as the legislation developed, predominantly by way of exempting agreements from the compass of the legislation, as in the section 21(2) procedure of the Restrictive Trade Practices Act 1976. This tendency arose because the basic approach of the legislation was to require registration of agreements of a particular form. In a Green Paper the authorities recognized that this had the drawbacks of, for example,

1 causing all agreements to be registered, some of the potentially more beneficial of which would then lapse
2 separate criteria for registration and for satisfying the public interest

but concluded that the form-based system ought to be retained with modifications. It is clear, however, that more fundamental policy revision is needed if criticisms of this approach to restrictive practices are to be answered.

Some commentators take the view that the big distinction lies not so much between judicial and administrative systems as between a form-based system and an effects-based system which examines how restrictions actually operate. However, all UK legislation requires effects to be assessed in the course of an investigation so the distinction is somewhat blurred. Furthermore, cases lead to precedents, and precedents indicate strongly what forms of agreements are likely to prove acceptable. Thus there seems to be little need for a fundamental revision of policy in this respect. A more significant distinction is to be found between judicial and administrative approaches. Experience indicates strongly that firms dislike the judicial manner in which restrictive practice cases are tried, and therefore sometimes go to considerable lengths to avoid such involvement. An administrative system would, therefore, promote cooperation, and also be more flexible, especially when associated with the 1980 Act powers of continuous supervision.

It can be argued that the legislative underpinning for the approach to restrictive practices is essential since, first, an administrative procedure alone would be uncertain in its impact and would do little to discourage firms from continuing with such practices, and, secondly, since legal precedent pins down certain practices as unacceptable, neither the firm nor the investigating body need spend time and money finding out whether they are acceptable or not. Nevertheless, substituting the legalistic approach for the administrative in its entirety could be counter-productive, given the costs to the firm of defending itself and the somewhat unpleasant experience of being on trial.

What is increasingly being stated is that there must be a realistic punishment if there is to be a deterrent effect. It has long been argued that under UK law a business accused of anti-competitive behaviour cannot be punished until it has been investigated, found guilty and subsequently broken undertakings not to offend again. In addition, there are no powers to impose penalties for past misconduct nor to provide damages for victims of abuse. In other words, at present, when a firm exploits its market power, the worst potential consequence is that it be forced to desist: there is no retribution as in other instances of illegal action.

In 1992, Michael Heseltine, the Secretary of State for Trade and Industry, published a Green Paper (*Abuse of Market Power — a Consultative Document on Possible Legislative Options*). In so doing, he was responding to complaints by the OFT that its investigatory powers and capacity to fine were inadequate and fell short of those of the European Union. However, it remained unclear whether the EU system should be adopted wholesale given the UK tradition of a case-by-case approach rather than an assumption that abuse must arise if specified conditions are met. For this reason, the Green Paper offered three options. The first was to strengthen existing legislation by giving the OFT greater powers to obtain evidence, including the right to enter and search premises without a magistrate's warrant. The OFT would also be allowed more scope to accept binding undertakings without a MMC investigation. However, the drawback of a weak deterrent effect would remain.

The second option was to repeal the existing legislation and to introduce an EU-style system making it an offence for companies to *abuse* market power. The OFT would be given powers to investigate and to establish a tribunal which could impose fines of up to £1 million. Applications for larger penalties could be made by the OFT to the High Court. Similar powers would be given to regulators of utilities. Companies that believed they were victims of market abuse would have the power to bring actions for damages and to seek interim relief through injunctions. However, a drawback could be a restriction on the ability of the authorities to examine cases involving duopoly or complex monopoly.

The third option was to implement a 'dual system' by introducing a prohibition on abuse of market power and repealing the Competition Act provisions on anti-competitive practices while keeping the relevant provisions of the Fair Trading Act. The latter would then be restricted to cases involving several companies.

Despite the potential confusion inherent in operating a dual system, Mr Heseltine expressed a preference for this latter option in order to simplify the relationship between UK and EU legislation. Nevertheless, it is possible to argue that this is a case of using a steamroller to crack a walnut in that, by the end of 1992, only 35 complaints of anti-competitive behaviour by a dominant firm had been investigated under the Competition Act. In 13 cases the complaint proved to be unfounded, and in a further 10 cases the company gave undertakings not to re-offend. Only 10 cases actually ended up before the MMC.

On the other hand, it is often alleged that the lack of a proper remedy causes some firms to feel that a complaint is a waste of time, while others prefer not to rock the boat by registering a complaint. They argue that by the time a decision gets taken in their favour they may anyway have been driven out of business. In any event, it is insufficient simply to show that abuse has occurred. What is needed is proof of intent, and that is often hard to come by, especially in cases of alleged predatory pricing. This is particularly true in the case of privatized utilities where they have been specifically enjoined to cut prices.

### 12.4.4   MMC or Cartel Office?

The MMC has attracted a good deal of criticism on the grounds that it is inappropriate to have a clear separation as is the case for the MMC between those who do the research and the part-time commissioners who make the decisions. The latter conduct the hearings at which the companies present their case, and it is argued that the commissioners can be more swayed by what they hear in evidence than by the facts uncovered by their researchers.

It is often advocated that a solution to this difficulty is to opt for an equivalent of the German Cartel Office which is staffed by full-time professionals. This, as noted elsewhere, also advocated as a model for the EU. A right of appeal would need to be retained, but what is more contentious is the claim that there should be no provision for Ministers to overrule decisions.

As an arm of competition policy, the control of mergers is intended to keep markets open. Arguably, an indicator of the strength of competition is the variability in market shares, and in particular the durability or otherwise of the shares of the largest firms in an industry following intervention by the competition authorities. Shaw and Simpson (1986) attempted to measure this by looking at 28 industries which had been examined by the MMC between 1959 and 1973, of which 11 had their entry barriers reduced through MMC recommendations ('policy' industries) while the other 17 had been left untouched ('untouched' industries). A control group was formed by 19 industries which had been scrutinized by the National Board for Prices and Incomes (NBPI) during the same period.

The researchers proceeded to trace the evolution of the market shares of the largest company, the second-ranked companies and a 'dominant' group representing the collective share of the largest 3 to 5 companies during the period. It was found that the leading companies suffered declines in market shares in most cases, with the average loss of the order of 6 percentage points from a base of 60 per cent. The intriguing point, however, was that there appeared to be little difference between the 11 'policy' industries (reductions of 7 per cent in terms of the median) and the 17 'untouched' industries (reductions of 6 per cent).

Turning to the second-ranked companies, losses in all three categories were so small as to be insignificant at 2 per cent, 0.5 per cent and 0.5 per cent respectively. In the case of dominant groups, however, clear differences emerged: in 'policy' industries such groups lost 7 per cent (from a base of 80 per cent) whereas in 'untouched' industries they lost only 2 per cent, and in the NBPI sample no losses at all were recorded. It accordingly appears that an active anti-trust policy of reducing entry barriers can serve to undermine the position of dominant groups.

## 12.5   The EU dimension

EU regulations are binding upon all Member States, but are an addition to, rather than a substitute for, each Member State's national regulations. In the event of any conflicts between Community and national decisions, the former over-rule the latter. Thus it is possible for a cartel to be proceeded against under both European and UK law, and for two punishments to be imposed. In practice, however, the UK European Communities Act permits the DGFT to set aside national proceedings where the European Commission either has taken, or intends to take, the matter in hand. To assist the DGFT in this respect, firms have been obliged since June 1973 to let the DGFT know within 30 days of any involvement with the European Commission.

Where the Commission has ruled against a restrictive practice, it cannot subsequently be approved under UK law. However, a restrictive practice which is acceptable to the Commission may still be condemned in the Restrictive Practices Court because it has adverse effects solely within the UK. The situation is more clear-cut with respect to monopolies and mergers since the MMC only has powers to make recommendations, which can then be held over pending the results of any similar proceedings being taken by the European Commission.

One difficulty here relates to the territorial reach of EU policy. UK practice is to claim jurisdiction only over those firms which carry on business in the UK. The Commission, the other hand, claims jurisdiction over all firms, wherever located, if the activities of those firms affect competition within the EU. Nevertheless, the existence of the EU regulations in the area of antitrust did not have much bearing upon UK policy prior to the much-increased emphasis upon merger cases discussed in detail below. Prior to the mid-1980s, EU policy was concerned primarily with the suppression of restrictive practices using criteria similar to those employed within the UK. However, since this was an area where UK policy was already relatively effective, few EU decisions involved UK producers. The Commission initially made little progress in respect of either monopolies or mergers, which was understandable in the light of the need to interpret ambiguous regulations and of the need for European firms to attain a size which would ensure their survival in the face of greatly intensified international competition.

We have commented upon the fact that, in respect of monopolies and mergers, the UK utilized an independent administrative tribunal and, in respect of restrictive practices, a court. However, the Commission took upon itself to act as both investigator, prosecutor and judge, subject to appeal to the Court of Justice.

### 12.5.1   EU legislation on restrictive practices

The EU rules on competition are embodied primarily in Articles 85 and 86 of the Treaty of Rome. Article 85 is concerned with restrictive practices and consists of three main clauses, the first of which states that 'agreements between undertakings, decisions by associations of under-takings and concerted practices which may affect trade between Member States and which have as their object the prevention, restriction and distortion of competition within the Common Market shall be prohibited'; the second of which states that prohibited practices will be void; and the third of which sets out the conditions governing exemption from prohibition.

The EU approach to restrictive practices is broadly similar to that of the UK, in that such practices are prohibited subject to exemption which can be obtained, for the most part, by passing through 'gateways'. However, the EU policy covers a wide range of agreements, and imposes heavier penalties, and its gateways relate only to agreements which improve either production, distribution or technical progressiveness, in which respect these benefits, where justified, must not be outweighed by other detriments which are associated with a reduction in the degree of competition. Certain exemptions can also be applied for, provided specified conditions can be met. An agreement must first contribute to an improvement in the production or distribution of goods and promote technical or economic progress. Secondly, it must allow the consumer a fair share of the resulting benefit, and, thirdly, it must not contain any restrictions which are not indispensable to the benefits to be achieved. Exemptions apply only under Article 85, and are for specific, though renewable, periods of time.

Article 85 was enacted by the implementation of Regulation 17 in 1962. This established an administrative machinery with enforcement powers vested in the European Commission, acting through a Directorate General for Competition. The Commission has powers to hold hearings *in camera*, to seize evidence, and to impose fines of up to ECU 1 million or 10 per cent of turnover on each party to a restrictive practice. Regulation 17 did not make registration compulsory, so that companies can choose between neglecting to register (and so running the risk of heavy punishment if found guilty by the Commission); claiming exemption under clause 3 of Article 85; or applying for 'negative clearance' whereby the Commission is asked to declare, without being irrevocably bound by so doing, whether Article 85 is relevant to the practice in question. Although there is no way of knowing for certain, it is commonly believed that a significant proportion of the practices covered by Article 85 have yet to be registered. An ambiguity arises in this respect because Article 85 only applies where the effect on trade between Member States is deemed to be 'significant'.

The Commission can either reach voluntary agreements with firms found guilty of malpractice, or impose legally binding sanctions. Negative clearances and exemptions may be subject to the imposition of conditions which, if breached, can cause them to be revoked. Both firms and Member States can appeal to the European Court of Justice against decisions taken by the Commission.

Article 86, which relates to monopolies, states that 'any abuse by one or more undertakings of a dominant position within the Common Market or a substantial part of it shall be prohibited as incompatible with the Common Market insofar as it may affect trade between Member States'. The Article cites four examples of such abuse, although the list of potential abuses is meant to be open-ended. A key factor was that the *holding* of a dominant position was not prohibited, only its *abuse*. However, although it has been argued that dominance can best be identified by examining the relationships between companies, the European Court of Justice understandably insisted that a dominant position be defined in relation to a *relevant market*.

Unlike in the UK, there is *no specific structural rule*, either pertaining to market share or any other indicator, to help clarify what is meant by *dominant*. According to the Commission in the Continental Can case (1973), firms enjoy a dominant position when 'they have power to behave independently' or when they can 'act without taking into account their competitors, purchasers or suppliers'. In practice, a market share of 40 per cent or more is now taken to be strongly indicative of dominance, but is not treated in isolation. The methodology used by the Commission to identify the relevant market is broadly similar to that utilized in the UK (Fishwick, 1989) in that it begins by specifying the substitutable products and the integrated geographical area. It then proceeds to measure shares in that market, looks at potential competition and, in the case of intermediate or component products, examines whether monopoly power is constrained by competition in the final or composite product market.

Dominant undertakings are treated more strictly than their smaller competitors in that forms of competitive behaviour, such as pricing below cost, are often treated as an abuse even though they may be acceptable if practised by the latter. No exemptions are permitted, but firms may apply for negative clearance as under Article 85. Where firms are adjudged to be abusing their dominant position then either voluntary agreements may be reached with the Commission, or the Commission may legally enforce its decision. Firms may, however, appeal to the European Court of Justice.

Article 86 was not used until 1971, perhaps because of difficulties in proving that a given firm is both in a dominant position and is abusing the position. Initially, it was used only nine times in seven years. Article 86 was also applied to the merger proposal involving Continental Can, which was prohibited but subsequently allowed on appeal to the Court of Justice. However, Article 86 did not appear to be satisfactory where merger cases were concerned.

To illustrate the more rule-governed approach of the USA, pragmatic measures are used. As noted earlier the Department of Justice there defines a market as the area over which producers, acting in concert, could hypothetically impose a five per cent price increase for a year, without it being undermined completely by new entry. Although the method is open to objections in that the five per cent figure and the one-year period are arbitrary, it has commanded a level of consensus.

## 12.5.2   EU merger control

The emergence of an EU Merger Control Regulation (MCR) to control this situation was hindered by legal and political factors. The legal issue was whether Article 86 was a sufficient basis for action against anti-competitive mergers. The Continental Can case (1972) established that Article 86 could be applied, but the situation clearly required legislation directly related to the issue. Political concerns centred on the thresholds to be employed, the smaller Member States seeking lower ones to cover larger numbers of mergers, while the UK and other larger states preferred higher ones so as to reserve more cases for their domestic antitrust agencies.

The MCR is concerned primarily with situations which create or strengthen a dominant position. Four principles are involved.

1 The MCR only applies where there is a 'European dimension'.
2 There must be some legal certainty necessitating pre-merger notification and procedural deadlines.
3 Authorizations for advantageous mergers (similar to the Article 85(3) rules) should be available.
4 Cases should be dealt with speedily and in close cooperation with Member States.

The term 'concentrations', as defined in Article 3, is in general use in the MCR so as to include not only mergers but also other situations where direct or indirect control is obtained even though a full merger has not taken place. It is defined such as to include partial mergers or joint ventures which are autonomous, but to exclude operations which have the purpose of coordinating the competitive behaviour of independent entities (which remain subject to Article 85). It therefore follows that the extent of control is a crucial test for applicability of the MCR. A concentration need not accordingly require the acquisition of shares or capital investment. Rather, a party has control if it may exercise a decisive influence on another by virtue of (a) ownership or the right to use all or part of the assets of the other party or (b) rights which confer decisive influence on the composition, voting or decisions of the other party's board or shareholders' meetings.

*Community dimension*

The EU has exclusive jurisdiction over concentrations with a Community dimension. The MCR defines this, utilizing both geographic and turnover criteria. As a result, some large mergers, the impact of which is primarily in a single Member State, are excluded while smaller mergers with a wider impact are included. A merger has a Community dimension where it involves 'undertakings' (which include the merging firms, parents and subsidiaries) with aggregate worldwide turnover (pre-tax) in excess of ECU 5 billion, and the aggregate EU-wide turnover of each of at least two of the undertakings exceeds ECU 250 million. Separate rules apply for financial institutions, banks and insurance companies.

Where, however, each of the undertakings has more than two-thirds of its EU-wide turnover in the same Member State, the merger is deemed not to have a Community dimension. This structure thus reserves jurisdiction to individual States whenever the primary impact is within their borders irrespective of the size of the merger. A legal presence within the EU is not required. The MCR thus applies technically to mergers between non-EU entities.

*Specified procedures*

The MCR provides for a highly-structured process of pre-merger notification, strict time deadlines for decisions and substantial penalties for non-compliance (see Fig. 12.3). Concentrations or mergers must be notified to the Commission using prescribed Form CO within one week after the signing of an agreement, a public bid or acquisition of a controlling interest. When notice has been given, the merger or concentration must be suspended for three weeks. Within one month of receiving complete notice, the Commission must either clear the merger or open formal proceedings should it decide that the merger falls within the application of the regulation. This period may be extended to six weeks if a Member State invokes the so-called 'German

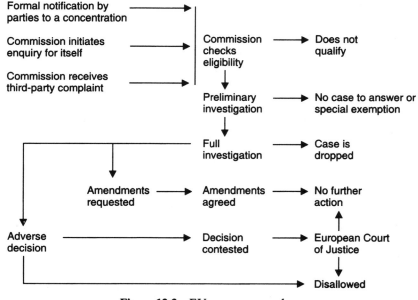

**Figure 12.3**   EU merger procedure

clause', which provides for a Member State to pursue its own actions if a distinct market within that State is affected and the Commission agrees.

Once formal proceedings have been initiated the Commission opens an examination which includes written proceedings, investigation, oral hearings and liaison with Member States. It has four months (subject to agreed extensions) to make the decision whether the merger creates or strengthens a market position harming competition and to determine if it is compatible with the market, based upon the justification criteria of Article 2(3). A clearance decision or a prohibition decision is then issued. The decision may be appealed to the European Court of Justice.

Failure to comply with these requirements could be very expensive, with directors and officers liable for fines of ECU 1000–50 000 and the firms themselves of up to 10 per cent of aggregate turnover. If the concentration is disapproved, it is not permitted to proceed. If the merger (or concentration) is completed and the Commission only considers it at a later date, whether because of a failure to follow the procedures or because of false or misleading information, a finding of incompatibility may lead to an order for separation and divestiture.

### Substantive considerations

Substantively, for the concentration to be suspect, it must create or strengthen a dominant position and as a result effective competition would be significantly impeded in the EU or a substantial part of it. In making the appraisal, the Commission is to take into account:

1 The need to preserve and develop effective competition within the EU in view of, among other things, the structure of all markets concerned and the actual or potential competition from undertakings located either within or outside the EU.
2 The market position of the undertakings concerned and their economic and financial power; the opportunities available to suppliers and users; their access to supplies or markets; any legal or other barriers to market entry; supply and demand trends for the relevant goods and services; the interests of the intermediate and ultimate consumers; and the development of technical and economic progress provided it is to consumers' advantage and does not form an obstacle to competition. These last two may form the basis of approval despite negative effects on the other criteria.

Within this analysis, market share is the starting point, and this is dependent upon definition of product and geographic market. The regulation itself gives no indication of how this is to be done, nor the levels which are suspect, other than the specification in Recital 15 that when the combined market share of the parties in the Community or a substantial part of it is less than 25 per cent, the concentration will be considered 'compatible', that is, compatible with the principles of competition.

### Member State role

During the deliberations surrounding the passage of the MCR, the Commission won the support of industry by its commitment to the idea of *one stop shopping* whereby mergers would be subject *either* to Community *or* to national merger control, but *not both*. In the end, one stop shopping survived, but with two principal exceptions. One is the distinct market exemption embodied in the German clause discussed above. The second is the 'legitimate interest' exemption whereby the Member State may take appropriate measures to protect certain legitimate interests such as public security, plurality of the media and prudential controls, particularly relative to control of financial institutions.

A Member State may also request the Commission to apply the MCR to a concentration which does not meet the thresholds. This is intended to allow intervention when a merger would have unacceptable consequences in only one State. The Commission has indicated its intent to limit application here to those mergers which would fall under its proposed reduced turnover standards.

In January 1990, a Merger Task Force was established within DGIV to handle the required reviews. In the first calendar year of implementation, 54 cases were notified. By the end of 1992, 115 cases had qualified for assessment under the MCR. The Commission has consistently urged that there be prenotification communication to explore issues which might arise, and to clarify and narrow information requirements prior to the completion of Form CO. According to Commission staff, no major case has yet proceeded in which such communication did not occur. Pending the publication of general guidelines, each case is handled individually.

Fewer than 10 per cent of qualifying mergers have been the subject of a full-scale proceeding under the MCR, and only one has produced a negative decision, as noted below. The bulk of decisions so far have been unpublished letter notices to the parties. Though these do not set precedents, they indicate the thinking of the Task Force on substantive application of the regulation. There has been a very permissive attitude on the part of the Commission to the issue of compatibility with the Common Market. Only in the case of *Aérospatiale–Alenia/De Havilland* (1991) was the agreement challenged as being incompatible (see Case Study below). The assessment of the compatibility of the concentration rests on two points: (1) does it create or strengthen a dominant position and (2) is there a resulting significant impediment to effective competition? Both have been addressed in the decisions, but a stronger focus has been on the first of the two.

### CASE STUDY: AÉROSPATIALE-ALENIA/DE HAVILLAND (1991)

The case is of particular interest because, prior to the rejection of the proposed merger between Aérospatiale–Alenia and De Havilland on 2 October 1991, the Commission had approved all 52 mergers which it had considered, attaching conditions only to five.

The takeover bid by France's state-owned Aérospatiale and Italy's state-owned Alenia for De Havilland, the Canadian turboprop subsidiary of Boeing, which wanted to get out of what was proving to be an unprofitable business, brought to a head the simmering issue as to whether the Franco-Italian preference for interpreting the public interest in terms of industrial policy and national champions or the British preference for open competition should prevail. For the first time, a takeover bid was judged on straightforward competition grounds.

The proposed takeover would have given the Franco/Italian joint venture 50 per cent of the world market and 67 per cent of the EU market for commuter turboprops of between 20 and 70 seats (and rather more in the 40–70 seat range). This would probably have had the effect of driving out of business two privately-owned EU companies, British Aerospace and Fokker of The Netherlands.

The awkward fact about this decision was that the merged companies would still have faced competition from a range of manufacturers of similar aircraft, mostly located in developing countries. Furthermore, developed countries were moving over to small jets such as those planned by Airbus Industrie and Daimler–Benz, the inclusion of which would have altered markedly the market share figures. Even more awkwardly, the Commission had itself approved, in February 1991, a merger of Aérospatiale's helicopter business with that of Germany's Messerschmitt–Bolkow–Blohm, despite the fact that the resulting joint venture would have 50 per cent of the EU market for civilian helicopters.

Given the record of approval for concentrations with high market shares, the denial of permission to merge in the Aérospatiale–Alenia/De Havilland case was somewhat unexpected. The Commission distinguished the situation on the basis of the limited substitute products, weak bargaining power of the buyers and the small market share of the next largest company in the market.

While a substantial role for Member States is specified in the MCR, their role to date has been somewhat limited. In *Steetley/Tarmac* (1992), for example, the UK government requested submission to its competition law authority under Article 9, and the Commission referred the case to the UK brick and tile markets. However, three requests by Germany were all turned down. The Commission also has the power to require modifications of agreements as a condition of approval.

A fundamental difficulty is that the 'public interest' is often perceived somewhat differently at a national level and this is reflected in the voting patterns of Commissioners. The replacement of Leon Brittan by Karel van Miert, a Flemish socialist on 1 January 1992 was expected to usher in a less market-driven philosophy. He stated that 'It is not wise to seek competition at all costs, and nothing but competition', and expressed a desire to take into consideration industrial, environmental, regional and social pressures. In the view of many critics, the political pressures can best be prevented by the creation of an independent EU cartel office whose decisions can only be revised by the Commission in exceptional circumstances.

It is true that the Commission has, as yet, only rejected one merger proposal out of hand. Nevertheless, a preliminary investigation followed by a full EU reference, not to mention the possibility of a national reference, leaves the companies in question in limbo for a considerable period of time (as in Nestlé/Perrier, 1992). Hence the failure so far to resolve jurisdictional conflicts, and the possible extension of the MCR to cover not merely duopolies but oligopolies (as in Nestlé/Perrier) leaves much to be resolved.

## Guide to further reading

Frazer (1992) is a useful overview, as is Swann (1979); the former covers the UK, the EU and America, while the latter deals mainly with the UK and USA. The European Commission issues an Annual report on Competition Policy, which is of interest. Montagnon (1990) covers European issues well.

# 13  Privatization

## 13.1  Introduction

For our purposes, the term 'privatization' can be said to encompass:

1 The disposal of state-owned industrial assets to private sector individuals/organizations via either a public offer for sale or a trade sale/management buy-out.
2 The disposal of other state-owned assets such as land and buildings.
3 The cessation of state controls over the private provision of goods and services (deregulation).
4 The contracting-out of services previously performed by central and local government agencies.
5 The imposition of 'user charges' and fees in respect of services previously supplied at zero cost.
6 The introduction of initiatives which seek to stimulate competitive outcomes in the absence of market prices.

This chapter focuses first upon the sale of the large utilities (gas, electricity, telecommunications and water) where the change in ownership allowed the government simultaneously to change the structure of the industry and to introduce a system of regulation. The second item for concern in this chapter is the process of deregulation, which was of course confined to industries which the state had not previously owned. Table 13.1 lists all sales involving the general public; a complete statistical analysis of the entire programme of asset disposals can be found in Curwen (1994).

The sale of state-owned companies has taken many forms. While the best known are the marketing of shares to the public, others include selling shares to financial institutions in the City (as with Amhurst International), selling subsidiaries to existing industrial firms (buy-ins) as with Rover which was bought by British Aerospace, and selling to incumbent management with or without the participation of other workers ('buy-outs'). An example of the last is the sale of National Freight. Occasionally companies were prepared for sale by the installation of a new management with the brief of cutting costs and raising efficiency. Some companies were broken up and sold in units such as National Bus or electricity generation, while others were sold entire like British Gas. As of late 1995, only Railtrack and the Post Office remain as large state-owned enterprises. Awaiting their turn are: Civil Aviation Authority, London Regional Transport, British Waterways, Nuclear Electric and Caledonian MacBrayne, the ferry company.

## 13.2  Ownership, competition and efficiency

There are, in principle, two main reasons for expecting an industry in public ownership to be inefficient. In the first place, whereas such industries are supposed to be operated in the public interest, there is every incentive for both politicians, who are responsible for strategy, and

**TABLE 13.1   Privatizations via public offer of shares, 1979–95**

| Company | Date | | % Sold[1] |
|---|---|---|---|
| Amersham International | February | 1982 | 99.0 |
| Anglian Water | December | 1989 | 97.0 |
| Associated British Ports | February | 1983 | 49.0 |
| | April | 1984 | 48.5 |
| BAA | July | 1987 | 95.6 |
| British Aerospace | February | 1981 | 51.6 |
| | May | 1985 | 59.0 |
| British Airways | February | 1987 | 100.0 |
| British Gas | December | 1986 | 97.0 |
| British Petroleum | October | 1979 | 5.2 |
| | September | 1983 | 7.2 |
| | November | 1987 | 36.8 |
| British Steel | December | 1988 | 99.0 |
| British Telecom | December | 1984 | 50.2 |
| | December | 1991 | 25.6 |
| | July | 1993 | 21.9 |
| Britoil | November | 1982 | 51.0 |
| | August | 1985 | 48.0 |
| Cable and Wireless | October | 1981 | 49.4 |
| | December | 1983 | 22.0 |
| | December | 1985 | 31.0 |
| East Midlands Electricity | December | 1990 | 96.0 |
| Eastern Electricity[2] | December | 1990 | 96.0 |
| Enterprise Oil | July | 1984 | 100.0 |
| Jaguar | August | 1984 | 99.0 |
| London Electricity | December | 1990 | 96.0 |
| Manweb | December | 1990 | 96.0 |
| Midlands Electricity | December | 1990 | 96.0 |
| National Power | March | 1991 | 60.7 |
| | March | 1995 | 39.0 |
| North West Water Group[3] | December | 1989 | 97.0 |
| Northern Electric | December | 1990 | 96.0 |
| Northern Ireland Electricity | June | 1993 | 96.5 |
| Northumbrian Water Group | December | 1989 | 97.0 |
| Norweb[3] | December | 1990 | 96.0 |
| PowerGen | March | 1991 | 59.3 |
| | March | 1995 | 39.0 |
| Rolls-Royce | May | 1987 | 97.0 |
| Scottish Hydro-Electric | June | 1991 | 96.0 |
| ScottishPower | June | 1991 | 96.0 |
| Seeboard | December | 1990 | 96.0 |
| Severn Trent | December | 1989 | 97.0 |
| South Wales Electricity[4] | December | 1990 | 96.0 |
| South West Water | December | 1989 | 97.0 |
| South Western Electricity | December | 1990 | 96.0 |
| Southern Electric | December | 1990 | 96.0 |
| Southern Water | December | 1989 | 97.0 |
| Thames Water | December | 1989 | 97.0 |
| Welsh Water | December | 1989 | 97.0 |
| Wessex Water | December | 1989 | 97.0 |
| Yorkshire Electricity | December | 1990 | 96.0 |
| Yorkshire Water | December | 1989 | 97.0 |

[1]May total more than 100% due to rights issues or less than 100% due to shares retained for employee's loyalty bonuses.
[2]Renamed Eastern Group in October 1994. [3]The take-over of Norweb by North West Water in September 1995 has led to a combined group known as United Utilities. [4]Renamed Swalec in November 1993.

managers, who are responsible for day-to-day running, to pursue their own interests instead of maximizing profit. Equally, pressure groups such as trade unions will attempt to pursue their own objectives, leading typically to wasteful investment and excessive manning and wage levels.

In addition, property rights theory argues that private companies are obliged to raise funds in the capital markets, thereby acquiring shareholders who would sell out to a predator if the company's performance was below an acceptable level. Public enterprises, on the other hand, can borrow from public funds without in effect ever needing to repay the loans since the government would be obliged to cancel any debt which became too large to be serviced. Public enterprise's immunity to takeover thus represented a severe disincentive to improving efficiency since this went unrewarded and failure to perform went unpunished. The proposed solution to the difficulty was to privatize public enterprise since this would both remove political control and introduce the disciplines of the private capital markets.

Unfortunately, it is difficult to prove that the theory works in practice. It is well known, for example, that countries whose companies are largely immune to hostile takeover bids, such as Germany and Japan, have outperformed the USA and UK, where such bids are commonplace and where short-termism is viewed as a consequent problem. These considerations make it difficult to claim that the act of privatization must, of itself, guarantee greater efficiency. Hence, it has long been held that ownership is not the critical factor but rather whether a firm is subject to the forces of competition in its product markets. Introduce competition where previously there was a monopoly, or so the argument runs, and efficiency will look after itself.

But if improvements in efficiency are the objective of the exercise, how are these to be measured? Profitability is not a particularly helpful guide for a variety of reasons, among them the fact that part of the public enterprise sector was profitable as a consequence of its monopoly power while another part was unprofitable as a consequence of government-imposed pricing rules or an obligation to provide 'social services' at a loss. Adjusting for these factors is problematic, as is the need to take account of the balance sheet 'adjustments' which took place prior to several privatizations.

For these reasons studies of efficiency have tended to concentrate upon costs, and in particular upon their relationship to changes in productivity. A review of the early studies is to be found in Curwen (1986, pp.128–38), where the evidence is found to be contradictory, not least because of the difficulty of setting up valid comparisons. These must either involve privatized companies pre- and post-privatization, or equivalent public and private enterprises.

In the former case there is only a small sample set available, either within or outside the UK, and there are difficulties in adjusting for differing periods of time, macroeconomic conditions and any restructuring which preceded privatization. In certain cases there is also the need to adjust for a post-privatization regulatory regime.

Where public corporations have been compared with the nearest equivalent private firms the latter have come out on top more often than not, but by no means universally. Nevertheless, as Stevens (1992, p.13) observes, few studies exist which have attempted to test the effect of ownership in a truly competitive environment. Where multi-sectoral and multi-country comparisons have been conducted, excluding sectors such as posts and railways, the results mostly support the hypothesis that in competitive environments privately-owned industrial companies outperform their public counterparts both in terms of productivity and profitability, a conclusion which is unaffected by adjustments to allow for differences in size and industry structure.

Two recent studies are worthy of mention. The first, an attempt to examine the effects of ownership on economic and financial performance, was undertaken at the University of York between 1986 and 1990. This study included only two cases of a transfer from the public to the

**TABLE 13.2  Summary of the York research results. Did performance improve as expected?**
(*Source*: Parker, 1991)

| Organization | Performance measure | | | |
| --- | --- | --- | --- | --- |
| | Employment function | Labour productivity | Total factor productivity | Financial ratios |
| Royal Mint | Confirmed | Confirmed | Confirmed | N/A |
| London Transport (1970 change) | Not confirmed | Not confirmed | Confirmed | Not confirmed |
| London Transport (1984 change) | Mainly confirmed | Confirmed | Confirmed | Confirmed |
| British Airways | Confirmed | Confirmed | Confirmed | Confirmed |
| British Aerospace (nationalization) | Mainly confirmed | Confirmed | Unclear | Not confirmed |
| British Aerospace (privatization) | Confirmed | Confirmed | Unclear | Confirmed |
| National Freight | Confirmed | Confirmed | Confirmed | Confirmed |
| Post Office Postal | Not confirmed | Confirmed | Unclear | Confirmed |
| Post Office Telecommunications | Mainly confirmed | Confirmed | Unclear | Unclear |
| HMSO | Confirmed | Unclear | Not confirmed | Confirmed |
| Royal Ordnance Factories | Not confirmed | Not confirmed | Unclear | Confirmed |
| Rolls-Royce | Not confirmed | Not confirmed | Not confirmed | Not confirmed |

N/A = not available

private sector (British Aerospace and National Freight) but also covered one prospective privatization, two ownership changes from the private to the public sector and a variety of significant changes of status within the public sector. These latter changes involved a reduction in direct political interference and a more commercially minded approach. The overall picture is shown in Table 13.2.

The central hypothesis was that 'as organizations in the public sector move away from political control and Exchequer financing towards more independent management their economic and financial performance improve'. Performance was measured in three ways: first in terms of employment efficiency; secondly in terms of labour and total factor productivity; and thirdly through an analysis of a basket of standard accounting ratios. Only changes in production efficiency were considered; wider social welfare effects were ignored including the implications for efficiency in competing firms.

Both labour and total factor productivity (TFP) were estimated for the four years before the status change and were compared with the figures for the four years after. The effect of changes in macroeconomic factors on productivity was removed by comparing the figures with changes in productivity in the UK economy, UK manufacturing and the public corporation sector. In the absence of information about hours worked, labour productivity was assessed by calculating the change in each organization's volume of output in relation to changes in the labour input. TFP was estimated on the basis of the rate of growth of output minus a weighted average of input growth rates, where the weights are the share of each input in total cost.

Six financial ratios were used: percentage return on capital employed; turnover to average net fixed assets employed; stocks (including work in progress) to turnover; debtors to turnover; labour's share in expenditure; and value added per employee.

In five out of the twelve status changes studied, improved performance was discernible. It was noted that these included all three of the organizations which were privatized or being prepared for privatization. Only one case appeared to be completely contrary to expectation in that the performance of Rolls-Royce improved after nationalization. However, this might have been a response to the 'shock effect' of its bankruptcy in 1971 which led to State ownership, since all of its performance indicators subsequently deteriorated.

Parker was led to conclude (Parker, 1991, p.159) that a shift from the public to the private sector 'may improve performance, but that this improvement is not guaranteed. Performance improvement may depend upon other factors than ownership.'

The second study was conducted on behalf of the World Bank, the findings of which were initially announced in June 1992. This examined three privatizations in each of four countries: Britain, Chile, Malaysia and Mexico.

Although the sample was small, it was noteworthy that the Bank's conclusion was that in 11 of the 12 cases studied privatization produced an increase in wealth that could not be attributed to any inherent bias in the choice of companies. Interestingly, and contrary to what is commonly held to be the case, some privatizations were successful even though there was little change in the extent of competition or in the nature of the regulatory regime. According to the study, more competition and better regulation would have produced a superior outcome for everyone bar shareholders, but it nevertheless concluded that privatization *per se* is sufficient to bring about a measurable improvement.

The general view has almost invariably been cautious, frequently emphasizing the argument that an element of enhanced competition post-sale is a necessary condition for improved efficiency (see, for example, the review of efficiency in Marsh, 1991).

## 13.3  Regulation

Since the privatized utilities were sold as integrated monopolies, it was clearly necessary to set up systems of regulation to prevent them from exploiting consumers. Policy-makers were aware of the pitfalls of the American system of regulation, which guaranteed US utilities a fair profit, defined as a given return on capital. Two undesirable consequences followed. One was that producers over-invested in order to boost their capital base (Averch and Johnson, 1962). Examples, from casual observation, include US airlines' purchase of expensive aircraft and power companies' drive into nuclear power in the 1970s. The other consequence was that producers had no general incentive to improve efficiency, since costs could simply be passed on to customers. The British 'price-cap' approach, devised by Professor Littlechild, currently regulator of the electricity industry, is to control the prices which the utilities charge, allowing the companies to keep any profits made by raising efficiency. The system used was to calculate an index of prices for each utility and to allow this to rise by the general level of retail prices less a certain amount: the RPI–X formula. X represented those anticipated efficiency gains which were to be passed on to customers, the rest remaining as profit (Armstrong, Cowan and Vickers, 1994).

When examined in detail, the difference between the two systems begins to recede. First, it should be recognized that rate-of-return regulation works through the control of prices themselves. Secondly, price-cap regulation begins by setting a price which gives the firm a fair rate of return. Thus at the start the two systems are the same; the differences emerge only in terms of the length of time for which prices remain constant (the 'regulatory lag') and the criteria for passing price changes. Viewed from afar, the British system requires prices to fall relative to the general price level by X per cent per year. In reality, only BT (British Telecommunications plc) had a simple RPI–X price cap. The gas, water and (parts of the) electricity industries have the formula RPI–X + K, where K represented cost factors which lie beyond the firm's control. For water these are the costs of environmental protection, while for the others they are the costs of bought-in fuels. Incentives for efficiency were thus restricted to only a part of the utilities' inputs. Analytically, the reason for this is that a price has two functions: it offers an incentive (firms keep cost savings) but it brings risk (costs can rise and cut into profits). It was felt that a fixed price would expose some operators to too much risk; but in reducing it, incentives were also reduced. (It may also be noted that regulation covers only a proportion of the outputs of the companies, although this proportion is climbing. At inception, only 50 per cent of BT's output was price regulated; the figure is today nearer 75 per cent.)

Thirdly and more importantly, incentives were undermined by the flexibility of the system. The price-cap system gives most incentives when it is totally fixed; this has proved not to be the case. Price formula are reviewed periodically, so that when a firm succeeds in cutting costs, its X-factor can be increased. Although price reviews should come every five years, regulators have the power to instigate them more frequently. In 1995, Littlechild reviewed electricity prices when he found firms were making large profits, only months after setting a price cap! What criteria are used in price reviews? It is nowhere stated, but the evidence suggests it is the companies' profits. It must of course be remembered that the initial caps are set with a view to establishing a fair return in the first place. Over the long run, it appears that only fair returns are allowed: a price-cap system converges toward the US-style system.

A point of weakness with regulatory regimes is the possibility of 'capture' in the sense that the regulators become so concerned with the affairs of the industry that they see all problems from the latter's standpoint and thus seek to preserve their monopoly powers and high prices (Laffont and Tirole, 1993). A natural method whereby this occurs is through an infusion of ex-industry personnel into the regulatory agencies. After all, they have the expertise which regulators initially lack. The price of its acquisition may be a loss of independence. To guard against these problems of lack of information and likelihood of capture, many have argued that regulation is not a viable long-run regime and should be replaced by (or extensively buttressed by) competition in the industries.

## 13.4  Regulation and competition

A major problem for regulators is 'information asymmetry': the fact that they know less about the costs of the operators than do the operators themselves. This places them at a considerable disadvantage in previewing prices. How may it be remedied? The broad answer is through competition, which may take many forms. One method is to allow operators to bid for the right to provide a service which they then run as profitably as possible. They exploit consumers (as monopolists) but return their excess profits to the public purse through a franchise fee. This method has not been used in the UK, although franchise-bidding is used for TV broadcasting. One tactic has been to maintain horizontal divisions in the industries. There are 12 water companies, for example, and 10 regional electricity distributors. Such divisions allow cost comparisons (so-called yardstick or benchmark competition) to be made between operators even though they do not compete directly against each other, being local monopolies. The more interesting direction has been to exploit the fact that the utilities consist of several stages of production; typically a network which supports or is supported by other services. While providing the network could not be done competitively, the other activities may be open to competition. Across the privatized sector, therefore, operators have been required to separate networks from other operations so that in principle other operators may hire the network to deliver services. The task for regulators has been to promote competition where possible. This is not as simple as simply declaring the networks open for use, since the network operator could clearly (in the absence of regulation) engage in anti-competitive practices such as predatory pricing or overcharging for access. Naturally this works in different ways in each industry.

In telecommunications, BT has for the most part a monopoly of the 'local loop', the network connecting houses and offices. Long-distance connections are, however, not monopolized and in the last few years many operators have entered this section of the business, typically companies which themselves have other networks along which they can lay cable, such as the waterways and the national electric grid, as well as the established competitor, Mercury. Clearly these long-distance operators need access to the BT loop, and much controversy has surrounded the terms on which this should be given, the so-called access price. Economic theory suggests that everything should be sold at its marginal cost; for telecommunications, the marginal cost of letting a long-distance call come into a local loop is often very small because (a) networks such as local loops have substantial fixed costs but low operating costs and (b) new technology with even lower marginal costs is often used. Pricing at marginal cost would therefore leave BT with a massive deficit (the 'access deficit'), leading BT to argue for some average cost-based charge. Baumol and Sidak (1994) argue for the 'Economic Component Pricing Rule' (ECPR) by which BT would be allowed to charge the marginal cost plus the profit which it foregoes by not using the equipment itself. This profit is the difference between the marginal costs and its own prices. The ECPR says nothing about the way this price ought to be set; by setting a high price, BT could argue that letting (say) Mercury use its equipment was imposing a heavy opportunity cost, and thus they could charge Mercury a high access price. Laffont and Tirole (1995) argue that the ECPR should be supplemented by price-cap regulation, that is, that the access charge should be included in the basket of services whose prices are regulated. In practice, the access price was settled by the industry regulator, who set it low enough to encourage competition.

In electricity, the expectation was that the generators would compete in offering power, reducing price to marginal cost. In the event, prices for bulk electricity were not infrequently surprisingly high, leading to suspicions of collusion or at least Cournot behaviour and to reviews by the regulator, who also enjoined the generators to sell plant with a view to creating more competition. The generators dragged their feet in these sales, but competition was in fact created through another route. A combination of new companies and the regional distribution companies were allowed to build new gas-fuelled power stations which competed with the established generators (the so-called 'dash for gas') of the early 1990s. In the mid-1990s, distribution companies were forced to hire their networks out to anyone wishing to deliver electricity to large users. Such a supplier would have to arrange to buy power, rent the relevant cables and deliver it to the user, thus challenging the distributor's local monopoly. The programme was to extend this facility to larger and larger numbers of users, even by 1998 down to the millions of domestic consumers. Industrial economists await the outcome with interest.

A similar situation exists in gas supply except that here there is only one firm covering the country. It too, however, now has to separate its gas delivery business from the operation of the network, and is having to make the latter available to any firm wishing to deliver gas to large users. Again, the threshold is to fall so that more consumers will have choice over their supplier. Intriguingly, the companies entering this business include the regional electricity distribution firms.

## 13.5   Deregulation

In the UK, deregulation in the strict sense of the abolition of government controls has been rather limited, simply because ownership was used instead of regulation. Long distance coaches and municipal buses have, however, been subjected to this process (Curwen, 1986, pp.279–284). Deregulation, defined more broadly to encompass the abolition of restrictive practices has been more common. Several professions such as the law and opticians had forbidden their members from advertising, with the tacit approval of the competition authorities. This practice was ended. More importantly, similar restrictive practices and cartels in the financial sector (banks, stockbrokers and building societies) were largely abandoned in the so-called 'Big Bang' of 1985. The result was a surge in lending as credit-giving institutions fought for business, creating a consumption-led boom which eventually had to be reined in.

Regulation had been much more common in the USA. In the late 1970s, partly under the influence of economic (especially neo-Austrian) ideas, the process of regulation went into reverse: road haulage, railways, telecommunications, banking, pipelines and air transport were all deregulated. This provided economists with a huge amount of data with which to estimate the benefits of deregulation or, conversely, the costs of the initial imposition of regulation.

Much work has been done. For example, Winston (1993) begins by noting the problems of the researcher in this area. Regulatory reform in the USA was a protracted process which proceeded in stages, even in single industries. This creates a difficulty in isolating the effects of deregulation from a background of great turbulence including energy price rises; booms and slumps; technological changes; switches in consumer tastes; the inauguration of NAFTA and so forth.

The main approach has nevertheless centred on the assessment of price reductions which, in combination with knowledge of quantities, allowed calculations to be made of the gains to consumers. In the case of air transport, for example, studies estimated that consumers benefited to the extent of between $4.3 billion and $6.5 billion annually at 1990 prices. There were also gains from deregulating road transport (trucking) of over $13 billion annually; of over $9 billion annually in respect of railways. These gains were largely in line with economic predictions.

In the savings and loans sector, deregulation allowed institutions to invest in a wider range of assets, which was expected to reduce risk. In the event, however, poor supervision by the authorities permitted the institutions to engage in excessive risks and ultimately to run up huge bad debts which had to be made good by the taxpayer. What economists had failed to predict was the ways in which services would improve in deregulated industries; for example, air transport developed the hub-and-spoke system and sophisticated computerized booking systems, while rail and road hauliers found more flexible ways to assemble loads.

Deregulation affected profits both positively and adversely. On the one hand it opens up new profitable opportunities, but on the other hand it makes entry much more open. As predicted by economists, wages fell in some deregulated industries, notably trucking. Overall, the gains were estimated at $36–46 billion. Neo-Austrians would also stress the dynamic gains to be had from creating an entrepreneurial culture; productivity should rise not in a single step but in increasingly rapid increments.

## 13.6   New ideas on privatization

Over the past decade and a half, many of the principles (frequently neo-Austrian) developed largely in industrial economics have found application in many areas of state activity which might at first sight appear to lie beyond their traditional boundaries. The foremost example is perhaps putting work out to tender rather than reserving it for in-house departments. Instances include refuse collection, cleaning and laundry, transport services (including running local buses), catering, maintenance and architectural and legal services for local authorities, the health service, schools and the armed forces. An irony here is that existing in-house departments were usually allowed to submit tenders. Such organizations enjoyed high success rates in winning contracts, partly because administrators often had considerable discretion over which tenders should be accepted. Low-priced tenders could thus be rejected on the grounds that the quality of service was too low. Certainly, in-house providers had the added advantage of experience. One problem with such systems which has emerged is that competition dwindles with time: organizations which tender unsuccessfully for contracts one year may simply not be in existence to tender for the next round, leaving the incumbent in a monopoly provider: a recreation of the initial situation.

In the early phases of privatization, private providers were able to takeover existing organizations and rewrite work contracts. The situation has been complicated for the government and private providers by court rulings that have preserved the rights of employees when an undertaking changes hands.

In the NHS, many GPs have been given budgets which they use to buy care for their patients from hospitals. Hospitals thus receive funds not by virtue of having costs (the old system) but by virtue of providing care. A hospital which GPs deem too expensive thus fails to attract demand and faces the prospect of closure. One consequence has been the closure of well know teaching hospitals in central London, to the dismay of many clinicians. From an economic perspective, of course, such outcomes are predictable given the high costs of land there. One unintended consequence of this reform has been the recruitment of administrators and accountants, and the situation remains controversial.

In the Civil Service proper, attempts are being made to introduce market relationships under the 'Next Steps' initiative of 1988. This lays down the principle that every government ministry should be divided into two: a relatively small central staff to monitor and advise on policy, and a larger agency whose role would be to administer policy. Since the latter is in theory a more routine job, it could be contracted out to private providers. Thus accountancy firms could compete for a contract for the work of tax collection, displacing the Inland Revenue, for example. Such policies seem likely to be beset with problems of incumbents' advantages and the diminuation over time of effective competition.

Other initiatives in this area include attempts to permit private firms to build motorways, recouping their costs from tolls, and a policy of bringing charges for State services into line with costs. Under the former heading no such projects are currently in prospect; under the latter, a prime case is that of prescription charges, changes which are normally attended by substantial political opposition.

## 13.7  Conclusion

Policy-makers need to be decisive in circumstances where theorists are inclined to caution. Industrial economics, particularly in its Neo-Austrian guise, extols the virtues of entrepreneurship and in large measure such ideas have informed public policy in Britain and, indeed, the rest of the world: many industrial economists would applaud. However, others would draw back from wholehearted endorsement of policy because of the warnings which their science brings. It tells of the dangers of strategic behaviour by incumbents and of the possibility of first-mover advantages, not to mention regulatory capture. Industrial economists have shown that the cost-based regulation of prices leads to inefficiency, implying that price-based regulation, which allows entrepreneurs to retain the benefits of reduced costs, is superior. However, recent events involving the electricity regulator demonstrate that the real world is a very messy place in practice, and it is clearly going to take much longer than was originally anticipated to work out how to generate an appropriate balance between the various interests when drawing the line between private and public sector activity.

## Guide to further reading

Laffont and Tirole (1993) is a comprehensive introduction to the theory; Armstrong, Cowan and Vickers (1994) and Bishop, Kay and Mayer (1994, 1995) cover both theory and the British experience. Parker and Stead (1991) discuss the application of neo-Austrian principles to the welfare state.

# 14   Industrial policy

## 14.1   Introduction

Few markets are truly 'free' in a textbook sense. While it is true that in comparing one country with another, there are enormous variations in the degree of government intervention: all governments engage in sufficient interference with the forces of the market to be said to have an industrial policy. In that respect it is unhelpful to treat domestic policies in isolation. In the first place, much of what can be described as UK industrial policy is organized on an EU-wide basis, and it has also to be recognized, in the second place, that industrial policy is designed specifically to affect relations between countries and trading blocs, and must accordingly take account of what, for example, the USA or Japan are themselves doing by way of their own industrial policies.

Chapter 12 was concerned with competition policy, yet it is evident that there is a fine dividing line between competition and industrial policy. It is equally evident that regional policy and industrial policy are closely interwoven, since much of the money spent by governments to sustain regional development is intended to influence firms to locate in depressed regions at the expense of depressed regions elsewhere. Finally, it is evident that industrial policy and trade policy are also closely interwoven, since industrial policy in the EU is designed in good part to achieve competitive advantage.

It is useful to set out the Commission's own definition (CEC, 1992b, p.42):

Industrial policy concerns the effective and coherent implementation of all those policies which impinge on the structural adjustment of industry with a view to promoting competitiveness. The provision of a horizontal framework in which industry can develop and prosper by remedying structural deficiencies and addressing areas where the market mechanism alone fails to provide the conditions necessary for success is the principal means by which the Community applies its industrial policy. Central to this approach are the three specific Community policies which promote competition within the Community: an open trade policy, completion of the internal market and an active competition policy.

The various policies that will be discussed below are therefore, of necessity, indicative rather than comprehensive, but they all share the common characteristics that they are microeconomic and designed to affect conditions of supply in a variety of markets. For the most part, they are also intended to improve the competitiveness of domestic (in a national or EU sense) firms in international markets, and in many cases they involve technologically advanced products. An indication of the range of instruments in use encompasses the creation of *national champions* in high-tech industries; the organization of crisis cartels; subsidies for R&D and for regional relocation; training support; support for small businesses; and barriers to trade of all kinds. All of these instruments are designed to create a pattern of production and trade which differs from that to be expected in a free market, and the justification for their use must, therefore, lie in the (regrettably often ill-founded) belief that government intervention will bring about an improved allocation of resources.

Broadly defined, the industrial policy of the EU has two strands. One is to create the best framework for development. This is essentially a free-market approach and in practice the central element is the creation of the Single European Market. This means the abolition of barriers to trade between EU Member States. Barriers still in existence in 1992, 35 years after the creation of the European Common Market, included different safety standards, different regulations covering food ingredients and labelling, public contracts and the non-recognition of professional qualifications. Thus British insurers could not trade in Germany because they lacked approval from the relevant German authorities, nor could British beer be sold there because it was not made in the approved German manner which stipulated that only malt, hops and water could be used. The Single European Market programme consisted of the mutual recognition of each Member State's standards by its partners. Thus if a product was of saleable standard in one country, it was automatically deemed to be saleable anywhere in the EU. The thinking behind this programme was that large free-trade areas encourage dynamism, by offering greater incentives to innovate and be competitive.

The other track pursued by the European Commission was to stimulate and assist, primarily by means of subsidies, industries which were not competitive by international standards. Today this takes the form largely of the R&D programmes such as EUREKA and ESPRIT. It is a policy which draws upon the tradition of the Member States such as the UK which in the 1960s and 1970s sought to follow this track alone: the policy of picking so-called national champions.

## 14.2   Picking winners: 'National Champions'

The governments of many Member States together with, at times, the Commission itself, have espoused the view that they have both the ability and the obligation to 'pick winners'; that is, to sponsor or favour one or more firms from an industry in the expectation that world-class status will be attained with high sales, profits and jobs. During the 1960s in the UK, this policy was pursued through the agency of the Industrial Reorganisation Corporation (IRC) which acted as an industrial introduction agency, helping leading firms to merge with their weaker brethren.

The underlying philosophy was that the superior management skills of the better firms would thus be shared across the industry. There was also the idea that UK firms were on the whole too small by international standards and thus deprived themselves of economies of scale. Companies were given state aid to finance mergers. The motor vehicle industry, for example, was reorganized by prompting Leyland Motors (a relatively successful lorry and bus manufacturer) to take over car-makers Austin and Morris to form British Leyland. The policy fell into abeyance during the early 1970s when the Conservatives returned to office, but was resumed between 1974 and 1979 with the creation of the National Enterprise Board (NEB). The NEB had a more technological brief than the IRC: its role was to identify and to assist, through the medium of cheap loans and equity finance, companies with technological promise.

To economists of a *laissez-faire*, and especially of a Neo-Austrian persuasion, this policy was anathema. Burton (1983), for example, argues forcefully that this policy distorted the competitive process, which in his view works through two quasi-biological mechanisms; mutation and selection. By mutation is meant the trying out of new ideas by entrepreneurs; the generation of alternatives. By selection is meant, brutally, that many of these new ideas are going to be failures. Only a few will survive the rigours of competition to become 'champions'. Certainly, the process requires someone to take a longer term perspective; to arrange the supply of finance needed to see a project through its inevitable initial adjustment difficulties. This role should be performed either by the entrepreneur or by the financial sector since, in either case, incentives are then in place to prompt agents to take correct decisions because their wealth is at stake.

Can governments (ministers and civil service advisers) do better, asks Burton, by supplying funds to enterprises which the financial sector has incorrectly identified as likely failures? Are civil servants better than bankers at picking winners? Burton argues that this is unlikely, given their respective backgrounds. Moreover, civil servants have no incentives to be correct because their salaries are not linked to their performance. By contrast, ministers faced a strong incentive to use NEB funds to help ailing firms stay in business, since their continued operation meant jobs and thus votes. The damning evidence is that this is indeed precisely what happened in the 1970s; as British Leyland lost sales and profits to competing car-makers, notably the Japanese, NEB funds were used to keep the company in business. It was finally taken into public ownership. The policy of picking winners was subsequently abandoned with the accession to office of the Conservatives in 1979, and British Leyland, later renamed Rover, was sold off first to British Aerospace and then to BMW, in the process being restored to prosperity.

Other Member States have pursued similar policies by other means, with varying levels of success. Indeed, foreign practices were often cited as justification for NEB-type intervention. For example, the Japanese approach during the 1950s and 1960s was to encourage the licensing of foreign (essentially American) technology so as to improve the capabilities of domestic firms. Credit and access to imports (which then required licences) were manipulated in order to boost the preferred firms. However, as Japanese firms developed their abilities to create their own technologies the State took a diminishing role, confining itself during the 1970s and 1980s to sponsoring joint research projects with industry.

In France, Italy and Spain, in contrast, public ownership was widely used as the means to create national champions. This was often backed by preferential purchasing from public organizations (a technique also used in the UK, but not necessarily successfully as in the vain attempt to foster a domestic computer industry by inducing public organizations to buy only ICL computers). The result was that, by 1970, the number of large firms in many EU industries was fewer than the number of large Member States. Nevertheless, according to the Cecchini Report (1988), this was still too many in that economies of scale were still going unrealized.

In order to tap these economies, the Report recommended the creation of a Single European Market (SEM), involving the abolition of preferential treatment for domestic firms. The intention was that the free play of market forces would force industries to consolidate around the most efficient producer. If the market happened to take the form of a natural monopoly, then competition would cease. In nearly all cases, however, the indications are that the EU as a whole can tolerate the existence of several producers (Cecchini, 1988; Emerson, 1988; Geroski, 1989) so competition can be sustained.

The other obvious risk of free markets is that firms with some standing in the minds of the public on account of their technological prowess, the size of their workforces or both, could be forced out of business by more efficient foreign producers. This remains the constant tension of industrial policy; to promote efficiency through the unleashing of market forces while ensuring that certain producers remain in existence through intervention. Thus, at the same time as the EU worked towards the SEM, it funded a wide range of schemes to subsidize industrial research and Member States continued to give State aids as discussed below.

## 14.3   State aids

Article 92 of the Treaty of Rome bans 'any aid granted by a Member State or through resources in any form whatsoever which distorts or threatens to distort competition by favouring certain undertakings or the production of certain goods.' The rationale is that subsidies reduce efficiency and distort trade in a similar way to protectionist measures, although exceptionally they may be justifiable, for example in the pursuit of social justice. Specifically, aid *is* deemed to be compatible where at least one of the following conditions applies:

- it is of a social character and given to individuals in a non-discriminatory manner;
- it is related to national disasters;
- it is concerned with German unification.

Aid *may* also be deemed to be compatible where it is related to specific activities or areas and where the EU as a whole can be seen to benefit, or ultimately because the European Council so wishes.

There is no generally agreed definition of a subsidy. The European Commission accordingly (CEC, 1991, p.13) opts for:

all forms of specific transfers from the government sector which directly or indirectly benefit enterprises, for which the government receives no equivalent compensation in return and which are granted with the purpose of changing market outcome.

The particular subset of all subsidies that are subject to EU policy is referred to as *State aids*, and these are basically subsidies that distort intra-EU competition. They are specified in EU law as amended by the Court of Justice. They are widely used in practice, as quantified below, for example to influence choices in respect of transport modes, fuels and employees and to promote research and development.

Subsidies do not merely encompass direct transfers to firms, although most of the empirical evidence relates to these as they can be derived from national accounts. Rather, they include grants; credit on preferential terms; tax concessions (tax expenditures); equity investments which would not be undertaken by a commercial investor; provision of public goods or services at below market prices; and public procurement at above market prices. They may be received directly by the party to be assisted or indirectly via either higher output prices or lower input prices generated via subsidies to other economic actors. They may be paid to producers or to consumers; linked to gross output, intermediate inputs or primary inputs; and directed at traded or non-traded goods.

The underlying theory, when couched in static terms, is ambiguous. In a perfect (and static) world, subsidies would lead to distortions and inefficiency; but in a world already subject to distortion, one more may actually improve the allocation of resources. More important is the dynamic case against subsidies, which is that they undermine incentives: firms in receipt of subsidies are thereby under less compulsion to adjust to new conditions. Concerned to take action on the issue, the Commission sought to activate a ruling by the Court of Justice that State aids should be repaid. The first steps were to discover the true extent of State aids. The latest results are shown in Table 14.1.

During the period 1988–90 some 40 per cent of EU aid went to manufacturing. In real terms the total was roughly ECU 40 billion in 1986, and had fallen to roughly ECU 34 billion by 1990, a slightly greater figure than for 1989. In terms of EU value added this represented a sharp reduction from 4.2 per cent in 1986 to 3.3 per cent in 1990. The overall picture can be seen

**TABLE 14.1   State aid to the manufacturing sector, annual averages 1988–1990 and 1986–1988 (in brackets)** (*Source*: Commission of the European Communities 1992a)

|  | In per cent of valued added | | In ECU per person employed | | In million ECU* | |
|---|---|---|---|---|---|---|
|  | *(1986–1988)* | *1988–1990* | *(1986–1988)* | *1988–1990* | *(1986–1988)* | *1988–1990* |
| Belgium | (4.3) | 4.1 | (1606) | 1655 | (1175) | 1211 |
| Denmark | (1.9) | 2.1 | (593) | 634 | (316) | 333 |
| Germany | (2.7) | 2.5 | (994) | 984 | (7869) | 7865 |
| Greece | (24.3) | 14.6 | (2983) | 1502 | (2074) | 1072 |
| Spain | (6.8) | 3.6 | (1749) | 936 | (4491) | 2499 |
| France | (3.8) | 3.5 | (1437) | 1380 | (6479) | 6106 |
| Ireland | (6.4) | 4.9 | (2114) | 1734 | (447) | 368 |
| Italy | (6.2) | 6.0 | (2139) | 2175 | (10760) | 11027 |
| Luxembourg | (2.3) | 2.6 | (988) | 1270 | (37) | 48 |
| Netherlands | (3.1) | 3.1 | (1215) | 1327 | (1101) | 1225 |
| Portugal | (2.2) | 5.3 | (302) | 758 | (245) | 616 |
| United Kingdom | (2.6) | 2.0 | (770) | 582 | (4101) | 3133 |
| EUR 12 | (4.0) | 3.5 | (1325) | 1203 | (38835) | 35503 |

*\*1986–88 averages in 1989 prices*

in Table 14.1. The Greek data are unreliable, but it seems certain that aid levels are disproportionately high. Italy, Portugal and Ireland are also well above the EU average, with Italy showing little tendency to cut its aid and the situation in Portugal deteriorating badly. The best performance belongs to the UK, which even managed to bring down the percentage from its low level in 1986.

The UK retains its place as the lowest aid-giver in terms of aid per person employed, with Italy giving out almost four times as much. It is evident, therefore, that the general downwards trend over the period has left significant differences between States. It may also be noted that three of the four biggest States, Germany, France and Italy, not merely give out the vast bulk of total aid, but that this proportion rose from 65 per cent in 1986 to 70 per cent in 1990. As the Commission observed (CEC, 1992a, p.13), this has negative effects on economic convergence within the EU.

The only manufacturing sector singled out by the Commission was shipbuilding. On average, one-third of value added in this sector was given out in aid throughout the period, but in 1988–90 it represented 85 per cent in Italy (up from 60 per cent in 1986–88) and 79 per cent in Portugal (up from 10 per cent), whereas it represented only 11 per cent in the UK (down from 24 per cent).

Grants and definitive tax reductions are by far the most frequently used form of aid in the EU. Grants are most popular because they are easy to legislate for and are very flexible. In 1988–90, 78 per cent of all aid to manufacturing in the UK consisted of grants, a figure matched only by Spain, but only 4 per cent consisted of tax reductions. Equity participation is primarily related to financial preparations for privatization, and accordingly constituted 8 per cent of total aid in the UK over the period. The Commission observes that this is the least transparent form of aid because it only constitutes aid where participation is carried out under circumstances which would induce private entrepreneurs to refrain from such an investment. The remainder of UK aid to manufacturing consisted of soft loans (3 per cent), guarantees (1 per cent) and tax deferrals (6 per cent, mainly in the form of accelerated depreciation) which were used in only three States.

The objectives of aid are classified in Table 14.2. This is a somewhat arbitrary breakdown in that, for example, aid for R&D may be transmitted via sector specific programmes. However, it would appear that some 40 per cent of aid to manufacturing is spent on horizontal objectives, although there is tremendous variability between States and also in relation to the balance between objectives. Overall, the UK is clearly the 'representative' State, but it is worth observing that it uses a relatively large amount of general investment aid about which the Commission has distinct reservations (CEC, 1992a, p.23).

Aid to particular sectors was heavily reduced between 1986 and 1990, most notably because of the phasing out of aids to restructure the steel industry. However, regional aid remained important. Article 92(3)a regions are those where the conditions of living are particularly low (Northern Ireland in the case of the UK). Leaving aside the special case of Berlin, the data indicate that, at least up to 1990, less aid was directed to such regions than to specific industries in difficulties, a fact which is somewhat incompatible with the EU's stated aspirations for improved cohesion.

The Commission has stated its clear preference for horizontal rather than sector-speciifc aids. The position in this respect improved in 1988–90 compared with 1986–88, but the early 1990s' recession once again brought to the fore the problems of, for example, the steel industry (see Case Study: The rescue plan for steel on p.203) which suggested that sectoral aids were returning to favour.

The other sectors where aid is widely given are agriculture, fisheries, transport and coal mining. It is worthy of note, given the debate concerning the privatization of British Rail, that in 1988–90 the UK provided State aid to the railways and inland waterways equal to 6 per cent of gross value added (down from 9.5 per cent in 1986–88) compared to an EU average of 12.5 per cent, and where the comparable figure in Germany was 29 per cent, in France 25 per cent and in Spain 26 per cent (CEC, 1992a, p.35).

Further, in the case of coal mining, the amount of aid rose sharply between 1986–88 and 1988–90 (from ECU 12 180 to ECU 40 071 per person employed in the UK, at which time it constituted 42 per cent of total aid compared to 40 per cent for manufacturing and 18 per cent for coal aid on average in the EU). The UK total was, however, only one-sixth that for Belgium and less than half that for France. While 68 per cent of the aid in the UK went to current production for restructuring, the comparable figure for Belgium was 14 per cent and for France was 7 per cent, where in both cases the great bulk of the aid went to pay for social/redundancy costs.

Recent years have seen the Commission attempting to extend its prerogatives into hitherto uncharted territory, much as it has done in relation to competition policy. Only non-discriminatory aid given to consumers and disaster relief are specifically permitted by the Treaty of Rome, although the Commission gave blanket approval in May 1992 to low levels of aid to small and medium-sized enterprises (SMEs). This means, however, that the Commission has a good deal of latitude in determining what is meant by compatibility in respect of, for example, State aid to public enterprises and state shareholdings.

As noted above, the current principle is that all enterprises should compete on a level playing field (CEC, 1992b, p.126), so if a private investor would have gone ahead then it is legitimate for the State to do so (CEC, 1992b, p.307). In cases involving Lanerossi and Fiat/Alfa/Romeo in the late 1980s, it was held that any investment should be judged from the long-term perspective of a conglomerate rather than from the short-term perspective of the capital markets, and a number of payments made to, for example, national airlines such as Sabena and Air France have recently been sanctioned on this basis (CEC, 1992b, p.179), as well as to Iberia in July 1992. In order to assist with the determination of whether aid is taking place, Member States

**TABLE 14.2 State aid (percentage) to the manufacturing sector 1988–1990, breakdown of aid according to sector and function**
(*Source*: Commission of the European Communities, 1992a)

| SECTORS/FUNCTION | B | DK | D | GR | E | F | IRL | I | L | NL | P | UK | EUR 12 |
|---|---|---|---|---|---|---|---|---|---|---|---|---|---|
| *Horizontal objectives* | 76 | 59 | 29 | 81 | 28 | 66 | 50 | 30 | 39 | 77 | 17 | 45 | 42 |
| Innovation: R&D | 13 | 35 | 12 | 1 | 9 | 17 | 4 | 4 | 8 | 35 | 1 | 8 | 10 |
| Environment | 0 | 4 | 2 | 0 | 1 | 0 | 0 | 0 | 1 | 2 | 0 | 2 | 1 |
| S.M.E. | 25 | 1 | 7 | 10 | 5 | 11 | 8 | 10 | 21 | 31 | 0 | 12 | 10 |
| Trade/Export | 14 | 8 | 2 | 22 | 1 | 36 | 38 | 6 | 2 | 1 | 0 | 15 | 11 |
| Economisation of | | | | | | | | | | | | | |
| Energy | 6 | 10 | 3 | 0 | 1 | 1 | 0 | 1 | 0 | 2 | 0 | 0 | 1 |
| General Investment | 12 | 0 | 0 | 10 | 5 | 1 | 0 | 2 | 8 | 4 | 1 | 9 | 3 |
| Other objectives | 6 | 0 | 2 | 37 | 6 | 0 | 0 | 7 | 0 | 0 | 14 | 0 | 5 |
| *Particular sectors* | 4 | 38 | 11 | 5 | 67 | 25 | 9 | 15 | 0 | 11 | 78 | 20 | 20 |
| Shipbuilding | 1 | 32 | 3 | 3 | 10 | 4 | 0 | 4 | 0 | 7 | 27 | 7 | 5 |
| Other sectors | 3 | 6 | 8 | 2 | 57 | 21 | 9 | 11 | 0 | 4 | 51 | 13 | 15 |
| *Regional objectives* | 21 | 3 | 61 | 15 | 5* | 9 | 42 | 55 | 61 | 12 | 5 | 34 | 38 |
| Regions under 92(3)c | 21 | 3 | 9 | – | – | 5 | – | 4 | 61 | 12 | – | 25 | 8 |
| Regions under 92(3)a | – | – | | 15 | 5 | 4 | 42 | 51 | – | – | 5 | 9 | 30 |
| Berlin/92(2)c | | | 52 | | | | | | | | | | |
| *Total* | 100 | 100 | 100 | 100 | 100 | 100 | 100 | 100 | 100 | 100 | 100 | 100 | 100 |

*Subdivision not available

202

have been asked to submit balance sheets and profit and loss accounts for all public enterprises with a turnover exceeding ECU 250 million (CEC, 1992b, p.128).

Particularly awkward issues arise where the Commission requires the repayment of aid, possibly well after the event, on the grounds that it conferred a hidden advantage. In a case involving the French nationalized car-maker Renault, the Commission alleged that State aid was not fully put to the use it had specified, and ruled in May 1990 that part would have to be repaid to the authorities. More recently, after an initial attempt was ruled out of order by the Court of Justice, British Aerospace was ordered to repay 'sweeteners' (plus interest) given to it by the UK government at the time of its purchase of Rover over and above what had been sanctioned by the Commission.

State aid is intensely politicized, so it is unsurprising that the Commission's decisions are almost invariably criticized by firms and the authorities in at least one State, and that it is sometimes forced to retract them, at least temporarily, as in the BAe/Rover case. This also happened when the Commission proposed in July 1992 that Asea Brown Boveri (ABB) should repay Spanish State aid. In July 1990, when ABB bought CCC, an electrical group, the latter's debts were written off, but ABB claimed that it had not gained from the aid and the Spanish government took the case to the Court of Justice, claiming procedural irregularities.

---

### CASE STUDY: THE RESCUE PLAN FOR STEEL

Overcapacity in the world steel industry has plagued the Community for well over a decade. Previous attempts to restore some semblance of equilibrium between supply and demand fell upon stony ground essentially because, other than in the UK where the privatization of British Steel resulted in the creation of a slimmed-down, much more efficient producer, Member States were totally unwilling to face up to the political consequences of shutting down publicly-owned steel works in areas of high unemployment.

The latest rescue plan began at the end of 1992, as an attempt to cut between 25 and 30 million tonnes of crude steel capacity from a total of 170 million tonnes. Up to 25 million tonnes of cuts were to be forthcoming from private sector producers, of which 10.5 million tonnes would be voluntary and financed by the Community. However, in the State-owned sector, plans to rationalize Ilva of Italy rapidly broke down, and Germany refused to shut down Eko Stahl in the east. In December, the Community accordingly agreed to offer £5.4 billion of aid to state-owned producers in return for a reduction in capacity of 5.5 million tonnes of finished product capacity in Italy, Spain, Portugal and eastern Germany.

Subsequently, complaints were made that a rescue plan for Klockner-Werke's Bremen mill amounted to State aid, and thus contravened the December announcement that there would be no further subsidies; Riva pulled out of a provisional agreement to buy Eko Stahl in spite of an agreed subsidy of £325 million; and a proposal to reduce production at privately-owned mills in Brescia, northern Italy, was rejected by the European Commission on the grounds that this would have involved bending rules on State aid, leaving the Commission open to legal action from unsubsidized steel producers as well as the US authorities with whom the Community was negotiating a multilateral steel agreement.

Unsurprisingly, the relatively efficient privately-owned mills were unwilling to deliver their required capacity cuts if their State-owned rivals maintained capacity. In any event, the demand for steel once again began to improve, so the incentive to pursue capacity reductions was much reduced. As a result, the rescue plan was officially pronounced dead. Unfortunately, it is in the nature of things that recession will return, probably in the not-too-distant future. Hence, given that Member States will continue to reject a market-driven solution, and that the renewal of the subsidy race will serve only to penalize the efficient producers and alienate the USA, which will possibly impose trade sanctions as a consequence, a further re-run of recent history can be reliably predicted. Clearly, it is difficult to level a playing field when it is made of steel.

## 14.4   Research and development

The 1980s saw the proliferation of schemes such as ESPRIT (information technology), RACE (telecommunications), BRITE (advanced technologies) and JESSI (semiconductors) collectively administered through a series of Framework Programmes. Current spending under these headings runs at 12 billion ECU over five years. The Commission funds 50 per cent of the costs of approved projects. These schemes were intended to remedy Europe's perceived weakness in high-tech industries, a weakness compounded by the fragmentation of research. This in turn can be traced back to the fact the the EU has in many advanced industries rather too many firms, an effect of the policy of husbanding national champions during the 1960s and 1970s. One objective of the EU's technology programme is therefore to encourage international cooperation between firms and between firms and universities. Projects are thus funded if and only if they have three or more partners from different countries and, ideally, if they have both industrial and academic partners too.

The programme focuses largely on research rather than commercial development. In part this is because of a concern over the anti-competitive implications of subsidizing rival firms to cooperate. This approach has, however, limited the commercial benefits (see *The Economist*, 9 January 1993). A study of EUREKA in June 1991 for example indicated that few products were being brought to market despite large expenditures, primarily by Member States, that JESSI has been almost permanently near to collapse and that the High-Definition Television (HDTV) project has proved to be misguided. This has not, however, prevented the Commission from wanting to devote more money to the development of flatscreen technology. Others such as Hobday (1989) see the EU programme as the catalyst for regeneration; the jury is still out.

## 14.5   Small and medium-sized enterprises

Aid for SMEs (companies which employ up to 500 people) started out as a means to overcome their main difficulties relative to their larger counterparts. In particular, SMEs were seen to have problems in raising capital, keeping up with a rapidly changing environment and learning how to expand beyond national markets. The Commission has long held that SMEs are an essential element in a healthy and competitive environment, and is prepared to tolerate a higher level of aid than for larger firms (Evans and Martin, 1991).

At the end of 1992, Member States operated some 420 national initiatives for SMEs, while the EU operated a further 70 EU-wide programmes according to a study by the Dutch Research Institute for Small and Medium-sized Businesses (see *Financial Times*, 3 November 1992). Given that 92 per cent of the 11.6 million enterprises in the EU in 1993 employed fewer than 10 people (and nearly 50 per cent only the owner), and account for some 70 per cent of total employment, it would be curious if industrial policy ignored their existence. Nevertheless, the EU itself is not involved financially, but prefers to offer help with information and cross-border cooperation. Currently there is a separate directorate for enterprise although it may be absorbed into the one for industry. Meanwhile, the enterprise programme, which expired at the end of 1993, is set to be rolled over for a further four years.

At a national level the UK is less active overall than France or Ireland, but compares well with Germany, Spain and Italy. It is particularly active in respect of start-ups and training, but does very little in respect of financial assistance.

## 14.6 Conclusion

The Single European Market is now officially in being. The timing was not altogether particularly auspicious, as it coincided with a widespread recession throughout the EU which has only recently begun to lift in many Member States. Unfortunately, this raises the possibility that further attempts to unwind State aids and other policies designed to favour one Member State in relation to others are likely to meet increased rather than the reduced resistance associated in priciple with the onset of the SEM.

The replacement of Sir Leon Brittan as Commissioner for Competition by Karel van Miert is inauspicious as the latter has indicated that he will take a softer line on State aids than his predecessor. It is also worth bearing in mind that the current enthusiasm for 'subsidiarity' may be twisted to justify more control at national level over decisions relating to specific sectors, decisions which are unlikely to have the welfare of the entire EU at heart.

The tensions inherent in reaching pan-EU agreement on anything are fairly accute in respect of industrial policy. The UK would have been happy to see any mention of the topic expunged from the Maastricht Treaty, but was outvoted. The others then all opted for majority voting on industrial policy matters, but the UK objected and unanimity prevailed. However, the other Member States are frequently at loggerheads, in relation, for example, to assisting the car industry with clean engine technology. If 'lean-burn' engine assistance were to be forthcoming from the EU then it would have to be open to all Member States. However, there are only some 10 car-makers in the EU capable of doing such research, and if the money were to go primarily to those lagging in the race, France and Italy would get the lion's share. Most States would get none, and Germany might feel that the end-result would be to erode its competitive advantage.

On a more optimistic note, there is the recent acknowledgement that, just possibly, the US authorities got it right when they used the forces of competition to resolve the future of HDTV and restricted themselves to the role of referee. Equally, the defeat of the Socialists in France may portend a more market-driven policy there, especially in relation to State enterprise, and the severe budgetary problems in Italy are forcing a more rational approach to the long-delayed restructuring of industry. Finally, recent moves by companies such as IBM to downsize may spell the end of an era when being big was much preferred to being flexible and responsive to consumer demands. Perhaps the Anglo-Saxon preference for freer markets will ultimately prevail, and national champions will fade into the mists of time; or then again, perhaps not.

## Guide to further reading

Jill Hills (1984) is a fascinating if now rather historical account of British attempts to build national champions in high-tech industries. Reading from Chapter 10 on innovation is in large measure relevant here also.

# Questions on Part III

1 Review your understanding of the following concepts:

| | |
|---|---|
| Intra-trade | Full-line forcing |
| Restrictive trade practices | Cartel |
| Bicester agreement | National champion |
| European Union's twin-track approach | Access deficit |
| Liberalization | Privatization |
| Rent-shifting | |

2 'The history of privatization in the UK is one large u-turn: the government sold the utilities as monopolies so as to make them attractive to buyers, then had second thoughts and spent years trying to break up these monopolies to promote competition.' To what extent is or was it a good policy?

3 Read the Silbertston report on the Multifibre agreement. Examine trends in the textile industry in the UK and another major EU country since its publication in 1984. Comment critically on the viewpoint taken by the report.

4 Find recent copies of the Annual Report of the Director-General of Fair Trading (for the UK; this describes the work of the MMC) and the Annual Report on Competition Policy (for the EU). Look for press comment on policy by both organizations in recent years. Critically examine the issues raised in this literature.

5 Find an MMC report on a merger from at least 10 years ago. Find out what has happened in the industry or sector over this time in terms of market shares, entry, technology and other relevant factors. Comment critically on the recommendations of the MMC using the wisdom of hindsight.

# Bibliography

Acs, Z. J. and Audretsch, D. B. (1988) 'Innovation in large and small firms: empirical analysis', *American Economic Review*, September.

Alberts, W. W. (1984) 'Do oligopolisits earn "non-competitive" rates of return?', *American Economic Review*, vol. 74, 624–632.

Alchian, A. and Demsetz, H. (1972) 'Production, information costs, and economic organization', *American Economic Review*, vol. 62, no. 5, 777–795.

Ansoff, I. (1965) *Corporate Strategy*, McGraw-Hill, New York.

Aoki, M. (1990) 'Towards an economic theory of the Japanese firm', *Journal of Economic Literature*, vol. XXVII, 1–27.

Armstrong, M., Cowan, S. and Vickers, J. (1994) *Regulatory Reform*, MIT Press, Cambridge MA.

Arrow, K. J. (1962) 'Economic welfare and the allocation of resources for invention' in *The Rate and Direction of Inventive Activity: economic and social factors*, Princeton University Press, Princeton, NJ, 609–25.

Auerbach, A. J. (1988) *Competition*, Blackwell, Oxford.

Auerbach, A. J. (ed.) (1988) *Mergers and Acquisitions*, University of Chicago Press, Chicago (A National Bureau of Economic Research project report).

Auerbach, A. J. and Reishus, D. (1988) 'Taxes and the merger decision' in Coffee, J. J., Lowenstein, L. and Rose-Ackerman, R. (eds) *Knights, Raiders and Takeovers*, Oxford University Press, 300–313.

Averch, H. and Johnson, L. (1962) 'Behaviour of the firm under regulatory constraint', *American Economic Review*, 52.

Axelrod, R. (1981) 'The emergence of cooperation among egoists', *American Political Science Review*, vol. 74, 624–632.

Bain, J. S. (1951) 'Relation of profit rate to industry concentration: American manufacturing, 1936–1940', *Quarterly Journal of Economics*, vol. 65, no. 3, 293–324.

Bain, J. S. (1956) *Barriers to New Competition*, Harvard University Press, Cambridge MA.

Baldwin, R. and Krugman, P. R. (1989) 'Persistent trade effects of large exchange rate shocks', *Quarterly Journal of Economics*, vol. 104, no. 4, 635–654.

Baldwin, W. L. and Scott, J. T. (1987) *Market Structure and Technological Change*, Harwood Academic, Switzerland.

Baumol, W. J. (1959) *Business Behaviour, Value and Growth*, Macmillan, London.

Baumol, W. J., Panzar, J. C. and Willig, R. D. (1982) *Contestable Markets and the Theory of Industry Structure*, Harcourt Brace Jovanovich, New York.

Baumol, W. J. and Sidak, G. (1994) 'Pricing of inputs sold to competitors', *Yale Journal on Regulation*, vol. 11, 171–202.

Bell, W. (1968) 'The effects of monopoly profits and wages on prices and consumer surplus in US manufacturing', *Western Economic Journal*, June.

Berle, A. A. and Means, G. C. (1932) *The Modern Corporation and Private Property*, Macmillan, New York.

Bertrand, J. (1883) 'Théorie mathématique de la richesse sociale', *Journal des Savants*, 499–508.

Best, M. (1990) *The New Competition: Institutions of Industrial Restructuring*, Polity Press, Oxford.

Bhagwati, J. (1970) 'Oligopoly theory, entry prevention and growth', *Oxford Economic Papers*, vol. 22, 297–310.

Bishop, M., Kay, J. and Mayer, C. (eds) (1994) *Privatization and Economic Performance*, Oxford University Press, Oxford.

Bishop, M., Kay, J. and Mayer, C. (eds) (1995) *The Regulatory Challenge*, Oxford University Press, Oxford.

Booz. Allen Acquisition Services (1989) 'Study on obstacles to takeover bids in the European Community', Commission of the European Communities DG XV-B-2, Brussels.

Bowles, S. (1985) 'The production process in a competitive economy: Walrasian, Neo-Hobbesian and Marxian models', *American Economic Review*, vol. 75, 16–36.

Brander, J. A. (1981) 'Intra-industry trade in identical commodities', *Journal of International Economics*, vol. 11, 1–14.

Brander, J. A. and Easton, J. (1984) 'Product line rivalry' *American Economic Review*, vol. 74, 323–334.

Brozen, Y. (1970) 'The antitrust task force deconcentration recommendation', *Journal of Law and Economics*, vol. 2.

Buckley, P. and Casson, M. (1976) *The Future of the Multinational Enterprise*, Macmillan, London.

Bulow, J., Geanakupulos, J. and Klemperer, P. (1985) 'Multi-market oligopoly and strategic substitutes', *Journal of Political Economy*, vol. 93, 488–511.

Burton, J. (1983) 'Picking losers? The political economy of industrial policy', *Hobart Paper 99*, Institute of Economic Affairs, London.

Camanor, W. S. and Wilson, T. (1974) *Advertising and Market Power*, Harvard University Press, Cambridge MA.

Caves, R. (1989) 'Mergers, takeovers, and economic efficiency: foresight vs. hindsight', *International Journal of Industrial Organization*, vol. 7, no. 1, 151–174.

Cecchini, P. (1988) *1992: The European challenge*, Wildwood House, Aldershot.

Chamberlin, E. H. (1933) *The Theory of Monopolistic Competition*, Harvard University Press, Cambridge MA.

Chandler, A. (1992) 'Organisational capabilities and the economic history of the industrial enterprise', *Journal of Economic Perspectives*, vol. 6, no. 3, 79–100.

Clarke, R., Davies, S. W. and Waterson, M. (1984) 'The profitability-concentration relation: market power or efficiency?', *Journal of Industrial Economics*, vol. 32, no. 4, 435–450.

Coase, R. (1937) 'The nature of the firm', *Economica*, *NS*, vol. 4, 386-405. Reprinted in Stigler, G. J. and Boulding, K. E. (eds) (1952), *Readings in Price Theory*, Richard D. Irwin, Chicago IL.

Collins, N. R. and Preston, L. E. (1969) 'Price-cost margins and industry structure', *Review of Economics and Statistics*, 51 (August), 226–242.

Comanor, W. and Liebenstein, T. (1969) 'Allocative efficiency, X-efficiency and the measurement of welfare loss', *Economica*, August, 304–309.

Commission of the European Communities (1991) Fair competition in the internal market: Community State Aid Policy, *European Economy 48*.

Commission of the European Communities (1992a) *Third Survey of State Aids in the European Community in the Manufacturing and Certain Other Sectors*, CEC, Brussels.

Commission of the European Communities (1992b) *XXIst report on Competition Policy 1991*, CEC, Brussels.

Connolly, R. A. and Hirschey, M. (1984) 'R&D, market structure and profits: a value-based approach', *Review of Economics and Statistics*, 66, 678–681.

Cosh, A. D., Hughes, M. S., Kumar, M. S. and Singh A. (1985) 'Institutional investment company performance and mergers: empirical evidence for the UK: a report to the Office of Fair Trading', Mimeo, Cambridge.

Cournot, A. (1838) *Recherches sur laes Principles Mathématiques de la Théorie des Richesse*. English edition, N. Bacon (ed.) (1897) *Researches into the Mathematical Principles of the Theory of Wealth*, Macmillan, New York.

Cowling, K. and Mueller, D. (1978) 'The social costs of monopoly', *Economic Journal*, vol. 88, 807–827.

Cowling, K. and Sugden, R. (1987) *Transnational Monopoly Capitalism*, Wheatsheaf, Brighton.

Cowling, K. and Sugden, R. (1993) 'Behind the market facade: an assessment of developments in the theory of the firm', University of Warwick discussion paper.

Cowling, K. and Waterston, M. (1976) 'Price-cost margins and market structure', *Economica*, 43 (August), 267–274.

Cowling, K., Stoneman, P., Cubbin, J., Cable, J., Hall, G., Comberger, S. and Dutton, P. (1980) *Mergers and Economic Performance*, Cambridge University Press, Cambridge.

Curwen (1986) *Public Enterprise*, Wheatsheaf, Brighton.

Curwen (1994) *Privatisation in the UK – the facts and figures*, Ernst & Young, London.

Cyert R. M. and March J. G. (1967) *A Behaviorial Theory of the Firm*, Prentice-Hall, Englewood Cliffs NJ.

Cyert, R. M. and Simon, H. A. (1971) 'Theory of the firm: behavioralism and marginalism', unpublished working paper, Graduate School of Industrial Administration, Carnegie-Mellon University.

d'Asprement, C., Gabszewicz, J. and Thisse, J. F. (1979) 'On Hotelling's stability in competition' *Econometrica*, vol. 17, 1145–1151.

Dasgupta, P. (1988) 'Patents, priority and imitation, or the economics of races and waiting games', *Economic Journal*, vol. 98, 66–80.

Dasgupta, P. and Stiglitz, J. (1980a) 'Industrial structure and the nature of innovative activity', *Economic Journal*, vol. 90, 266–93.

Dasgupta, P. and Stiglitz, J. (1980b) 'Uncertainty, industrial structure and the speed of R&D', *Bell Journal of Economics*, 1–28.

Dasgupta, P. and Stoneman, P. (eds) (1987) *Economic Policy and Technological Performance*, Cambridge University Press, Cambridge.

Davies, S. (1979) *The Diffusion of Process Innovations*, Cambridge University Press, Cambridge.

Demsetz, H. (1969) 'Information and efficiency: another viewpoint', *Journal of Law and Economics*, vol. 12, 1–22.

Demsetz, H. (1973) 'Industry structure, market rivalry and public policy', *Journal of Law and Economics*, vol. 16, no. 1, 1–10.

Demsetz, H. (1974) 'Two systems of belief about monopoly' in Goldschmidt, H. J., Mann, H. M. and Weston, J. F. (eds) *Industrial Concentration: the New Learning*, Little, Brown, Boston MA.

Department of Trade and Industry (1988) *Review of Mergers Policy*, HMSO.

Dixit, A. K. (1980) 'The role of investment in entry deterrence', *Economic Journal*, vol. 90, 95–106.

Dixon, H. (1986) 'Cournot and Bertrand outcomes as equilibria in a strategic measure', *Economic Journal*, Conference Supplement, 59–70.

Doyle, P. (1968) 'Advertising expenditure and consumer demand', *Oxford Economic Papers*, vol. 20, 295–415.

Dunning, J. H. (1988) *Explaining International Production*, Unwin, London.

*Economist, The* (1993) 'Europe's Technology Policy', 9 January.

Emerson, M. (1988) *The Economics of 1992*, Oxford University Press, Oxford.

Ergas, H. (1986) 'Does technology policy matter?', Centre for European Policy Studies, no. 29.

Eskin, G. J. (1975) 'A case for test marketing experiments', *Journal of Advertising Research*, vol. 15, 27–33.

Eskin, G. J. and Baron, P. H. (1977) 'Effect of price and advertising in test market experiments', *Journal of Marketing Research*, vol. 14, 499–508.

Evans, A. and Martin, S. (1991) 'Socially acceptable distortion of competition: Community Policy on State aid', *European Law Review*, vol. 16, no. 2, 79–111.

Fairburn, J. A. and Kay, J. A. (1989) *Mergers and Mergers Policy*, Oxford University Press, Oxford.

Firth, M. (1980) 'Takeovers, shareholders returns and the theory of the firm', *Quarterly Journal of Economics*, vol. 94, 236–260.

Fishwick, F. (1989) 'Definition of monopoly power in the antitrust policies of the United Kingdom and the European Community', *The Antitrust Bulletin* (Fall), 451–488.

Franks, J. R. and Harris, R. S. (1986) 'Shareholder wealth effects of corporate takeovers: the UK experience 1955–85', London Business School and University of North Carolina at Chapel Hill Working Paper.

Franks, J. R. and Mayer, C. (1989) *Risk, Regulation and Investor Protection: The Case of Investment Management*, Clarendon Press, Oxford.

Frazer, T. (1992) *Monopoly Competition and the Law*, Harvester Wheatsheaf, London.

Freeman, C. (1989) 'R&D, technical change and investment in the UK' in Green, F. (1989) *The Restructuring of the UK Economy*, Harvester Wheatsheaf, Brighton.

Freeman, C. (1991) *Technology and the Future of Europe: Global Competition and the Environment in the 1990s*, edited by C. Freeman, M. Sharp and W. Walker, Pinter, London.

Friedman, J. W. (1977a) *Oligopoly Theory*, Cambridge University Press, Cambridge.

Friedman, J. W. (1977b) *Oligopoly and the Theory of Games*, North-Holland, New York.

Friedman, J. W. (1991) *Game Theory With Applications to Economies*, 2nd edition, Oxford University Press, New York.

Friedman, M. (1953) 'Methodology of positive economics' in Friedman, M. (1953) *Essays in Positive Economics*, University of Chicago Press, Chicago.

Fudenberg, D. and Tirole, J. (1983a) 'Capital as commitment: strategic investment to deter mobility', *Journal of Economic Theory*, vol. 31, 227–250.

Fudenberg, D. and Tirole, J. (1983b) 'Learning by doing and market performance', *Bell Journal of Economics*, vol. 14, 522–530.

Fudenberg, D., Gilbert, R., Stiglitz, J. and Tirole, J. (1983) 'Pre-emption, leap-frogging and competition in patent races', *European Economic Review*, vol. 2, 3–31.

Galbraith, J. K. (1961) *Affluent Society*, Hamish Hamilton, London

Galbraith, J. K. (1968) *New Industrial State*, Penguin, Harmondsworth.

Gaskins, D. W. (1971) 'Dynamic limit pricing: optimal pricing under threat of entry', *Journal of Economic Theory*, vol. 3, 306–322.

Geroski, P. A. (1984) 'On the relationship between aggregate merger activity and the stock-market', *European Economic Review*, vol. 23, 223–233.

Geroski, P. A. (1989) 'European industrial policy and industrial policy in Europe', *Oxford Review of Economic Policy*, vol. 5, no. 2.

Gilbert, R. and Newbery, D. (1982) 'Pre-empitve patenting and the persistence of monopoly', *American Economic Review*, vol. 72, 514–526.

Grabowski, H. G. and Mueller, D. C. (1978) 'Industrial research and development, intangible capital stocks and firm profit rates', *Bell Journal of Economics*, 9, 328–343.

Greenaway, D. (ed.) (1985) *Current Issues in International Trade*, Macmillan, London.

Grossman, G. M. and Shapiro, C. (1987) 'Dynamic R&D competition', *Journal of Economics*, vol. 97, 372–387.

Gupta, V. K. (1983) 'A simultaneous determination of structure, conduct and performance in Canadian manufacturing', *Oxford Economic Papers*, 35, 281–301.

Haldi, J. and Whitcomb, D. (1967) 'Economies of scale in industrial plants', *Journal of Political Economy*, vol. 75, 373–385.

Hall, B. H. (1987) 'The effect of takeover activity on corporate R&D', NEBT working paper referenced in Jarrel, Brickley and Netter, *Journal of Economic Perspectives*, winter 1988, p.55.

Handy, C. (1993) *The Age of Unreason*, 2nd edition, Century Business, London.

Hannah, L. and Kay, J. A. (1977) *Concentration in Modern Industry*, Macmillan, London.

Hannah, L. and Kay, J. A. (1981) 'The contribution of mergers to concentration and growth – a reply to Professor Hart', *Journal of Industrial Economics*, vol. 29, 305–319.

Harberger, A. (1954) 'Monopoly and resource misallocation', *American Economic Review*, vol. 45, May, 77–87.

Harris, C. and Vickers, J. (1985a) 'Patent races and the persistence of monopoly', *Journal of Industrial Economics*, vol. 33, 461–481.

Harris, C. and Vickers, J. (1985b) 'Perfect equilibrium in a model of race', *Review of Economic Studies*, vol. 52, 193–209.

Hart, P. E. and Clarke, R. (1980) *Concentration in British Industry 1935–75*, Cambridge University Press, Cambridge.

Hart, P. E. and Morgan, E. (1977) 'Market structure and economic performance in the UK', *Journal of Industrial Economics*, 25, 177–193.

Hart, P. E., Utton, M. A. and Walshe, G. (1973) *Mergers in British Industry*, Cambridge University Press, Cambridge.

Hay, D. A. and Morris, D. J. (1991) *Industrial Economics and Organization*, 2nd edition, Oxford University Press, Oxford.

Hills, J. (1984) *Information Technology and Industrial Policy*, Croom Helm, London.

Hirschey, M. (1985) 'Market structure and market value', *Journal of Business*, 58, 89–98.

HMSO (1955) 'Collective discrimination. A report on exclusive dealing, collective boycotts, aggregated rebates and other discriminatory trade practices', Cm 9504, HMSO, London.

Hobday, M. (1989) 'European semi-conductor industry: resurgence and rationalisation', *Journal of Common Market Studies*, vol. 28, no. 2, December, 155–186.

Holl, P. (1975) 'Effect of control type on the performance of the firm in the UK', *Journal of Industrial Economics*, vol. 23, 257–272.

Hotelling, H. (1929) 'Stability in competition', *Economic Journal*, vol. 39, 41–57.

Hughes, A. and Kumar, M. S. (1985) 'Mergers, concentration and mobility amongst the largest UK non-financial corporations, 1972–82: a report to the Office of Fair Trading', Mimeo, Department of Applied Economics, Cambridge.

Jacquemin, A. (1989) *International and Multinational Strategic Behaviour*, Kyklos.

Jacquemin, A., de Ghellinck, E. and Huveneers, C. (1980) 'Concentration and profitability in a small open economy', *Journal of Industrial Economics*, vol. 29, 131–144.

Johnson (1993) *European Industries: Structure, Conduct and Performance*, Edward Elgar, Aldershot.

Kamerschen, D. (1966) 'An estimation of welfare losses from monopoly in the American economy', *Western Economic Journal*, Summer.

Kamien, M. I. and Schwartz, N. L. (1982) *Market Structure and Innovation*, Cambridge University Press, Cambridge.

Kay, J. (1993) *Foundations of Corporate Success*, Oxford University Press, Oxford.

Kirzner, I. M. (1973) *Competition and Entrepreneurship*, University of Chicago Press, Chicago.

Kreps, D. M. (1991) *Game Theory and Economic Modelling*, Oxford University Press, Oxford.

Kreps, D. M. and Scheinkman, J. A. (1983) 'Quantity precommitment and Bertrand competition yield Cournot outcomes', *Bell Journal of Economics*, vol. 14, no. 2, 326–337.

Kreps, D. M. and Wilson, R. (1982) 'Reputation and imperfect information', *Journal of Economic Theory*, 27 (August), 253-279.

Kreps, D. M., Milgrom, P. R., Roberts, J. and Wilson, R. (1982) 'Rational cooperation in the finitely repeated Prisoners' Dilemma', *Journal of Economic Theory*, vol. 27, no. 2, 245–252.

Krugman, P. R. (1987) 'Is free trade passé?', *Journal of Economic Prospects*, vol. 1, no. 2, 131–144.

Kuenhn, D. A. (1975) *Takeovers and the Theory of the Firm*, Macmillan, London.

Kumar, M. S. (1985) 'Growth, acquisition activity, and firm size: evidence from the United Kingdom', *Journal of Industrial Economics*, vol. 33, 327–338.

Kwoka, J. E. (1981) 'Does the choice of concentration measure really matter?', *Journal of Industrial Economics,* vol. 29, no. 4, 445–453.

Laffont, J. J. and Tirole, J. (1993) *Theory of Incentives in Procurement and Regulation*, MIT Press, Cambridge MA.

Laffont, J. J. and Tirole, J. (1995) 'Creating competiton through interconnection', mimeo.

Lambin, J. J. (1976) *Advertising, Competition and Market Conduct in Oligopoly over Time*, New-Holland, Amsterdam.

Landau, R. and Rosenberg, N. (1986) 'The positive sum strategy: harnessing technology for economic growth' in Baily, M. and Chakrabarti, A. (1988) *Innovation and the Productiviy Crisis*, Brookings, Washington DC.

Larner, R. J. (1966) 'Ownership and control in the 200 largest non-financial corporations', *American Economic Review*, vol. 56, 777–787.

Leibenstein, H. (1966) 'Allocative efficiency vs, "X-efficiency"', *American Economic Review*, vol. 56, no. 3, 392–415.

Levin, R. C. (1986) 'A new look at the patent system', *American Economic Review*, vol. 76, no. 2, 199–202.

Levin, R. C., Cohen, W. M. and Mowery, D. C. (1985) 'R&D appropriability, opportunity and market structure: new evidence on some Schumpeterian hypotheses', *American Economic Review Papers and Proceedings*, vol. 75, no. 2, 20–24.

Levine, P. and Aaronovitch, S. (1981) 'The financial characteristics of firms and theories of merger activity', *Journal of Industrial Economics*, vol. 30, 149–172.

Levy, D. T. (1985) 'Specifying the dynamics of industry concentration', *Journal of Industrial Economics*, vol. 34, no. 1, 55–68.

Littlechild, S. (1981) 'Misleading calculations of social cost of monopoly', *Economic Journal*, vol. 91, June, 348–363.

Lukacs, P. (1995) 'Price-cost margins', University of Leeds mimeo.

Machlup, F. (1967) 'Theories of the firm: marginalist, behavioural and managerial', *American Economic Review*, vol. 57, 1–83.

Magenheim, E. B. and Mueller, D. C. (1988) 'Are acquiring firm shareholders better-off after an acquisition?' in J. J. Coffee, L. Lowenstein, and S. Rose-Ackerman (eds), *Knights, raiders and targets: the impact of the hostile takeover*, Oxford University Press, New York.

Manne, H. G. (1965) 'Mergers and the market for corporate control', *Journal of Political Economy*, 73 (April), 110–120.

Mansfield, E., Schwartz, M. and Wagner, S. (1981) 'Imitation costs and patents: an empirical study', *Economic Journal*, 91 (December), 907–918.

Marglin, S. (1974) 'What do bosses do? The origins and functions of hierarchy in capitalist production', *Review of Radical Political Economy*, vol. 6, 33–60.

Marris, R. (1964) *Economic Theory of Managerial Capitalism*, Macmillan, London.

Marris, R. and Mueller, D. C. (1980) 'The corporation, competition, and the invisible hand', *Journal of Economic Literature*, vol. 18, no. 1, 32–63.

Marsh, (1991) 'Privatisation under Mrs Thatcher: an Extension to the Debate', *Public Administration*, vol. 70, no. 2, 287–291.

Marshall, A. (1920) *Principles of Economics*, 8th edition, Macmillan, London.

Martin, S. (1979) 'Advertising, concentration, and profitability: the simultaneity problem', *Bell Journal of Economics*, vol. 10, no. 2, 639–647.

Martin, S. (1988) 'Market power and/or efficiency?', *Review of Economics and Statistics*, vol. 70, no. 2, 331–335.

Martin, S. (1989) Product differentiation and the stability of non-cooperative collusion, mimeo, October.

Martin, S. (1991) 'Direct foreign investment in the United States', *Journal of Economic Behavior and Organization*, 16, 283–93.

Martin, S. (1993) *Advanced Industrial Economics*, Basil Blackwell, Oxford.

Masson, R. T. and Shannan, J. (1984) 'Social costs of oligopoly and the value of competition', *Economic Journal*, vol. 94, 520–535.

McConnell, J. J. and Muscarella, C. J. (1985) 'Corporate capital expenditure decisions and the market value of the firm', *Journal of Financial Economics*, 14, 399–422.

Meeks, G. and Meeks, J. G. (1981) 'Profitability measures as indicators of post-merger efficiency', *Journal of Industrial Economics*, vol. 34, no. 4, 335–345.

Meeks, S. (1977) *Disappointing Marriage*, Cambridge University Press, Cambridge.

Metcalfe, J. S. (1988) 'The diffusion of innovation' in G. Dosi and L. Soete (eds) *Technological Change and Economic Theory*, Pinter, London.

Milgrom, P. and Roberts, J. (1987) 'Informational asymmetries, strategic behaviour and industrial organization', *American Economic Review (Papers and Proceedings)*, vol. 77, 184–193.

Montagnon, P. (1990) *European Competition Policy*, Chatham House Papers, Royal Institute of International Affairs, Pinter, London.

Morck, R., Shleifer, A. and Vishny, R. W. (1988) 'Characteristics of targets of hostile and friendly takeovers' in *Corporate Takeovers*, edited by A. Auerbach, University of Chicago Press, Chicago.

Mueller, D. C. (ed.) (1980) *The Determinants and Effects of Mergers*, Oelgeschlager, Gunn and Hain, Cambridge MA.

Mueller, D. C. (1985) 'Mergers and market share', *Review of Economics and Statistics*, vol. 47, no. 2, 259–67.

Mueller, D. C. (1986) *Profits in the Long Run*, Cambridge University Press, Cambridge.

Mundell, R. A. (1962) 'Free trade, protection and customs unions', *American Economic Review*, vol. 52, 622.

Murray, F. (1987) 'Flexible specialisation in the third Italy', *Capital and Class*, vol. 19.

Nabseth, L. and Ray G. F. (1974) *Diffusion of New Industrial Processes*, Cambridge University Press, Cambridge.

Needham, D. (1978), *The Economics of Industrial Structure, Conduct and Performance*, Holt, Rhinehart & Wilson.

Nelson, R. (1964) 'Advertising as information', *Journal of Political Economy*, vol. 82, 729–784.

Nelson, R. R. and Winter, S. G. (1982) *An Evolutionary Theory of Economic Change*, Belknap Press of Harvard University Press, Cambridge MA.

Nerlove, M. and Arrow, K. J. (1962) 'Optimal advertising policy under dynamic conditions', *Economica*, vol. 29, 129–142.

Neven, D. J. (1990) 'EEC towards 1992: some distributional aspects', *Economic Policy*, April.

Newbould, G. D. (1970) *Management and Merger Activity*, Guthstead Ltd., Liverpool.

Newel, A. and Simon, H. (1972) *Human Problem-Solving*, Prentice-Hall International, Englewood Cliffs NY.

Norman, G. and La Manna, M. (1992) *New Industrial Economics: recent developments in industrial organization oligopoly and game theory*, Edward Elgar.

Northcott, J. and Walling, A. (1988) 'The impact of micro electronics', Policy Studies Institute, London.

O'Brien, D. (1982) 'Competition policy in Britain: the silent revolution', *The Antitrust Bulletin*, Spring.

Packard, V. (1957) *Hidden Persuaders*, D. McKay, New York.

Parish, R. and Ng, Y. K. (1972) 'Monopoly, x-efficiency and the measurement of welfare loss', *Economica*, vol. 39, 301–308.

Parker, D. (1991) 'Privatisation ten years on: a critical analysis of its rationale and results', *Economics*, vol. XXVII, no. 4, 155–163.

Parker, D. and Stead, R. (1991) *Profit and Enterprise – the Political Economy of Profit*, Harvester Wheatsheaf, London.

Patel, P. and Pavitt, K. (1987) 'Elements of British technological competitiveness', *National Institute Economic Review*, November, no. 122, 4/87, 72–83.

Pavitt, K., Robson, M. and Towsend, J. (1987) 'The size distribution of innovating firms in the UK, 1945–83', *Journal of Industrial Economics*, March, vol. 35, no. 3, 297–316.

Peltzman, S. (1977) 'The gains and losses from industrial concentration', *Journal of Law and Economics*, vol. 20, 229–264.

Penrose, E. T. (1959) *Theory of the Growth of the Firm*, Basil Blackwell, Oxford.

Phillips, A. (1972) 'An econometric study of price fixing, market structure and performance in British industry in the early 1950s' in Cowling, K. (ed.) (1972) *Market Structure and Corporate Behaviour*, Gray Mills.

Phlips, I. (1971) *Effects of Industrial Concentration*, North-Holland, Amsterdam.

Pickering, J. (1974) 'The abolition of Resale Price Maintenance in Great Britain', *Oxford Economic Papers*, March.

Pickering, J. F. and Cockerill, T. A. J. (1984) *The Economic Management of the Firm*, Barnes & Noble, New Jersey.

Piggott, J. and Cook, M. (1993) *International Business Economics: A European Perspective*, Longman, UK.

Piore, M. J. and Sabel, C. F. (1984) *The Second Industrial Revolution*, Basic Books, New York.

Porter, M. E. (1976a) 'Interbrand choice, media mix and market performance', *American Economic Review*, 66, 398–406.

Porter, M. E. (1976b) *Interbrand Choice, Strategy and Bilateral Market Power*, Harvard University Press, Cambridge MA.

Posner, R. (1975) 'The social costs of monopoly and regulations', *Journal of Political Economy*, vol. 83, 807–827.

Prais, S. (1976) *Evolution of Giant Firms in Britain*, Cambridge University Press, Cambridge.

Prais, S. (1980) *Responsibility of Parent Companies for their Subsidiaries*, Organization for Economic Cooperation and Development.

Pratten, C. F. (1971) *Economies of Scale in Manufacturing Industry*, Cambridge University Press, Cambridge.

Pryor, F. L. (1972) 'An international comparison of concentration ratios', *Review of Economics and Statistics,* vol. 54, no. 2, 130–139.

Radice, H. (1971) 'Control type, profitability and growth in large firms: an empirical study', *Economic Journal*, vol. 81, 547–562.

Ravenscraft, D. J. (1983) 'Structure-profit relationships at the line of business and industry level', *Review of Economics and Statistics*, vol. 65, 22–31.

Ravenscraft, D. J. (1987) 'The 1980s' merger boom: an industrial organisation perspective' in Browne, L. E. and Rosengren, E. S. (eds) *The Merger Boom*, Federal Reserve Bank of Boston.

Ravenscraft, D. J. and Scherer, F. M. (1987) *Mergers, Sell-offs, and Economic Efficiency*, Brookings Institution, Washington DC.

Ravenscraft, D. J. and Scherer, F. M. (1989) 'The profitability of mergers', *International Journal of Industrial Organization*, vol. 7, no. 1, 101–116.

Ray, G. F. (1984) *Diffusion of Mature Industrial Processes*, Cambridge University Press, Cambridge.

Reekie, W. D. (1981) *The Economics of Advertising*, Macmillan, London.

Rees, J., Briggs, R. and Oakley, R. (1984) 'The adoption of new technology in the American machinery industry', *Regional Studies*, vol. 18, no. 6, 489–504.

Rees, R. (1993) 'Collusion equilibrium in the Great Salt Duopoly', *Economic Journal*, vol. 103, 833–848.

Rose, N. L. (1987) 'Labor rent sharing and regulation: evidence from the trucking industry', *Journal of Political Economy*, vol. 95, no. 6, 1146–1178.

Salamon, G. L. (1985) 'Accounting rates of return', *American Economic Review*, vol. 75, no. 3, 495–504.

Salinger, M. A. (1984) 'Tobin's $q$, unionization and the concentration-profits relationship', *Rand Journal of Economics*, vol. 15, no. 2, 159–170.

Scherer, F. M. (1967) 'Research and development resource allocation under rivalry', *Quarterly Journal of Economics*, August, 359–394.

Scherer, F. M. (1979) 'The welfare economics of product variety: an application to the ready-to-eat cereals industry', *Journal of Industrial Economics*, vol. 28, no. 2, 113–134.

Scherer, F. M. (1980) *Industrial Market Structure and Economic Performance*, Rand McNally, Chicago IL.

Scherer, F. M., Beckenstein, A., Kaufer, E. and Murphy, R. D. (1975) *The Economics of Multi-Plant Operation: an international comparisons study*, Harvard University Press, Cambridge MA.

Schmalensee, R. C. (1972) *The Economics of Advertising*, American Elsevier, North Holland.

Schmalensee, R. C. (1988) 'Industrial economics: an overview', *Economic Journal,* vol. 98 (September), 643–681.

Schmalensee, R. C. (1989) 'Inter-industry studies of structure and performance' in Schmalensee, R. C. and Willig, R. D. (eds), *Handbook of Industrial Organization*, vol. II, North-Holland, Amsterdam.

Schmalensee, R. C. and Willig, R. D. (eds) (1989) *Handbook of Industrial Organization*, North-Holland, Amsterdam.

Schumpeter, J. (1953) *Capitalism, Socialism and Democracy*, Allen & Unwin, London.

Schumpeter, J. (1954) *History of Economic Analysis*, Oxford University Press, Oxford.

Schwartzman, D. (1960) 'The burden of monopoly', *Journal of Political Economy*, vol. 68, 77–87.

Selten, R. (1978) 'The chain store paradox', *Theory and Decision*, vol. 9, 127–159.

Shaked, A. and Sutton, J. (1984) 'Natural oligopolies and international trade', in H. Kierzkowski (ed.) Monopolistic Competition and International Trade, Clarendon Press, Oxford.

Shaw, R. and Simpson, P. (1986) 'The persisitence of monopoly: an assessment of the effectiveness of the UK MMC', *Journal of Industrial Economics*, vol. 34, no. 4, 355–373.

Shepherd, W. G. (1982) 'Causes of increased competition in the US economy 1939-80', *Review of Economics and Statistics*, vol. 14, no. 4, 613–626.

Shepherd, W. G. (1984) 'Contestibility vs. competition', *American Economic Review*, vol. 74, no. 4, 572–587.

Shleifer, A. and Vishny, R. W. (1987) 'Value maximisation and the acquisition process', *Journal of Economic Perspectives*, vol. 2, no. 1, 7–20.

Shubik, M. (1959) 'Edgeworth Market Games' in *Contributions to the Theory of Games*, R. D. Luce and A. W. Tucker (eds), Princeton University Press, Princeton.

Siegfried, J. J. and Tiemann, T. K. (1974) 'The welfare costs of monopoly: an inter-industry analysis', *Economic Inquiry*, June.

Simon, H. A. (1979) 'Rational decision making in business organizations', *American Economic Review*, vol. 69, 493–513.

Singh, A. (1971) *Takeovers: Their Relevance to the Stock Market and the Theory of the Firm*, Cambridge University Press, Cambridge.

Singh, A. (1975) 'Takeovers, economic natural selection and theory of the firm: evidence from the UK experience', *Economic Journal*, 85 (September), 497–515.

Slade, M. E. (1987) 'Interfirm rivalry in a repeated game: an empirical test on tacit collusion', *Journal of Industrial Economics*, vol. 35, no. 4, 499–516.

Sleuwaegen, L. and Dehandschutter, W. (1986) 'The critical choice between the concentration ratio and the H-index in assessing industry performance', *Journal of Industrial Economics*, vol. 35, no. 2, 193–208.

Smith, A. and Venables, A. J. (1988) 'Completing the internal market in the European Community', *European Economic Review*.

Stead, R. (1994) 'Mergers' in B. Atkinson (ed.) *Developments in Economics*, Causeway Press, Preston.

Steedman, H. and Wagner, K. (1988) 'Productivity, machinery and skills: clothing manufacturing in Britain and Germany', *National Institute of Economic Review*, no. 128, 40–57.

Steiner, R. L. (1973) 'Does advertising lower consumer prices?', *Journal of Marketing*, vol. 37, 24.

Stevens, G. (1992) *Privatization: the Lessons of Experience*, World Bank, Washington DC.

Stigler, G. (1956) 'The statistics of monopoly and mergers', *Journal of Political Economy*, vol. 64, 33–40.

Stoneman, P. (ed.) (1995) *Handbook of the Economics of Industrial Innovation and Technological Change*, Blackwell, Oxford.

Stoneman, P. (1987) *The Economic Analysis of Technology Policy*, Oxford University Press, Oxford.

Strickland, A. D. and Weiss, L. W. (1976) 'Advertising, concentration and price-cost margins', *Journal of Political Economy*, vol. 84, no. 5, 1109–1121.

Sugden, R. and Pitelis, C. N. (1986) 'The separation of ownership and control in the theory of the firm', *International Journal of Industrial Organization*, vol. 4. 69–86.

Sutton, J. (1991) *Sunk Costs and Market Structure*, MIT Press, Cambridge MA.

Swann, D. (1979) *Competition and Consumer Protection*, Penguin, London.

Teece, D. (1980) 'Economies of scope and the scope of the enterprise', *Journal of Economic Behavior and Organization*, 1, 223–247.

Teece, D. (1982) 'Towards an economic theory of the multiproduct firm', *Journal of Economic Behavior and Organization*, vol. 3, 39–63.

Thaler, R. H. (1994) 'Financial decision-making under uncertainty', *American Economic Review*, vol. 84, no. 2, 186–192.

Thwaites, A. T. (1982) 'Some evidence of regional variations in the introduction and diffusion of industrial products and processes within British manufacturing industry', *Regional Studies*, vol 16, no. 5, 371–381.

Tirole, J. (1988) *The Theory of Industrial Organization*, MIT Press, Cambridge MA.

Tullock, G. (1967) 'The welfare loss of tariffs, monopolies and theft', *Western Economic Journal*, vol. 5, 224–232.

Tyson, L. D. (1992) *Who's Bashing Whom? Trade Conflict in High Technology Industries*, Institute for International Economics, Washington DC.

US Attorney General (1988) *Horizontal Merger Guidelines*, USA.

Utton, M. A. (1974a) 'Aggregate versus market concentration: a note', *Economic Journal*, vol. 84, 150–155.

Utton, M. A. (1974b) 'On measuring the effects of industrial mergers', *Scot. Journal of Political Economics*, vol. 21, 13–28.

Utton, M. A. (1982) *Political Economy of Big Business*, Martin Robertson, Oxford.

Venables, A. (1985) 'International trade, industry policy and imperfect competition', CEPR Discussion Papers, 74.

Vickers, J. (1988) 'Strategic competition among the few', *Oxford Review of Economic Policy*, vol. 1, no. 3, 39–62.

von Stackelberg, H. (1934) *Marketform and Gleichgewicht*, Julius Springer, Vienna.

Wahlroos, B. (1984) 'Monopoly welfare losses under uncertainty', *Southern Economic Journal*, vol. 51, 429–442.

Weiss, L. W. (1974) 'The concentration-profits relationship and antitrust' in Goldschmidt, H. J., Mann, H. M. and Weston, J. F. (eds) *Industrial Concentration: the new learning*, Little, Brown, Boston MA.

Wender, J. T. (1971) 'Collusion and entry', *Journal of Political Economy*, vol. 79, 258–277.

Wildsmith, R. J. (1973) *Managerial Theories of the Firm*, Martin Robertson, London.

Williamson, O. E. (1965) *Economics of Discretionay Behaviour: Managerial Objectives in a Theory of the Firm*, Kershaw, New York.

Williamson, O. E. (1981) 'The modern corporation, origins, evolution, attributes', *Journal of Economic Literature*, vol. 19, no. 4, 1537–1568.

Winston, C. (1993) 'Economic deregulation: days of reckoning for microeconomists', *Journal of Economic Literature*, vol. 31, no. 3, 1263–1289.

Wittink, D. R. (1977) 'Advertising increases sensitivity to price', *Journal of Advertising Research*, vol. 17, 39–42.

Worcester, D. A. (1973) 'New estimates of the welfare loss to monopoly in the US 1956–69', *Southern Economic Journal*, October.

# Index